New York State Coach
March-to-March Edition
Mathematics
Grade 5

Coach™
America's Best for Student Success®

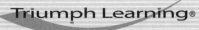

Triumph Learning®

A Haights Cross Communications ®️ Company

New York State Coach, March-to-March Edition, Mathematics, Grade 5
125NY
ISBN-10: 1-59823-455-2
ISBN-13: 978-1-59823-455-8

Author: Jerome D. Kaplan, Ed.D.
Cover Image: Eduoard Berne/Getty Images

Triumph Learning® 136 Madison Avenue, 7th Floor, New York, NY 10016
Kevin McAliley, President and Chief Executive Officer

Table of Contents

GRADE 4 POST-MARCH LESSONS

GRADE 5 PRE-MARCH LESSONS

To the Student

This book will help you get ready for the Grade 5 New York State Math Test.

The *New York State Coach, March-to-March Edition, Mathematics, Grade 5* is divided into three parts. The first part is called **Grade 4 Post-March Lessons**. These are the lessons that are part of Grade 4, but were taught after the March Test last year. The second part is the **Grade 5 Pre-March Lessons**. These two parts will get you ready for the New York State Grade 5 Math Test. The third part is called **Grade 5 Post-March Lessons**. These are lessons that will get you ready for next year's Grade 6 New York State Math Test. They are taught after the March Test. The names Pre-March and Post-March come from the month when math tests are given.

The main parts of the lessons are Examples. Examples begin with math questions similar to test questions and explain step by step how to find answers to the questions.

You will practice three types of questions just like those on the test. One type is the multiple-choice question (MCQ). After each MCQ there are four answers. Only one is correct. Choose the one answer that is correct.

The test also has a number of questions that have two parts. These are called Short-Response Questions (SRQ). The first part of an SRQ asks for a short answer. The second part asks you to explain how you got the answer to the first part.

The third type of question is like the SRQ except longer. This type is called an Extended-Response Question (ERQ). The word "extended" tells us that it is like the SRQ, but longer. Each ERQ is made up of several related parts. One or more parts ask you to write complete answers. Another part may ask you to draw a diagram or give a full explanation of your solution to the question.

This book has many features that will help you—Examples in all lessons; an interactive Check It Out with the Coach in every lesson; and Progress Checks. A Glossary at the end of the book helps with special vocabulary and explains many concepts.

When you finish this book, you will be ready for the New York State Math Test.

This table shows you the schedule for the New York State Grade 5 Math Test.

Day 1 Session 1	26 multiple-choice questions	45 minutes, plus an additional 10 minutes prep time
Day 2 Session 2	4 short-response questions and 4 extended-response questions	50 minutes, plus an additional 10 minutes prep time

Correlation Chart of New York State Grade 4 Post-March and Grade 5 Pre- and Post-March Math Indicators to *Coach* Lessons

NEW YORK STATE GRADE 4 MATH INDICATORS (Post-March)		*COACH* LESSON
STRAND 1: NUMBER SENSE AND OPERATIONS		
Number Systems: *Students will understand numbers, multiple ways of representing numbers, relationships among numbers, and number systems.*		
4.N.7	Develop an understanding of fractions as locations on number lines and as divisions of whole numbers	2
4.N.8	Recognize and generate equivalent fractions (halves, fourths, thirds, fifths, sixths, and tenths) using manipulatives, visual models, and illustrations	1
4.N.9	Use concrete materials and visual models to compare and order unit fractions or fractions with the same denominator (with and without the use of a number line)	3
4.N.10	Develop an understanding of decimals as part of a whole	4
4.N.11	Read and write decimals to hundredths, using money as a context	4
4.N.12	Use concrete materials and visual models to compare and order decimals (less than 1) to the hundredths place in the context of money	5
Operations: *Students will understand meanings of operations and procedures, and how they relate to one another*		
4.N.19	Use a variety of strategies to multiply two-digit numbers by two-digit numbers (with and without regrouping)	6
4.N.23	Add and subtract proper fractions with common denominators	7
4.N.24	Express decimals as an equivalent form of fractions to tenths and hundredths	8
4.N.25	Add and subtract decimals to tenths and hundredths using a hundreds chart	9
STRAND 2: ALGEBRA		
Equations and Inequalities: *Students will perform algebraic procedures accurately.*		
4.A.2	Use the symbols $<$, $>$, $=$, and $\neq$ (with and without the use of a number line) to compare unit fractions and decimals (up to hundredths)	10
STRAND 3: GEOMETRY		
Geometric Relationships: *Students will identify and justify geometric relationships, formally and informally.*		
4.G.6	Draw and identify intersecting, perpendicular, and parallel lines	12
4.G.7	Identify points and rays when drawing angles	11
4.G.8	Classify angles as acute, obtuse, right, and straight	11
STRAND 5: STATISTICS AND PROBABILITY		
Collection of Data: *Students will collect, organize, display, and analyze data.*		
4.S.1	Design investigations to address a question from given data	13
4.S.2	Collect data using observations, surveys, and experiments and record appropriately	13
Analysis of Data		
4.S.4	Read and interpret line graphs	14

NEW YORK STATE GRADE 5 MATH INDICATORS (Pre-March)	COACH LESSON
STRAND 1: NUMBER SENSE AND OPERATIONS	
Number Systems: *Students will understand numbers, multiple ways of representing numbers, relationships among numbers, and number systems.*	
5.N.1 Read and write whole numbers to millions	15
5.N.2 Compare and order numbers to millions	16
5.N.3 Understand the place value structure of the base ten number system 10 ones = 1 ten 10 tens = 1 hundred 10 hundreds = 1 thousand 10 thousands = 1 ten thousand 10 ten thousands = 1 hundred thousand 10 hundred thousands = 1 million	15
5.N.4 Create equivalent fractions, given a fraction	17
5.N.5 Compare and order fractions including unlike denominators (with and without the use of a number line)	18
5.N.6 Understand the concept of ratio	19
5.N.7 Express ratios in different forms	19
5.N.8 Read, write, and order decimals to thousandths	20, 21
5.N.9 Compare fractions using <, >, or =	18
5.N.10 Compare decimals using <, >, or =	21
5.N.11 Understand that percent means part of 100, and write percents as fractions and decimals	22
Number Theory	
5.N.12 Recognize that some numbers are only divisible by one and themselves (prime) and others have multiple divisors (composite)	23
5.N.13 Calculate multiples of a whole number and the least common multiple of two numbers	24
5.N.14 Identify the factors of a given number	24
5.N.15 Find the common factors and the greatest common factor of two numbers	24
Operations: *Students will understand meanings of operations and procedures, and how they relate to one another.*	
5.N.16 Use a variety of strategies to multiply three-digit by three-digit numbers *Note: Multiplication by anything greater than a three-digit multiplier/multiplicand should be done using technology*	25
5.N.17 Use a variety of strategies to divide three-digit numbers by one- and two-digit numbers *Note: Division by anything greater than a two-digit divisor should be done using technology.*	26
5.N.18 Evaluate an arithmetic expression using order of operations including multiplication, division, addition, subtraction and parentheses	27
5.N.19 Simplify fractions to lowest terms	17
5.N.20 Convert improper fractions to mixed numbers, and mixed numbers to improper fractions	28
5.N.21 Use a variety of strategies to add and subtract fractions with like denominators	29

NEW YORK STATE GRADE 5 MATH INDICATORS (Pre-March)		*COACH* LESSON
5.N.22	Add and subtract mixed numbers with like denominators	29
5.N.23	Use a variety of strategies to add, subtract, multiply, and divide decimals to thousandths	30, 31
Estimation: *Students will compute accurately and make reasonable estimates.*		
5.N.24	Round numbers to the nearest hundredth and up to 10,000	32, 33
5.N.25	Estimate sums and differences of fractions with like denominators	34
5.N.26	Estimate sums differences, products, and quotients of decimals	35
5.N.27	Justify the reasonableness of answers using estimation	36
STRAND 2: ALGEBRA		
Variables and Expressions: *Students will represent and analyze algebraically a wide variety of problem solving situations.*		
5.A.1	Define and use appropriate terminology when referring to constants, variables, and algebraic expressions	37
Equations and Inequalities		
5.A.6	Evaluate the perimeter formula for given input values	38, 40
Patterns, Functions, and Relations: *Students will recognize, use, and represent algebraic patterns, relations, and functions.*		
5.A.7	Create and explain patterns and algebraic relationships (i.e., 2, 4, 6, 8,…) algebraically: $2n$ (doubling)	39
5.A.8	Create algebraic or geometric patterns using concrete objects or visual drawings (i.e., rotate and shade geometric shapes)	39
STRAND 3: GEOMETRY		
Shapes: *Students will use visualization and spatial reasoning to analyze characteristics and properties of geometric shapes.*		
5.G.1	Calculate the perimeter of regular and irregular polygons	38, 40
Geometric Relationships: *Students will identify and justify geometric relationships, formally and informally.*		
5.G.2	Identify pairs of similar triangles	42
5.G.3	Identify the ratio of corresponding sides of similar triangles	42
5.G.4	Classify quadrilaterals by properties of their angles and sides	43
5.G.5	Know that the sum of the interior angles of a quadrilateral is 360 degrees	44
5.G.6	Classify triangles by properties of their angles and sides	43
5.G.7	Know that the sum of the interior angles of a triangle is 180 degrees	44
5.G.8	Find a missing angle when given two angles of a triangle	44
5.G.9	Identify pairs of congruent triangles	41
5.G.10	Identify corresponding parts of congruent triangles	41

NEW YORK STATE GRADE 5 MATH INDICATORS (Pre-March)		COACH LESSON
Transformational Geometry: *Students will apply transformations and symmetry to analyze problem solving situations.*		
5.G.11	Identify and draw lines of symmetry of basic geometric shapes	45
STRAND 4: MEASUREMENT		
Units of Measurement: *Students will determine what can be measured and how, using appropriate methods and formulas.*		
5.M.1	Use a ruler to measure to the nearest inch, $\frac{1}{2}$, $\frac{1}{4}$, and $\frac{1}{8}$ inch	46
5.M.2	Identify customary equivalent units of length	47
5.M.3	Measure to the nearest centimeter	46
5.M.4	Identify equivalent metric units of length	47
5.M.5	Convert measurement within a given system	47
Tools and Methods		
5.M.6	Determine the tool and technique to measure with an appropriate level of precision: lengths and angles	46, 48
Units: *Students will use units to give meaning to measurements.*		
5.M.7	Calculate elapsed time in hours and minutes	49
5.M.8	Measure and draw angles using a protractor	48
Estimation: *Students will develop strategies for estimating measurements.*		
5.M.9	Determine personal references for customary units of length (i.e., your pace is approximately 3 feet, your height is approximately 5 feet, etc.)	50
5.M.10	Determine personal references for metric units of length	50
5.M.11	Justify the reasonableness of estimates	51
STRAND 5: STATISTICS AND PROBABILITY		
Collection of Data: *Students will collect, organize, display, and analyze data.*		
5.S.1	Collect and record data from a variety of sources (i.e., newspapers, magazines, polls, charts, and surveys)	52
Organization and Display of Data		
5.S.2	Display data in a line graph to show an increase or decrease over time	53
Analysis of Data		
5.S.3	Calculate the mean for a given set of data and use to describe a set of data	54
Predictions from Data: *Students will make predictions that are based upon data analysis.*		
5.S.4	Formulate conclusions and make predictions from graphs	55

NEW YORK STATE GRADE 5 MATH INDICATORS (Post-March)	COACH LESSON
STRAND 2: ALGEBRA	
Variables and Expressions: *Students will represent and analyze algebraically a wide variety of problem solving situations.*	
5.A.2 Translate simple verbal expressions into algebraic expressions	56
Variables and Expressions: *Students will perform algebraic procedures accurately*	
5.A.3 Substitute assigned values into variable expressions and evaluate using order of operations	57
Equations and Inequalities	
5.A.4 Solve simple one-step equations using basic whole-number facts	58
5.A.5 Solve and explain simple one-step equations using inverse operations involving whole numbers	58
STRAND 3: GEOMETRY	
Coordinate Geometry: *Students will apply coordinate geometry to analyze problem solving situations.*	
5.G.12 Identify and plot points in the first quadrant	59
5.G.13 Plot points to form basic geometric shapes (identify and classify)	60
5.G.14 Calculate perimeter of basic geometric shapes drawn on a coordinate plane (rectangles and shapes composed of rectangles having sides with integer lengths and parallel to the axes)	60
STRAND 5: STATISTICS AND PROBABILITY	
Probability: *Students will understand and apply concepts of probability.*	
5.S.5 List the possible outcomes for a single-event experiment	61
5.S.6 Record experiment results using fractions/ratios	62
5.S.7 Create a sample space and determine the probability of a single event, given a simple experiment (i.e., rolling a number cube)	61

Competencies Analysis and Correlation Chart of *Coach* Lessons to Practice Test 1 and Practice Test 2

Practice Test Question	STANDARDS and INDICATORS					Coach Lessons
	N	A	G	M	S	
SESSION 1						
Multiple Choice						
1	5.N.17					26
2				5.M.2, 5.M.5		47
3	5.N.12					23
4	4.N.8					1
5				5.M.6, 5.M.8		48
6			5.G.2			42
7	5.N.11					22
8					5.S.3	54
9	5.N.8					20
10		5.A.8				39
11			5.G.6			43
12					5.S.4	55
13				5.M.3, 5.M.6		46
14		4.A.2				10
15			5.G.10			41
16		5.A.1				37
17	5.N.19, 5.N.22					17, 29
18	5.N.1					15
19			5.G.4			43
20	5.N.4					17
21	5.N.18					27
22	5.N.25					34
23	5.N.5, 5.N.9					18
24	5.N.14, 5.N.15					24
25		5.A.6	5.G.1			38, 40
26			5.G.7, 5.G.8			44
SESSION 2						
Short Response						
27	5.N.6, 5.N.7					19
28		5.A.7				39
29			5.G.11			45
30	5.N.13					24
Extended Response						
31				5.M.7		49
32			4.G.6, 4.G.7, 4.G.8			11, 12
33	5.N.23, 5.N.24, 5.N.26, 5.N.27					30, 31, 32, 33, 35, 36
34					5.S.2	53

Practice Test 1

Session 1

1 Divide: $25\overline{)302}$

A 12 R1

B 12 R2

C 120 R1

D 120 R2

2 A rowboat is 4 yards long. What is the length of the rowboat in inches?

F 12 inches

G 48 inches

H 144 inches

J 148 inches

3 How many prime numbers are there between 1 and 10?

A 4

B 5

C 6

D 7

4 What two fractions name the part of the marbles that are black?

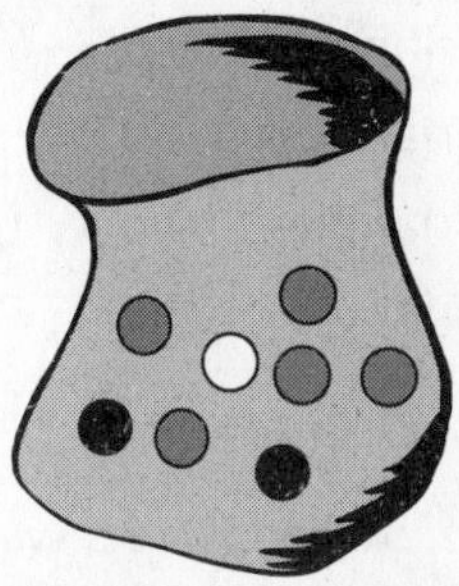

F $\frac{2}{6}$ and $\frac{1}{3}$

G $\frac{2}{4}$ and $\frac{1}{2}$

H $\frac{6}{8}$ and $\frac{3}{4}$

J $\frac{2}{8}$ and $\frac{1}{4}$

5 What is the measure of the angle shown below?

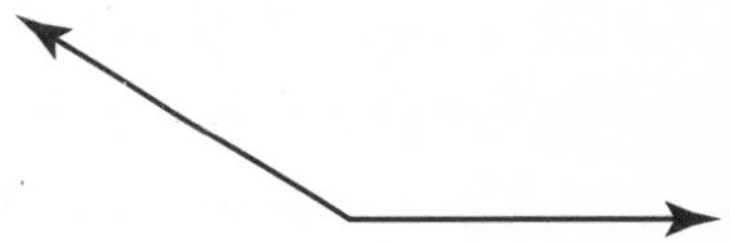

A 30°

B 35°

C 145°

D 150°

Go On

6 Which of these triangles appear to be similar triangles?

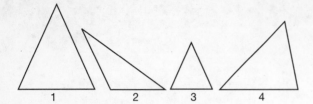

1   2   3   4

F   Triangles 1 and 2

G   Triangles 1 and 3

H   Triangles 2 and 4

J   Triangles 3 and 4

7 One hundred tickets were sold for a raffle. If Joe bought 7 of the 100 tickets, what percent of the tickets did he buy?

A   7%

B   17%

C   70%

D   107%

8 Below are the heights, in inches, of five members of a girls' basketball team.

59, 60, 63, 62, 61

What is the mean of these heights?

F   60 inches

G   61 inches

H   62 inches

J   63 inches

9 This table shows the weights of three puppies.

Puppy	Weight (in kg)
Pauly	4.995
Dottie	5.43
Biddy	5.2

Which shows these puppies in order from the puppy with the lowest weight to the puppy with the greatest weight?

A   Biddy, Dottie, Pauly

B   Dottie, Pauly, Biddy

C   Pauly, Biddy, Dottie

D   Pauly, Dottie, Biddy

10 Yvonne is creating a pattern by shading squares on grids. Below are the first five figures in her pattern.

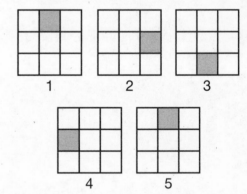

1   2   3

4   5

If she continues this pattern, what should Figure 6 look like?

F   H

G   J

Go On

11 A triangle has one angle that measures 90°. Which of the following must be true?

    A It is a right triangle.

    B It is an obtuse triangle.

    C It is an acute triangle.

    D It is an equilateral triangle.

12 A salesperson kept track of the number of new cars that she sold from January to May.

New Cars Sold by Salesperson

If the number of cars she sells continues to increase at the same rate, what is the best prediction for the number of cars the salesperson will sell in July?

    F 35

    G 40

    H 45

    J 50

13 What is the length of this line segment to the nearest centimeter?

_____

    A 1 cm

    B 2 cm

    C 3 cm

    D 4 cm

14 Which sentence is true?

    F $0.21 = 0.24$

    G $0.21 > 0.24$

    H $0.21 < 0.24$

    J $0.21 \neq 0.21$

15 Triangle *JKL* is congruent to triangle *PQR*. Which two angles are corresponding angles of these triangles?

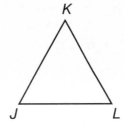 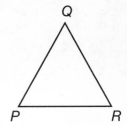

    A $\angle L$ and $\angle K$

    B $\angle L$ and $\angle P$

    C $\angle L$ and $\angle Q$

    D $\angle L$ and $\angle R$

Go On

16 In the expression below, which is the constant?

$$3x + 7$$

F   3

G x

H   +

J   7

17 Elizabeth spent $1\frac{1}{4}$ hours raking leaves and $1\frac{1}{4}$ hours reading. How much time in all did she spend doing these two activities?

A $\frac{1}{4}$ hour

B $2\frac{1}{2}$ hours

C $2\frac{3}{4}$ hours

D $3\frac{1}{4}$ hours

18 In the year 2000, the population of Buffalo, New York was 292,648. What is another way to express this number?

F   twenty-nine thousand, six hundred forty-eight

G   two hundred nine thousand, six hundred forty-eight

H   two hundred ninety thousand, six hundred forty-eight

J   two hundred ninety-two thousand, six hundred forty-eight

19 Octavius drew a quadrilateral that has two pairs of parallel sides and no right angles. The quadrilateral he drew also has four congruent sides. Which kind of quadrilateral did he draw?

A   rhombus

B   square

C   trapezoid

D   rectangle

20 Alexis measured the length of an eraser as $\frac{6}{8}$ inch. What is another way to express that length?

F $\frac{1}{6}$ inch

G $\frac{2}{4}$ inch

H $\frac{3}{4}$ inch

J $\frac{4}{6}$ inch

21 If $z = 3$, what is the value of the expression $4z + 6 \div 3$?

A   7

B   9

C   14

D   15

Go On

Test 1: Session 1

22 Which is the best estimate of $\frac{9}{10} - \frac{3}{10}$?

F　0

G　$\frac{1}{2}$

H　1

J　$1\frac{1}{2}$

23 Which symbol makes this sentence true?

$$\frac{2}{3} \underline{\hspace{1.5cm}} \frac{5}{9}$$

A　$>$

B　$=$

C　$<$

D　$\times$

24 There are 54 tiles in a bag. Cynthia wants to divide the tiles into equal groups, with no tiles left over. Which of the following shows groups into which she could divide the tiles?

F　groups of 6 tiles each

G　groups of 7 tiles each

H　groups of 8 tiles each

J　groups of 10 tiles each

25 Corey traced a picture of a stop sign. The picture was a regular octagon with sides that were 2 centimeters long.

Corey wants to glue a piece of red yarn along the entire perimeter of the octagon. How long will this piece of yarn need to be?

A　10 centimeters

B　12 centimeters

C　14 centimeters

D　16 centimeters

26 What is the measure of the unknown angle in this triangle?

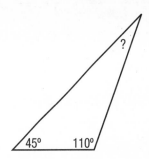

F　70°

G　45°

H　30°

J　25°

STOP

Session 2

27 There are only green and yellow markers in a box. The ratio of green to yellow markers in the box is 7 to 6.

Part A

If there are a total of 39 markers in the box, how many green markers are in the box? How many yellow markers are in the box?

Show your work.

Number of green markers _____

Number of yellow markers _____

Part B

On the lines below, explain how you found your answer.

_____

_____

_____

28 Hazel is creating a number pattern that follows the rule 8*n*, where *n* represents the position of the number in the pattern.

Part A

What should be the first five numbers in Hazel's pattern?

Answer _____

Part B

Use words, tables, and/or numbers to explain how you used the rule 8*n* to determine the first five numbers in the pattern.

_____

_____

Go On

29 Look at the trapezoid shown below. This trapezoid has two right angles.

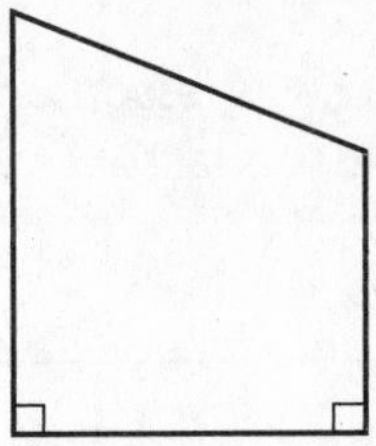

Part A

How many lines of symmetry does this trapezoid have? If it has one or more lines of symmetry, draw them above.

Answer _____ lines of symmetry

Part B

On the lines below, explain how you know that your answer for Part A is correct.

_____

_____

_____

30 Jodi is a camp counselor. She can divide the campers in her cabin into equal groups of 3 or equal groups of 9, with no campers left over.

Part A

What is the least possible number of campers in her cabin?

Show your work.

Answer _____

Part B

On the lines below, explain how you found your answer.

_____

_____

_____

Go On

31 Enrique takes music lessons in the afternoon.

Part A

He begins his guitar lesson at 3:45 P.M. His lesson ends at 4:25 P.M.
How many minutes does his guitar lesson last?

Answer _____ minutes

Part B

His voice lesson is just as long as his guitar lesson, but it begins at 4:35 P.M.
At what time does his voice lesson end?

Answer _____

Part C

On the lines below, explain how you found your answer for Parts A and B.

_____

_____

_____

_____

_____

Go On

Test 1: Session 2

32   A designer created a new logo for the Westland Tigers.
She labeled several points as shown below.

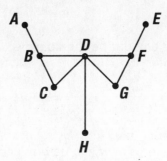

Part A

Name a pair of line segments that appear parallel.
Name a pair of line segments that appear perpendicular.

Parallel _____

Perpendicular _____

Part B

Name the line segments that form ∠ACD.

Answer _____

Part C

Name an angle that appears to be an acute angle.
Name an angle that appears to be an obtuse angle.
Name an angle that appears to be a right angle.
Name an angle that appears to be a straight angle.

Acute _____

Obtuse _____

Right _____

Straight _____

Go On

33   Mr. Dalton works at a restaurant. He plans to buy 12.1 pounds of red peppers at a cost of $2.80 per pound. This price includes tax.

Part A

What is a good estimate of the amount he should expect to pay?

Estimate _____

Part B

On the lines below, explain in words how you determined your estimate for Part A.

_____

_____

_____

Part C

What will be the exact cost of the red peppers? Show your work.

Show your work.

Exact Cost _____

Part D

Is the exact cost you found for Part C a reasonable answer? Use your estimate from Part A to explain.

_____

_____

_____

Go On

Test 1: Session 2

34 Every week, Ethan's class works on 20 challenge problems. This table shows how many challenge problems Ethan solved correctly each week.

Challenge Problems Solved Correctly

Week	1	2	3	4	5
Number of Correct Challenge Problems	2	5	8	10	15

Part A

Draw a line graph on the grid below to show the data in the table. Be sure to title your graph, label each axis, and choose an appropriate scale for the vertical axis.

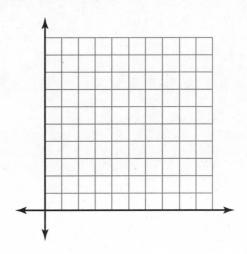

Part B

Use words and/or numbers to explain how you chose the scale for the vertical axis of your line graph in Part A.

_____

_____

_____

Part C

Look at the line graph you drew for Part A. What trend is shown by the line graph?

_____

_____

STOP

Strand 1: Number Sense and Operations

Equivalent Fractions

4.N.8 Recognize and generate equivalent fractions (halves, fourths, thirds, fifths, sixths, and tenths) using manipulatives, visual models, and illustrations

A **fraction** can name a part of a whole or a part of a set. A fraction has two numbers: a **numerator** and a **denominator**.

$$\frac{2}{5}$$ ← numerator
← denominator

EXAMPLE 1

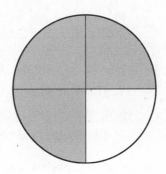

Name the fraction of the circle that is shaded.

STRATEGY   **Determine the number for the part and the number for the whole.**

STEP 1   How many parts are shaded?

There are 3 parts shaded.

This is the numerator.

STEP 2   How many parts are there in the circle?

There are 4 parts in the circle.

This is the denominator.

STEP 3   Name the fraction.

The fraction is $\frac{3}{4}$.

SOLUTION $\frac{3}{4}$ **of the circle is shaded.**

Equivalent fractions are fractions that have the same value.

EXAMPLE 2

What are two ways to name the shaded part of this rectangle?

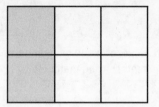

STRATEGY   **Think of the rectangle as divided in two different ways.**

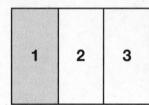

STEP 1   How much is shaded when you think of 3 equal parts?
The shaded part is $\frac{1}{3}$.

STEP 2   How much is shaded when you think of 6 equal parts?
The shaded part is $\frac{2}{6}$.

SOLUTION   **You can name the shaded part as $\frac{1}{3}$ or $\frac{2}{6}$. $\frac{1}{3}$ and $\frac{2}{6}$ are equivalent fractions.**

How do you write an equivalent fraction for $\frac{6}{10}$?

Let's check it out.

Think of rectangles divided two ways.

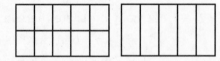

Shade the rectangle divided into 10 parts to show $\frac{6}{10}$.

Shade the rectangle divided into 5 parts to show the same amount.

What fraction of the rectangle divided into 5 parts is shaded? _____

The fraction _____ is equivalent to $\frac{6}{10}$.

Sample Test Questions

1 What does the number 6 in the fraction $\frac{5}{6}$ represent?

    A the numerator

    B the number for the part

    C the number for the whole

    D the equivalent fraction

2 What fraction of the square is shaded?

    F $\frac{1}{4}$

    G $\frac{2}{4}$

    H $\frac{3}{4}$

    J $\frac{4}{4}$

3 What are two ways to name the shaded part of the rectangle?

    A $\frac{1}{2}$ and $\frac{4}{8}$

    B $\frac{1}{3}$ and $\frac{2}{6}$

    C $\frac{1}{4}$ and $\frac{2}{8}$

    D $\frac{6}{8}$ and $\frac{3}{4}$

4 Which is **not** equivalent to one-half?

    F $\frac{2}{4}$

    G $\frac{3}{6}$

    H $\frac{5}{8}$

    J $\frac{5}{10}$

5 Which fraction is equivalent to $\frac{2}{5}$?

    A $\frac{1}{10}$

    B $\frac{5}{2}$

    C $\frac{1}{4}$

    D $\frac{4}{10}$

6 A circle has 6 equal sections. Fred shaded 3 of the sections. What is an equivalent way to write the fraction of the sections that are shaded?

    F $\frac{1}{2}$

    G $\frac{1}{3}$

    H $\frac{1}{6}$

    J $\frac{2}{3}$

7 Which fraction is equivalent to $\frac{4}{6}$?

    A $\frac{1}{3}$

    B $\frac{2}{3}$

    C $\frac{3}{6}$

    D $\frac{1}{2}$

8 Which fraction is **not** equivalent to the others?

F $\frac{1}{2}$

G $\frac{2}{4}$

H $\frac{1}{3}$

J $\frac{3}{6}$

9 What is an equivalent way to name the shaded part of the diagram?

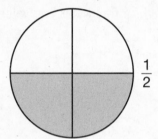

$\frac{1}{2}$

Answer _____

10 Look at the two rectangles. The shaded regions of the rectangles show equal parts. Write fractions to describe the shaded regions of the two rectangles.

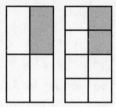

Answer _____

Short-Response Question

11 Look at the rectangle.

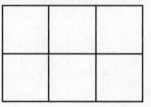

Part A

Shade an even number of parts on this rectangle and write the fraction that represents the shaded part.

Part B

Write an equivalent fraction with 3 in the denominator for the shaded part in Part A. Explain why the fractions are equivalent.

_____

_____

LESSON 2

Strand 1: Number Sense and Operations

Fractions on a Number Line

4.N.7 Develop an understanding of fractions as locations on number lines and as divisions of whole numbers

You can show fractions on a number line. The denominator tells you how many equal parts there are between whole numbers.

To show fourths, divide the length from 0 to 1 into 4 equal parts.

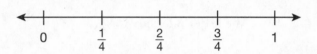

For fourths, each part is $\frac{1}{4}$ of the distance from 0 to 1.

EXAMPLE 1

What fraction does X stand for on this number line?

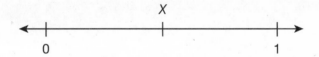

STRATEGY

Find the number of equal parts.

STEP 1   Look at the length from 0 to 1 on the number line.

STEP 2   How many equal parts are shown between 0 and 1?

There are 2 equal parts between 0 and 1.

STEP 3   What fraction stands for each part?

Each part is $\frac{1}{2}$.

STEP 4   What fraction does X stand for?

X is at the first tick mark, so *X* stands for $\frac{1}{2}$.

SOLUTION

The letter *X* stands for $\frac{1}{2}$.

EXAMPLE 2

What fraction does *X* stand for on this number line?

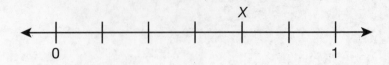

STRATEGY

Find the number of equal parts.

STEP 1   How many equal parts are shown between 0 and 1? What fraction stands for each part?

There are 6 equal parts.

Each part is $\frac{1}{6}$ of the distance from 0 to 1.

STEP 2   What fraction does *X* stand for?

X is at the fourth tick mark. *X* stands for $\frac{4}{6}$.

SOLUTION

The letter *X* stands for $\frac{4}{6}$.

What fraction does *B* stand for on this number line?

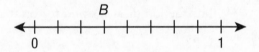

Let's check it out.

How many equal parts are shown between 0 and 1? _____

What fraction stands for each part? _____

At which tick mark is *B*? _____

What fraction does *B* stand for? _____

The letter *B* on the number line represents the fraction _____.

Sample Test Questions

1 What fraction does *K* stand for on the number line?

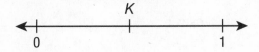

A 0

B $\frac{1}{3}$

C $\frac{1}{2}$

D 1

Use this number line for Questions 2–4.

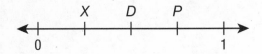

2 What fraction does letter *D* stand for on the number line?

F $\frac{1}{4}$

G $\frac{2}{4}$

H $\frac{3}{4}$

J $\frac{4}{4}$

3 What fraction does letter *P* stand for on the number line?

A $\frac{1}{4}$

B $\frac{2}{4}$

C $\frac{3}{4}$

D $\frac{4}{4}$

4 What fraction does letter *X* stand for on the number line?

F $\frac{1}{4}$

G $\frac{2}{4}$

H $\frac{3}{4}$

J $\frac{4}{4}$

5 On which number line does *W* show $\frac{1}{4}$?

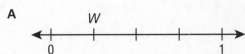

6 On which number line does *T* show $\frac{4}{4}$?

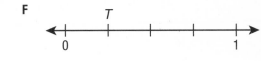
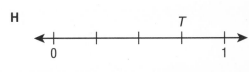
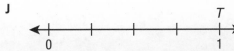

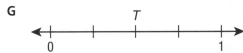

7 What fraction does *Y* stand for on the number line?

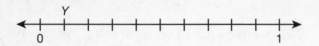

A $\frac{1}{2}$ C $\frac{1}{8}$

B $\frac{1}{5}$ D $\frac{1}{10}$

8 What fraction does *Z* stand for on the number line?

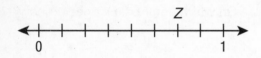

F $\frac{5}{6}$ H $\frac{6}{10}$

G $\frac{6}{8}$ J $\frac{7}{8}$

9 What fraction does *W* stand for on this number line?

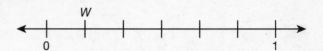

Answer _____

10 What fraction does *Q* stand for on this number line?

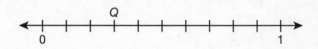

Answer _____

Short-Response Question

11 Ming draws this number line and the letter *R*.

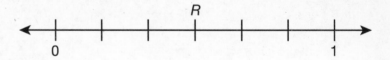

Part A

What fraction is represented by the letter *R*?

Answer _____

Part B

Use what you know about fractions on a number line to explain why your answer is correct. Use words and/or numbers in your explanation.

_____

_____

LESSON 3

Strand 1: Number Sense and Operations

Using Models to Compare Fractions

4.N.9 Use concrete materials and visual models to compare and order unit fractions or fractions with the same denominator (with and without the use of a number line)

You can use models and number lines to compare and order fractions.

EXAMPLE 1

Which is greater, $\frac{3}{8}$ or $\frac{7}{8}$?

STRATEGY

Use models.

STEP 1   Make a model of each fraction.

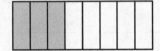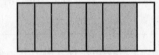

STEP 2   Decide which model has the greater part shaded.
The model of $\frac{7}{8}$ has the greater part shaded.

SOLUTION

$\frac{7}{8}$ is greater than $\frac{3}{8}$. You can write $\frac{7}{8} > \frac{3}{8}$.

EXAMPLE 2

Which is greater, $\frac{1}{2}$ or $\frac{1}{3}$?

STRATEGY

Use models.

STEP 1   Make a model of each fraction.

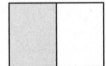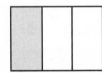

STEP 2   The model of $\frac{1}{2}$ has the greater part shaded.

SOLUTION

$\frac{1}{2}$ is greater than $\frac{1}{3}$. You can write $\frac{1}{2} > \frac{1}{3}$.

EXAMPLE 3

Order these fractions from least to greatest.

$$\frac{8}{10} \qquad \frac{3}{10} \qquad \frac{9}{10}$$

STRATEGY **Use a number line.**

STEP 1   The fractions have the same denominator, so you can show them on the same number line.

STEP 2   Order the fractions.

The fraction farthest to the left is the least fraction.

The fraction farthest to the right is the greatest fraction.

SOLUTION **The fractions in order from least to greatest are $\frac{3}{10}, \frac{8}{10}, \frac{9}{10}$.**

Which fraction is greater, $\frac{1}{4}$ or $\frac{1}{6}$?

Let's check it out.

Shade this circle to show $\frac{1}{4}$.

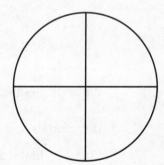

Shade this circle to show $\frac{1}{6}$.

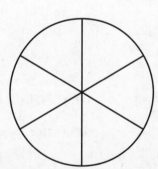

Which model has the greater part shaded? _____

Compare the fractions: _____

Sample Test Questions

1 Which diagram's shaded part(s) shows the greatest fraction?

A

B

C

D

2 Which is a correct statement based on the shaded sections of this diagram?

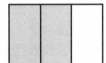 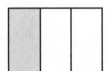

F $\frac{2}{3} > \frac{1}{3}$

G $\frac{2}{3} < \frac{1}{3}$

H $\frac{2}{3} > \frac{1}{4}$

J $\frac{1}{3} = \frac{1}{3}$

3 Which fraction makes this statement true?

$$\frac{3}{6} < \underline{\hspace{1.5cm}}$$

A $\frac{1}{6}$

B $\frac{2}{6}$

C $\frac{3}{6}$

D $\frac{4}{6}$

4 Which is a correct statement based on this diagram?

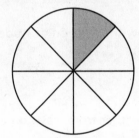 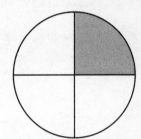

F $\frac{1}{8} > \frac{1}{4}$

G $\frac{1}{4} > \frac{1}{8}$

H $\frac{1}{4} = \frac{1}{8}$

J $\frac{1}{4} > \frac{2}{4}$

5 Which of the following are in order from greatest to least?

A $\frac{1}{6}, \frac{4}{6}, \frac{5}{6}$

B $\frac{4}{6}, \frac{1}{6}, \frac{5}{6}$

C $\frac{5}{6}, \frac{4}{6}, \frac{1}{6}$

D $\frac{5}{6}, \frac{1}{6}, \frac{4}{6}$

6 Which of these are in order from least to greatest?

F $\frac{7}{8}, \frac{5}{8}, \frac{6}{8}$

G $\frac{3}{4}, \frac{5}{4}, \frac{2}{4}$

H $\frac{6}{10}, \frac{8}{10}, \frac{1}{10}$

J $\frac{2}{5}, \frac{3}{5}, \frac{4}{5}$

7 Which symbol ($<$, $>$ or $=$) makes the statement true?

$$\frac{7}{10} \underline{\hspace{2cm}} \frac{5}{10}$$

Answer _____

8 Which of these fractions is the least?

$\frac{4}{8}$ $\frac{7}{8}$ $\frac{1}{8}$ $\frac{3}{8}$

Answer _____

Short-Response Question

9 These fractions show the fraction of students in three grades that play on the soccer team.

$\frac{3}{6}$ $\frac{1}{6}$ $\frac{5}{6}$

Part A

Put the fractions in order from least to greatest.

Answer _____

Part B

Use what you know about ordering fractions to explain why your answer is correct. Use words, drawings, and/or numbers in your explanation.

_____

_____

_____

_____

LESSON

4

Strand 1: Number Sense and Operations

Decimals

4.N.10 Develop an understanding of decimals as part of a whole

4.N.11 Read and write decimals to hundredths, using money as a context

Like fractions, **decimals** are another way to show a part of a whole.

The decimal 0.4 means the same as $\frac{4}{10}$, or four tenths.

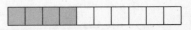

The decimal 0.24 means the same as $\frac{24}{100}$, or twenty-four hundredths.

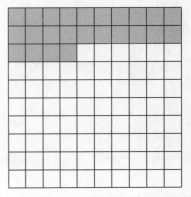

The decimal 1.51 means the same as $1\frac{51}{100}$, or one and fifty-one hundredths.

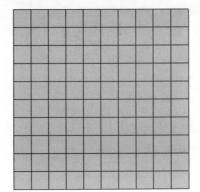 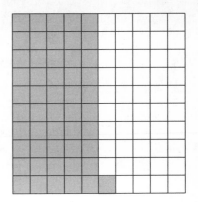

You can use a place-value chart to read and write a decimal.

Tens	Ones	.	Tenths	Hundredths
	1	.	5	1

NOTE: To read a decimal, separate the whole number from the decimal part with "and." So read 1.51 as one and fifty-one hundredths.

EXAMPLE 1

Write the word name for the decimal represented by the shaded grids.

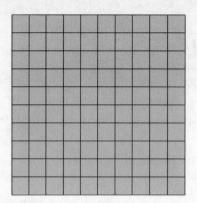 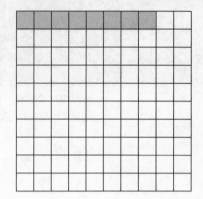

STRATEGY

Use a place-value chart.

STEP 1   What number is represented by the shaded parts?

The shaded parts show 1 whole (1 one) and 8 hundredths.

STEP 2   Write the decimal.

1.08

STEP 3   Write the word name.

The word name is "one and eight hundredths."

SOLUTION

The model shows 1.08, or one and eight hundredths.

EXAMPLE 2

Look at the bills and coins. How can you write this amount as a decimal?

STRATEGY

Count the dollars and cents.

STEP 1   How many dollars?

There are 6 dollars.

STEP 2   How many cents?

1 quarter is 25 cents; 1 nickel is 5 cents; 2 pennies are 2 cents.

There are 32 cents.

SOLUTION

The amount written as a decimal is $6.32.

NOTE: Be sure to use the dollar sign ($) when writing money amounts.

How do you write the number represented by the shaded part of this figure?

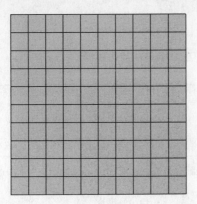 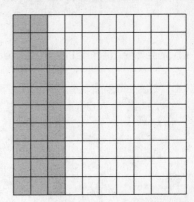

Let's check it out.

How many ones are shown by this model? _____

How many hundredths are shown by this model? _____

Write the decimal. _____

Write the word name for this decimal. _____

Sample Test Questions

1   Choose the decimal represented by the shaded grids.

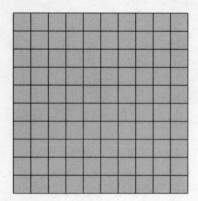 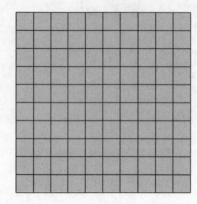 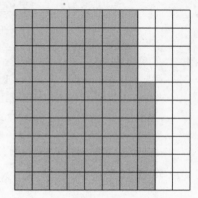

     A   2.67   **C**   2.86

     B   2.76   **D**   27.6

---

2   Sanjay carried a package weighing 9.23 pounds. What does the 3 stand for?

     F   3

     G   0.3

     H   0.03

     J   0.003

3   What is the decimal name for the shaded part of this figure?

     A   0.3

     B   0.31

     C   0.03

     D   1.3

4   What decimal is the same as $7\frac{5}{100}$?

     F   7.5

     G   7.05

     H   7.005

     J   75.0

5   What is the correct way to write the number represented below?

> 8 tenths
> 2 tens
> 1 hundredth
> 3 ones

     A   2,381

     B   238.1

     C   23.81

     D   2.381

6 Which of the following shows the money amounts as a decimal?

F $0.164   H $11.64

G $1.164   J $116.4

7 How do you write the word form for 3.65?

A Three hundred sixty-five hundredths

B Three sixty-five hundredths

C Three and sixty-five tenths

D Three and sixty-five hundredths

8 What is the word form for 12.06?

F Twelve and six tenths

G Twelve and six hundredths

H Twelve and sixty tenths

J Twelve and sixty hundredths

9 What does the digit 9 represent in 6.39?

Answer _____

10 What decimal is 0.1 less than 8.74?

Answer _____

Short-Response Question

11 Ella wants to use grids to show a decimal.

Part A

Shade the two grids to show 1.62.

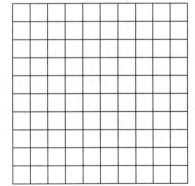 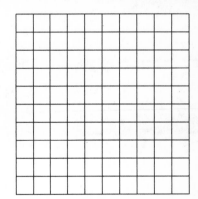

Part B

Use what you know about decimals to explain why your answer is correct.
Use words and/or numbers in your explanation.

_____

_____

LESSON
5

Strand 1: Number Sense and Operations

Comparing Decimals

4.N.12 Use concrete materials and visual models to compare and order decimals (less than 1) to the hundredths place in the context of money

EXAMPLE 1

Place these decimals in order from greatest to least:

0.42, 0.2, 0.48

STRATEGY **Use models.**

STEP 1 Shade a grid to model each decimal.

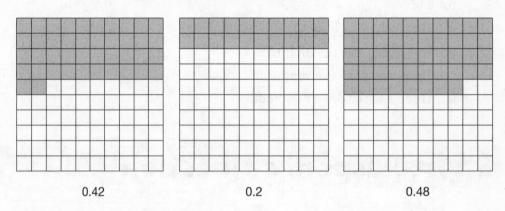

0.42   0.2   0.48

STEP 2 Compare the models.

The model for 0.2 has the least number of shaded squares.

The model for 0.48 has more shaded squares than 0.42.

SOLUTION **The decimals in order from greatest to least are: 0.48, 0.42, 0.2**

NOTE: You can use symbols to list the decimals: $0.48 > 0.42 > 0.2$

EXAMPLE 2

Enrico found a quarter and a dime in his pocket. Eva found a quarter, two nickels, and three pennies in her pocket. How much did each person find? Who found more money?

STRATEGY **Use coins to model each money amount.**

STEP 1 Model Enrico's money.

Enrico found $0.35.

STEP 2   Model Eva's money.

Eva found $0.38.

STEP 3   Compare the models.

$0.38 > $0.35   Eva has more money.

SOLUTION   **Enrico found $0.35. Eva found $0.38. Eva found more money.**

Which decimal is greater, 0.45 or 0.54?

Let's check it out.

Use this grid to model 0.45.

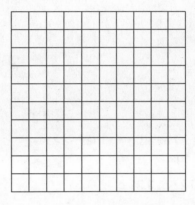

Use this grid to model 0.54.

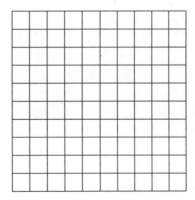

Which grid has more shaded squares? _____

Which decimal is greater? _____

Sample Test Questions

1 Kim has the following amounts of money: $0.80, $0.90, and $0.75. Which shows the correct ordering?

    A $0.75 < $0.90 < $0.80

    B $0.80 < $0.90 < $0.75

    C $0.75 < $0.80 < $0.90

    D $0.90 < $0.80 < $0.75

2 Which represents the greatest amount of money?

    F $0.75

    G $0.60

    H $0.51

    J $0.62

3 Tim found the mass of a raisin 4 times and got these readings:

    0.24 g, 0.26 g, 0.22 g, 0.21 g

Which measurement is the least?

    A 0.24 g

    B 0.26 g

    C 0.22 g

    D 0.21 g

Use the following information to answer Questions 4 and 5.

Stuart keeps a record of how far he walks each day. This table shows last week's record.

Day	Distance
Monday	0.85 mile
Tuesday	0.9 mile
Wednesday	0.4 mile
Thursday	0.35 mile
Friday	0.6 mile

4 On which day did Stuart walk the least?

    F Monday

    G Tuesday

    H Wednesday

    J Thursday

5 On which day did he walk the most?

    A Monday

    B Tuesday

    C Wednesday

    D Thursday

6 Which shows the correct order?

F   0.27 > 0.21 > 0.38

G   0.27 > 0.21 > 0.2

H   0.27 > 0.2 > 0.3

J   0.27 > 0.22 > 0.24

7 Which of the following shows the decimals in order from greatest to least?

A   0.76, 0.7, 0.62

B   0.62, 0.7, 0.76

C   0.7, 0.62, 0.76

D   0.62, 0.76, 0.7

8 Which of these money amounts is the greatest?

F $0.71

G $0.09

H $0.76

J $0.60

9 Write a number that is 0.1 greater than 0.25.

Answer _____

10 Write a money amount that is $0.01 less than $0.38

Answer _____

Short-Response Question

11 These decimals show the prices of a pack of the same kind of mints at three different stores.

$0.70 $0.65 $0.69

Part A

Write the three prices in order from least to greatest.

Answer _____

Part B

Use what you know about comparing and ordering decimals to explain why your answer is correct. Use words and/or numbers in your explanation.

_____

_____

_____

LESSON

6

Strand 1: Number Sense and Operations

Multiplying Two-Digit Numbers by Two-Digit Whole Numbers

4.N.19 Use a variety of strategies to multiply two-digit numbers by two-digit numbers (with and without regrouping)

This lesson shows how to multiply by two–digit whole numbers.

EXAMPLE

Multiply 59 × 27.

STRATEGY

Multiply and regroup.

STEP 1   Set up the problem.

$$
\begin{array}{r}
59 \\
\times\ 27 \\
\hline
\end{array}
$$

STEP 2   Multiply the 7 by the top number (59).

Regroup as necessary.

$$
\begin{array}{r}
6 \\
59 \\
\times\ 27 \\
\hline
413
\end{array}
$$

STEP 3   Multiply the 2 by the top number (59).

$$
\begin{array}{r}
1 \\
6 \\
59 \\
\times\ 27 \\
\hline
413 \\
+\ 118 \\
\end{array}
$$

STEP 4   Add to find the product.

$$
\begin{array}{r}
1 \\
6 \\
59 \\
\times\ 27 \\
\hline
413 \\
+\ 118 \\
\hline
1{,}593
\end{array}
$$

SOLUTION

The product is 1,593.

What is the product of 26 × 34?

Let's check it out.

$$\begin{array}{r} 26 \\ \times\ 34 \\ \hline \end{array}$$

After you set up the problem, what is the first step? _____

What is the product of 4 × 26? _____

What number do you write on the first line of the answer? _____

What is the product of 3 × 26? _____

What number do you write on the second line of the answer? _____

How do you align the two numbers? _____

What is the sum? _____

The product of 34 × 26 is _____.

Sample Test Questions

1 23 × 21 = _____

A 231

B 243

C 443

D 483

2 Multiply: 46 × 32

F 1,362

G 1,372

H 1,462

J 1,472

3 29 × 28 = _____

A 792

B 802

C 812

D 912

4 32 × 94 = _____

F 2,808

G 2,908

H 3,008

J 3,108

5 60 × 24 = _____

 A 1,404

 B 1,440

 C 1,464

 D 1,600

6 Multiply: 37 × 37

 F 1,369

 G 1,381

 H 1,401

 J 1,419

7 89 × 12 =

 Answer _____

8 48 × 35 =

 Answer _____

Short-Response Question

9 Iliana needs to find the product of these two numbers:

 42 × 36

 Find the product of 42 and 36.

 Show your work.

 Answer _____

LESSON

7

Strand 1: Number Sense and Operations

Adding and Subtracting Fractions with Common Denominators

4.N.23 Add and subtract proper fractions with common denominators

The fractions $\frac{4}{7}$ and $\frac{1}{7}$ have denominators that are the same number, so these fractions have a **common denominator**.

To add fractions with common denominators, add the numerators and put the sum over the common denominator.

To subtract fractions with common denominators, subtract the numerator of the second fraction from the numerator of the first fraction and put the difference over the common denominator.

EXAMPLE 1

Marty and Hans have the job of mowing the football field at school. So far, Marty has mowed $\frac{3}{10}$ of the field and Hans has mowed $\frac{1}{10}$ of the field. How much of the field have they mowed all together?

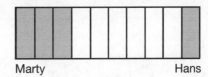

Marty   Hans

STRATEGY

Do the fractions have common denominators?
If they do, add the numerators.

STEP 1   What are the denominators of the two fractions?

     Both fractions have the denominator 10.

STEP 2   Add the numerators.

     Put the sum over the common denominator 10.

     $\frac{3}{10} + \frac{1}{10} = \frac{4}{10}$

SOLUTION

Marty and Hans have mowed $\frac{4}{10}$ of the football field.

EXAMPLE 2   How much more of the field did Marty mow than Hans?

STRATEGY   **Check whether the fractions have the same denominator.
If they do, subtract the numerators.**

STEP 1   Check the denominators.

$\frac{3}{10}$ and $\frac{1}{10}$ have common denominators.

STEP 2   Subtract the numerators.

Put the difference over the common denominator 10.

$\frac{3}{10} - \frac{1}{10} = \frac{2}{10}$

SOLUTION   **Marty mowed $\frac{2}{10}$ more of the field than Hans.**

CHECK IT OUT with the Coach™

What is the sum of $\frac{3}{8}$ and $\frac{2}{8}$?

Let's check it out.

Do the fractions have a common denominator? _____

What is sum of the numerators? _____

What is the denominator in the sum? _____

$\frac{3}{8} + \frac{2}{8} = $ _____

Sample Test Questions

1 $\frac{2}{4} + \frac{1}{4} = $ _____

A $\frac{1}{4}$ C $\frac{3}{4}$

B $\frac{2}{8}$ D $\frac{3}{8}$

2 $\frac{5}{6} - \frac{1}{6} = $ _____

F   0   H $\frac{5}{6}$

G $\frac{4}{6}$ J $\frac{6}{6}$

3   Joanna ate $\frac{1}{8}$ of a pizza and her sister Dana ate $\frac{3}{8}$ of the same pizza. How much of the pizza did they eat all together?

A $\frac{1}{8}$ C $\frac{3}{8}$

B $\frac{2}{8}$ D $\frac{4}{8}$

4 $\frac{3}{13} + \frac{2}{13} = $ _____

F $\frac{5}{26}$ H $\frac{4}{13}$

G $\frac{1}{13}$ J $\frac{5}{13}$

---

5 Waldo took $\frac{1}{6}$ of the stickers from a pack and Alicia took $\frac{3}{6}$ of the stickers. How much more of the pack did Alicia take than Waldo?

A $\frac{4}{6}$ C $\frac{2}{6}$

B $\frac{2}{3}$ D $\frac{1}{6}$

6 $\frac{7}{10} - \frac{1}{10} = $ _____

F $\frac{6}{10}$ H $\frac{8}{10}$

G $\frac{7}{10}$ J $\frac{9}{10}$

7 Angela spent $\frac{1}{3}$ of an hour on a science report. She spent another $\frac{1}{3}$ of an hour on a social studies report. What fraction of an hour did she spend on the two reports?

A $\frac{2}{6}$ C $\frac{2}{3}$

B $\frac{2}{5}$ D $\frac{4}{3}$

8 $\frac{5}{9} + \frac{2}{9} = $ _____

F $\frac{3}{9}$

G $\frac{4}{9}$

H $\frac{6}{9}$

J $\frac{7}{9}$

9 Two-fifths of the students in the fourth grade joined the band. One-fifth of the students in the fourth grade joined the chorus. What fraction of the students in fourth grade joined the band or chorus?

Answer _____

10 Doug got $\frac{4}{9}$ of the answers on his history test correct. Fran got $\frac{7}{9}$ of the answers correct. How much more of the test did Fran get correct than Doug?

Answer _____

Short-Response Question

11 Reyna needs to add $\frac{2}{8}$ and $\frac{5}{8}$ to decide what fraction of her sticker book is full.

Part A

Add $\frac{2}{8} + \frac{5}{8}$.

Answer _____

Part B

Use what you know about adding fractions to explain why your answer is correct. Use words and/or numbers in your explanation.

_____

_____

LESSON

8

Strand 1: Number Sense and Operations

Fraction-Decimal Equivalences

4.N.24 Express decimals as an equivalent form of fractions to tenths and hundredths

Fractions and decimals are different ways to express a number.

You can write an equivalent decimal form for a fraction.

EXAMPLE 1   What is the decimal that is equivalent to the fraction $\frac{17}{100}$?

STRATEGY   **Consider the meaning of the fraction.**

STEP 1   What does the fraction $\frac{17}{100}$ mean?

$\frac{17}{100}$ means seventeen hundredths.

STEP 2   What decimal means the same as seventeen hundredths?

The decimal 0.17 means seventeen hundredths.

SOLUTION   **The decimal equivalent of $\frac{17}{100}$ is 0.17.**

This table summarizes some common fraction–decimal equivalences.

Fraction		Decimal
$\frac{1}{100}$	=	0.01
$\frac{1}{10}$	=	0.1
$\frac{1}{5}$	=	0.2
$\frac{1}{4}$	=	0.25
$\frac{1}{2}$	=	0.5
$\frac{3}{4}$	=	0.75

EXAMPLE 2   What is the decimal that is equivalent to the fraction $\frac{3}{4}$?

STRATEGY   **Find $\frac{3}{4}$ on the table.**

SOLUTION   **The decimal that is equivalent to $\frac{3}{4}$ is 0.75.**

CHECK IT OUT with the **Coach**™

What is the decimal that is equivalent to $\frac{2}{10}$?

Let's check it out.

What does the fraction $\frac{2}{10}$ represent?_____

What decimal represents the same amount? _____

$\frac{2}{10}$ = _____

Sample Test Questions

For each fraction, choose the decimal that is equivalent. Use the fraction-decimal equivalent table if you need to.

1 $\frac{4}{10}$

    A   40

    B   4

    C   0.4

    D   0.04

2 $\frac{33}{100}$

    F   0.033

    G   0.33

    H   3.3

    J   33

3 $\frac{60}{100}$

    A   0.06

    B   0.60

    C   6.0

    D   60

4 $\frac{1}{2}$

    F   0.12

    G   0.25

    H   0.5

    J   0.75

5 $\frac{9}{100}$

    A   0.009

    B   0.09

    C   0.9

    D   9

6 $\frac{1}{4}$

    F   0.14

    G   0.25

    H   0.41

    J   0.5

7   What decimal is equivalent to $\frac{1}{5}$?

Answer _____

8   What decimal is equivalent to $\frac{45}{100}$?

Answer _____

Short-Response Question

9 $\frac{8}{10}$ of Luke's friends are coming to his birthday party.

Part A

Write $\frac{8}{10}$ as a decimal.

Answer _____

Part B

Use what you know about fraction-decimal equivalences to explain why your answer is correct. Use words and/or numbers in your explanation.

_____

_____

_____

_____

LESSON 9

Strand 1: Number Sense and Operations

Adding and Subtracting Decimals with Tenths and Hundredths

4.N.25 Add and subtract decimals to tenths and hundredths using a hundreds chart

You can use models to add and subtract decimals.

EXAMPLE 1

Add 0.57 + 0.33.

STRATEGY

Make a model to add.

STEP 1   Use a grid to model 0.57.

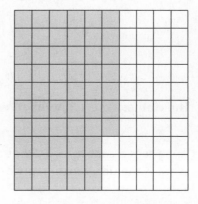

STEP 2   Use the same model to add 0.33.

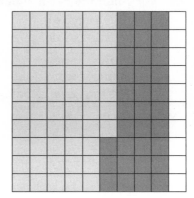

STEP 3   Write the total number of shaded parts as a decimal.

0.90

SOLUTION   **0.57 + 0.33 = 0.90**

You can also add and subtract decimals without using models. Align the decimal points and add or subtract as with whole numbers. Start at the right and regroup as necessary. Place the decimal point in the sum or difference.

EXAMPLE 2

It takes 0.45 of an hour for Frank's washing machine to wash a load of clothes. It takes 1.05 hours for the drier to dry the clothes. How long does it take for a load of clothes to wash and dry?

STRATEGY

Follow the steps for adding decimals.

STEP 1   Set up the problem and align the decimal points.

$$
\begin{array}{r}
0.45 \\
+\ 1.05 \\
\hline
\end{array}
$$

STEP 2   Add from right to left, regrouping as necessary.
Put the decimal point in the sum.

$$
\begin{array}{r}
1 \\
0.45 \\
+\ 1.05 \\
\hline
1.50
\end{array}
$$

SOLUTION

The clothes take 1.5 hours to wash and dry.

EXAMPLE 3

Anna sees a coat for $79.59 at one store and for $72.99 at another store. What is the difference in price?

STRATEGY

Follow the steps for subtracting decimals.

STEP 1   Align the decimal points and subtract.

$$
\begin{array}{r}
\$79.59 \\
-\ 72.99 \\
\hline
\end{array}
$$

STEP 2   Subtract from right to left, regrouping as necessary.
Put the decimal point in the difference.

$$
\begin{array}{r}
8\ 15 \\
\$79.59 \\
-\ 72.99 \\
\hline
6.60
\end{array}
$$

SOLUTION

The difference in price is $6.60.

What is 3.2 + 4.6?

Let's check it out.

What numbers do you add first? _____

What numbers do you add next? _____

Do the math.

Where do you put the decimal point in the answer? _____

3.2 + 4.6 = _____

Sample Test Questions

1 3.6 + 2.9 = _____

  A 5.5

  B 5.8

  C 6.4

  D 6.5

2 4.3 − 2.7 = _____

  F 1.6

  G 2.1

  H 2.4

  J 2.6

3 1.35 + 3.4 = _____

  A 1.69

  B 4.69

  C 4.75

  D 4.79

4 Marian spent 2.4 hours writing a report and 0.8 hours editing it. How much time did it take her to complete the report?

  F 3.1 hours

  G 3.2 hours

  H 3.8 hours

  J 4.2 hours

5 Dwight drove 9.32 miles to visit his brother, then 2.57 miles to visit his sister. How many miles did he drive in all?

  A 6.75

  B 11.89

  C 21.56

  D 35.02

6 Niki walked 10.4 km and ran 4.6 km yesterday. How much farther did she walk than run?

  F 5.8 km

  G 5.9 km

  H 6.8 km

  J 15.0 km

7 Rebecca's living room is 7.84 yards long and 4.81 yards wide. How many yards longer is the room than it is wide?

    A 2.85 yards

    B 3.03 yards

    C 3.13 yards

    D 3.2 yards

8 Melba earned $15.65 babysitting on Friday. She earned $29.50 on Saturday. How much did she earn on the two days?

    F $13.85

    G $44.70

    H $45.15

    J $46.05

9 Mario has two dogs. One weighs 3.4 pounds and the other weighs 4.75 pounds. How much do the two dogs weigh altogether?

Answer _____

10 Felix brought two computers to the repair shop. The Acme computer weighed 16.56 pounds and the Apex computer weighed 13.2 pounds. How much more did the Acme computer weigh than the Apex computer?

Answer _____

Short-Response Question

11 Aaron biked 6.07 miles on Friday. He biked 4.32 miles on Saturday.

Part A

How much farther did Aaron bike on Friday than on Saturday?

    Answer _____

Part B

Use what you know about adding and subtracting decimals to explain why your answer is correct. Use words and/or numbers in your explanation.

_____

_____

_____

LESSON

10

Strand 2: Algebra

Comparing Fractions and Decimals Using Symbols

4.A.2 Use the symbols $<$, $>$, $=$, and $\neq$ (with and without the use of a number line) to compare unit fractions and decimals (up to hundredths)

You are already familiar with these symbols: $=$, $<$, and $>$. The symbol $\neq$ is also used in number sentences. It means "not equal to."

$$63 \neq 75 \qquad \frac{1}{4} \neq \frac{1}{10} \qquad 0.21 \neq 0.04$$

EXAMPLE 1

Write $<$, $>$, or $=$ to make this open sentence true.

0.65 _____ 0.4

STRATEGY

Choose the symbol that makes the sentence true.

STEP 1   Compare the decimals.

0.65 is greater than 0.4. (See Lesson 5 on comparing decimals.)

STEP 2   Choose the correct symbol.

The $>$ symbol means "greater than."

0.65 $>$ 0.4

SOLUTION

The $>$ symbol makes the sentence true.

EXAMPLE 2

Write $>$, $=$, or $\neq$ to make this sentence true.

$\frac{1}{4}$ _____ 0.3

STRATEGY

Choose the symbol that makes the sentence true.

STEP 1   Change the fraction to a decimal.

$\frac{1}{4} = 0.25$ (See Lesson 8 on fraction-decimal equivalence.)

STEP 2   Compare the decimals.

0.25 is not equal to 0.3.

0.25 is not greater than 0.3.

STEP 3   Choose the correct symbol.

0.25 $\neq$ 0.3   So, $\frac{1}{4} \neq 0.3$

SOLUTION

The $\neq$ symbol makes the sentence true.

EXAMPLE 3

Which number makes this open sentence true?

$$\underline{\hspace{2cm}} > \frac{1}{2}$$

A $\frac{1}{10}$

B $\frac{1}{4}$

C   0.5

D   0.8

STRATEGY

Check each answer choice.

STEP 1   Compare $\frac{1}{10}$ and $\frac{1}{2}$.

$\frac{1}{10}$ is less than $\frac{1}{2}$.

Choice A is not correct.

STEP 2   Compare $\frac{1}{4}$ and $\frac{1}{2}$.

$\frac{1}{4}$ is less than $\frac{1}{2}$.

Choice B is not correct.

STEP 3   Compare 0.5 and $\frac{1}{2}$.

The decimal equivalent to $\frac{1}{2}$ is 0.5, so 0.5 and $\frac{1}{2}$ are equal.

Choice C is not correct.

STEP 4   Compare 0.8 and $\frac{1}{2}$.

$\frac{1}{2} = 0.5$ $0.8 > 0.5$

SOLUTION

The correct answer is Choice D.

CHECK IT OUT with the **Coach**™

Does the symbol <, >, or = make the open sentence $\frac{1}{2}$ _____ 0.4 true?

Let's check it out.

What is the decimal equivalent for $\frac{1}{2}$? _____

Is that decimal greater than, less than, or equal to 0.4? _____

Which symbol makes the open sentence true? _____

$\frac{1}{2}$ _____ 0.4

Sample Test Questions

1 Which symbol makes the open sentence true?

$$\frac{1}{2} \underline{\hspace{1cm}} \frac{1}{8}$$

A <

B >

C =

D +

2 Which number makes this open sentence true?

$$\underline{\hspace{1cm}} > \frac{1}{4}$$

F 0.14

G $\frac{1}{5}$

H 0.25

J 0.35

3 Which symbol makes the open sentence true?

$$0.6 \underline{\hspace{1cm}} 0.7$$

A >

B =

C ≠

D +

4 Which symbol makes the open sentence true?

$$\frac{1}{4} \underline{\hspace{1cm}} \frac{1}{3}$$

F <

G >

H =

J ×

5 Which number makes this open sentence true?

$$0.4 < \underline{\hspace{1cm}}$$

A 0.04

B $\frac{1}{2}$

C 0.35

D 0.4

6 Which symbol makes the open sentence true?

$$0.16 \underline{\hspace{1cm}} \frac{1}{5}$$

F <

G >

H =

J ×

7 Which number makes this open sentence true?

$$\frac{1}{5} < \underline{\hspace{1cm}}$$

A $\frac{1}{8}$

B $\frac{1}{6}$

C $\frac{1}{5}$

D $\frac{1}{4}$

8 Which number does **not** make this open sentence true?

_____ > 0.45

F 0.4

G 0.48

H 0.54

J $\frac{1}{2}$

9 Which symbol makes the open sentence true?

0.2 _____ 0.02

Answer _____

10 Which symbol makes the open sentence true?

$\frac{1}{4}$ _____ 0.25

Answer _____

Short-Response Question

11 Tamika sees this open sentence in her math book.

$\frac{1}{4}$ _____ 0.18

Part A

Write a symbol to make the open sentence true.

Answer _____

Part B

Use what you know about completing open sentences to explain why your answer is correct. Use words and/or numbers in your explanation.

_____

_____

_____

_____

LESSON 11

Strand 3: Geometry

Angles

4.G.7 Identify points and rays when drawing angles
4.G.8 Classify angles as acute, obtuse, right, and straight

PARTS OF ANGLES

An **angle** is formed when two rays or two line segments meet at a common point.

The common point is the **vertex**.
The two rays or two line segments
are called the sides.

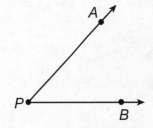

This diagram shows ∠APB. Point P is the vertex. $\overrightarrow{PA}$ and $\overrightarrow{PB}$ are the sides. When an angle is named, the vertex is always the middle letter of the name. An angle can also be named by its vertex only. So this angle can be named ∠APB, ∠BPA, or ∠P.

TYPES OF ANGLES

There are four different types of angles.

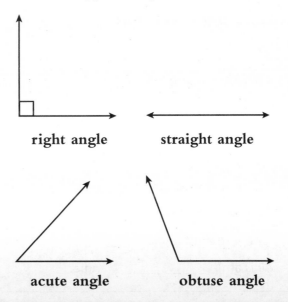

right angle   straight angle

acute angle   obtuse angle

EXAMPLE 1

Identify the vertex and
sides of this angle.

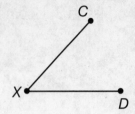

STRATEGY

Identify the sides. Then identify the vertex.

STEP 1   Identify the sides of the angle.

The line segments *XC* and *XD* are the sides of the angle.

STEP 2   What point identifies the vertex?

The sides meet at point *X*.

SOLUTION

The sides of this angle are $\overline{XC}$ and $\overline{XD}$. The vertex is point *X*.

EXAMPLE 2

What type of angle is ∠Z?

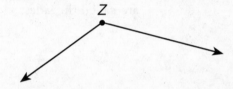

STRATEGY

Compare ∠Z to the other types of angles.

STEP 1   Is ∠Z a right angle?

∠Z does not form a square corner. It is not a right angle.

STEP 2   Is ∠Z a straight angle?

∠Z does not form a straight line. It is not a straight angle.

STEP 3   Is ∠Z smaller or greater than a right angle?

∠Z is greater than a right angle. It is obtuse.

SOLUTION

∠Z is an obtuse angle.

What kind of angle is ∠B?

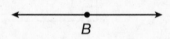

Let's check it out.

Is ∠B a right angle? _____

Is ∠B an acute angle? _____

Is ∠B an obtuse angle? _____

Is ∠B a straight angle? _____

∠B is a(n) _____ angle.

Sample Test Questions

Use this angle to answer Questions 1 and 2.

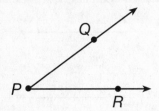

1 Which letter represents the vertex of the angle?

  A   P

  B   Q

  C   R

  D   S

2 Which of the following represents the sides of the angle?

  F $\overrightarrow{PQ}$ and $\overrightarrow{PS}$

  G $\overrightarrow{PS}$ and $\overrightarrow{PR}$

  H $\overrightarrow{PS}$ and $\overrightarrow{QR}$

  J $\overrightarrow{PQ}$ and $\overrightarrow{PR}$

3 Which choice best defines an acute angle?

  A   an angle that forms a straight line

  B   an angle that is larger than a right angle

  C   an angle that forms a square corner

  D   an angle that is smaller than a right angle

4 Which of the following best describes this angle?

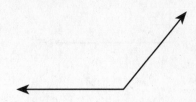

  F   acute

  G   obtuse

  H   right

  J   straight

5 Which of the following best describes this angle?

  A   acute

  B   obtuse

  C   right

  D   straight

6 Which of the following is a right angle?

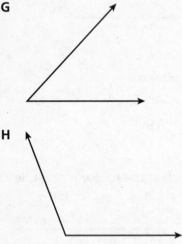

7 What type of angle is shown below?

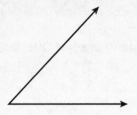

Answer _____

8 What type of angle is shown below?

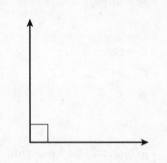

Answer _____

Short-Response Question

9 Hmong must draw an acute angle in a triangle.

Part A

Draw an acute angle. Label the vertex Point *G* and sides $\overrightarrow{GH}$ and $\overrightarrow{GK}$.

Part B

Use what you know about angles to explain why your answer is correct.
Use words and/or numbers in your explanation.

_____

LESSON

12

Strand 3: Geometry

Parallel and Perpendicular Lines

4.G.6 Draw and identify intersecting, perpendicular, and parallel lines

Here are some types of lines you should know.

Lines that cross each other are **intersecting** lines.

Lines that are always the same distance apart are **parallel** lines.

Lines that intersect at right angles are **perpendicular** lines.

EXAMPLE 1

Which line is parallel to line *q*?

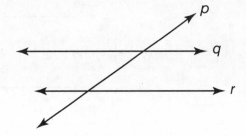

STRATEGY

Use the definition of parallel lines.

Look for a line that is always the same distance apart from line *q*.

Line *r* is always the same distance from line *q*.

SOLUTION

Line *r* is parallel to line *q*.

EXAMPLE 2

Which line is perpendicular to line *a*?

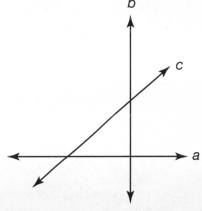

STRATEGY   **Use the definition of perpendicular lines.**

Perpendicular lines intersect at right angles.

Find the square corners.

Line *b* intersects line *a* at right angles.

SOLUTION   **Line *b* is perpendicular to line *a*.**

EXAMPLE 3   Draw two lines that are parallel.

STRATEGY   **Use a ruler.**

STEP 1   Draw a line.

STEP 2   Measure to draw points that are the same distance from the line.

STEP 3   Draw the second line.

SOLUTION   **The two lines are parallel.**

CHECK IT OUT with the Coach

How do you draw intersecting lines?

Let's check it out.

What are intersecting lines? _____

Draw the first line.

Draw the second line.

How do you know that the two lines intersect? _____

Sample Test Questions

Use this diagram to answer Questions 1 and 2.

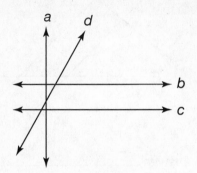

1 Which two lines are parallel?

A *a* and *b*   **C** *b* and *c*

B *a* and *c*   **D** *b* and *d*

2 Which two lines do **not** intersect?

F *a* and *b*   **H** *b* and *c*

G *a* and *d*   **J** *c* and *d*

Use this diagram to answer Questions 3 and 4.

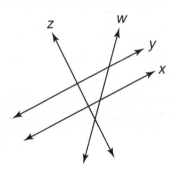

3 Which two lines are perpendicular?

A *w* and *y*

B *y* and *x*

C *w* and *z*

D *x* and *z*

4 Which two lines do **not** intersect?

F *w* and *y*

G *y* and *x*

H *w* and *z*

J *x* and *z*

5 Which segment is perpendicular to $\overline{MN}$?

A $\overline{NP}$

B $\overline{PQ}$

C $\overline{QN}$

D $\overline{MP}$

6 Which edge is parallel to edge *ZW*?

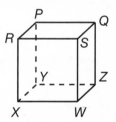

F $\overline{PQ}$

G $\overline{SW}$

H $\overline{XY}$

J $\overline{YZ}$

7 Which segment is perpendicular to $\overline{PQ}$?

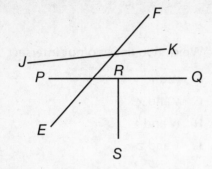

Answer _____

8 Which segment appears to be parallel to $\overline{GH}$?

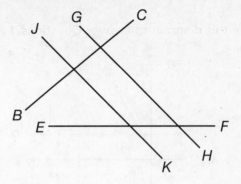

Answer _____

Short-Response Question

9 Pamil must draw perpendicular lines for a map.

Part A

Draw two perpendicular lines.

Part B

Use what you know about lines to explain why your answer is correct.
Use words and/or numbers in your explanation.

_____

_____

_____

LESSON
13

Strand 5: Statistics and Probability

Collecting Data to Answer Questions

4.S.1 Design investigations to address a question from given data
4.S.2 Collect data using observations, surveys, and experiments and record appropriately

You can collect data through observations, surveys, and experiments.
A survey is conducted by asking people questions. An experiment involves
an action that tests an idea. Often data are recorded in **tables** that organize
the data in columns.

EXAMPLE 1

Martina thinks that red is the most common car color in the school parking
lot. How can she collect data to investigate this question?

STRATEGY   **Collect data through observation.**

STEP 1   List all of the possible colors in a table.

STEP 2   Observe the color of each car in the parking lot.

STEP 3   Use tally marks to record the color of each car in the table.

SOLUTION   **This table shows the results of Martina's observations.**

Color	Tally	Number
Black	卌卌	10
Blue	卌	5
Gray	|||	3
Red	卌卌卌	15
White	卌|||	8

EXAMPLE 2

Tran wants to know how often a number cube will land on the number 3. How can he collect data to investigate this question?

STRATEGY

Conduct an experiment.

STEP 1   List the possible outcomes.

The possible outcomes are 1, 2, 3, 4, 5, and 6.

STEP 2   Toss a number cube 100 times.

STEP 3   Use tally marks to record the outcomes in a table.

SOLUTION

This table shows the results of Tran's experiment.

Cube Number	Tally	Number
1	ЖЖЖ	15
2	ЖЖЖ III	18
3	ЖЖЖ I	16
4	ЖЖЖ II	17
5	ЖЖЖ I	16
6	ЖЖЖ III	18

CHECK IT OUT with the Coach™

Suppose you want to know which kind of movie the students in your class like best. How would you investigate this question and collect the data?

Let's check it out.

Would you use observations, a survey, or an experiment to investigate your question? Explain. _____

_____

What question would you ask? _____

Who would you ask? _____

Make a table that you would use to record the results.

Sample Test Questions

1 Carly wants to know which singer is most popular at her school. What is the best way she could collect data to answer this question?

    A Play music in the hallway and wait for people to say that they like it.

    B Pick one student and look through his or her music collection.

    C Ask students, "Do you like music?"

    D Ask students, "Who is your favorite singer?"

2 Paco wants to know if heads or tails comes up more often when he flips a coin. What is the best way he can collect data to answer this question?

    F Ask people if they think heads or tails is more common.

    G Flip a coin once and observe the result.

    H Flip a coin 50 times and record the results in a table.

    J Find 50 coins lying on the ground and count how many are heads side up.

3 Keirnan wants to know if dogs or cats are the more popular pet in his apartment building. Which of the following would be the **least** useful way to collect data to answer his question?

    A Count the number of dogs and cats on each floor.

    B Ask 100 people, "What kind of pet do you have?"

    C Buy a dog and observe what happens.

    D Count the pets as people enter the building.

4 Lin collects these data. Which question did she most likely investigate?

Grade	Tally	Number
1	JHT JHT JHT IIII	19
2	JHT JHT JHT II	17
3	JHT JHT JHT JHT II	22
4	JHT JHT JHT JHT	20
5	JHT JHT JHT JHT IIII	24
6	JHT JHT JHT IIII	19

    F Do students like being in fourth grade?

    G How many students are in each grade?

    H How old are students in the fourth grade?

    J How many students are in fourth grade?

5 Lana investigates the most popular snack food among fourth graders. Which table most likely shows her results?

A

Snack	Tally	Number
Pretzel	卌 卌 III	13
Peanuts	卌 卌	10
Cookie	卌 卌 卌 I	16
Popcorn	卌 卌 II	12

C

Friend	Tally	Number
Ann	卌 卌 III	13
Bill	卌 卌	10
Carlos	卌 卌 卌 I	16
Donna	卌 卌 II	12

B

Grade	Tally	Number
1	卌 卌 III	13
2	卌 卌	10
3	卌 卌 卌 I	16
4	卌 卌 II	12

D

Food	Tally	Number
Meatloaf	卌 卌 III	13
Lasagna	卌 卌	10
Turkey	卌 卌 卌 I	16
Tacos	卌 卌 II	12

6 One way to collect data is to ask people questions. This is called taking a _____.

Answer _____

7 One way to record data in a table is to draw a _____ for each response to your question.

Answer _____

Short-Response Questions

8   Suppose you want to know the most popular color among students in your class.

Part A

Summarize how you would investigate this question and collect the data.

_____

_____

Part B

Use what you know about collecting data to explain why your answer is correct.
Use words and/or numbers in your explanation.

_____

_____

9   Suppose you want to know if most of the trees at your school are maple trees.

Part A

Summarize how you would investigate this question and collect the data.

_____

_____

Part B

Use what you know about collecting data to explain why your answer is correct.
Use words and/or numbers in your explanation.

_____

_____

LESSON 14

Strand 5: Statistics and Probability

Line Graphs

4.S.4 Read and interpret line graphs

A **line graph** uses line segments to shows trends or changes in data over time.

This graph shows the amount of TV watched by a student over five weeks.

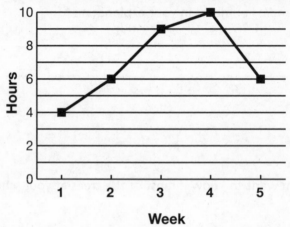

Number of Hours of TV Watched Over 5 Weeks

EXAMPLE 1

During which weeks did the number of hours increase? Decrease?

STRATEGY

Look at the shape of the graph.

STEP 1   During which weeks does the line go up from left to right?

The line goes up from Week 1 to Week 4.

STEP 2   During which weeks does the line go down from left to right?

The line goes down from Week 4 to Week 5.

SOLUTION

The number of hours increased from Week 1 to Week 4. They decreased from Week 4 to Week 5.

EXAMPLE 2   How many more hours of TV did the student watch during Week 4 than during Week 2?

STRATEGY   **Identify the number of hours for the two weeks and subtract.**

STEP 1   Find Week 4 and go up to the square.

STEP 2   Read the number on the scale at the left across from the square.
   The student watched 10 hours in Week 4.

STEP 3   Find the number of hours for Week 2.
   The student watched 6 hours in Week 2.

STEP 4   Subtract:
   10 hours − 6 hours = 4 hours

SOLUTION   **The student watched 4 more hours of TV during Week 4 than during Week 2.**

This graph shows the number of students in Ms. Lopez's class each day during a school week. How many students were in class on May 5?

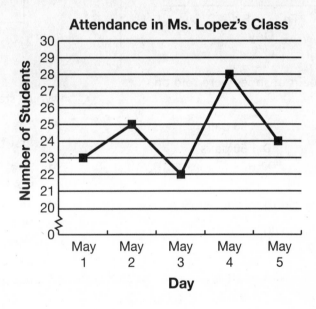

Let's check it out.

Where is May 5 on the graph?

Find the dot for May 5.

What number on the left scale lines up with the dot for May 5? _____

There were _____ students in class on May 5.

Sample Test Questions

This graph shows the number of pairs of shoes sold by a store during a four-day sale. Use this graph for Questions 1–3.

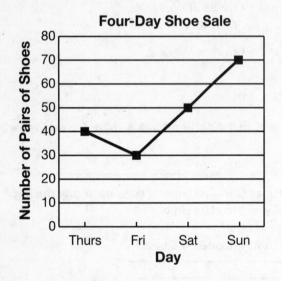

Four-Day Shoe Sale

This graph shows the value of a new car over the first five years after purchase. Use this graph for Questions 4 and 5.

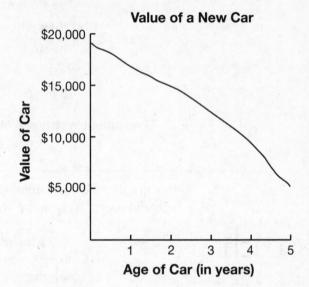

Value of a New Car

1 How many pairs of shoes were sold on Saturday?

A 30 pairs   C 50 pairs

B 40 pairs   D 60 pairs

2 On which day did the store sell 70 pairs of shoes?

F Thursday

G Friday

H Saturday

J Sunday

3 How many more pairs of shoes did the store sell on Sunday than on Thursday?

A 30 pairs

B 50 pairs

C 70 pairs

D 100 pairs

4 Which statement fits the graph?

F The value of a car increases in the first five years.

G The value of a car remains roughly the same for the first five years.

H The value of a car decreases in the first five years.

J The value of a car increases and decreases several times over the first five years.

5 What is the best estimate of the value of the car after 5 years?

A $0

B $1,000

C $5,000

D $10,000

This graph shows the daily high temperature during a week in August. Use this graph for Questions 6–8.

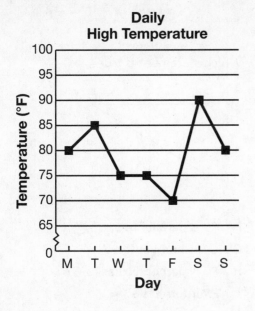

Daily High Temperature

6 What was the high temperature on Tuesday?

F 80°F

G 85°F

H 90°F

J 95°F

7 On which day was the high temperature the same as on Monday?

Answer _____

8 Between which two days did the high temperature decrease by exactly 5° Fahrenheit?

Answer _____

Short-Response Question

9 This graph shows the number of hours Teresa worked each week for a month.

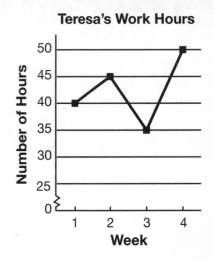

Teresa's Work Hours

Part A

How many hours did she work during Week 3?

Answer _____ hours

Part B

Use what you know about line graphs to explain why your answer is correct. Use words and/or numbers in your explanation.

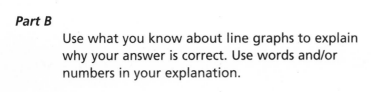

Progress Check for Lessons 1–14

1 Choose the decimal represented by the shaded grid.

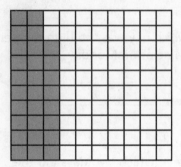

A   0.18

B   0.28

C   0.38

D   0.72

2 Which of the following shows fractions in order from least to greatest?

F $\frac{3}{8}, \frac{5}{8}, \frac{6}{8}$

G $\frac{6}{8}, \frac{5}{8}, \frac{3}{8}$

H $\frac{3}{8}, \frac{6}{8}, \frac{5}{8}$

J $\frac{6}{8}, \frac{3}{8}, \frac{5}{8}$

3 What number makes this sentence true?

$0.3 <$ _____

A   0.09

B $\frac{1}{10}$

C $\frac{1}{2}$

D   0.25

4 Which statement is true?

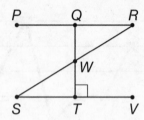

F $\overline{PR}$ is parallel to $\overline{SR}$

G $\overline{QT}$ is parallel to $\overline{SV}$

H $\overline{PR}$ is perpendicular to $\overline{QT}$

J $\overline{PR}$ intersects $\overline{SV}$

5 What fraction is represented by Point Z on the number line?

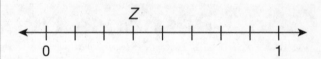

A $\frac{1}{2}$

B $\frac{3}{7}$

C $\frac{3}{8}$

D $\frac{4}{9}$

6 What decimal is equivalent to $\frac{7}{100}$?

F   0.007

G   0.07

H   0.7

J   0.71

7 Lonnie used $\frac{3}{8}$ cup of sugar for a cake and $\frac{1}{8}$ cup for icing. How much sugar did he use?

A $\frac{2}{8}$ cup C $\frac{4}{16}$ cup

B $\frac{4}{8}$ cup D $\frac{8}{10}$ cup

8 $34 \times 27 =$ _____

F 898 H 907

G 901 J 918

9 Maria wants to know what type of vegetable is most popular in her class. What is the best way she can collect data to answer this question?

A See what kind of vegetable is being served in the cafeteria

B Ask students to name their favorite vegetable

C Offer students two vegetables and see which one they pick

D Ask students if they like vegetables

10 Which of the following is a right angle?

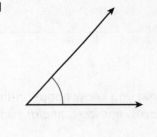

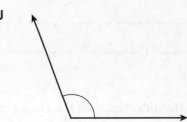

Short-Response Questions

11 On Monday Del had $\frac{5}{6}$ of a book left to read. On Tuesday he read $\frac{1}{6}$ of the book.

Part A

Subtract $\frac{1}{6}$ from $\frac{5}{6}$ to find the amount of the book Del had left to read.

Answer _____ of the book

Part B

Use what you know about subtracting fractions to explain how you know your answer is correct. Use words, numbers, and/or pictures in your explanation.

_____

_____

_____

Short-Response Questions

12   Chris walked 1.7 miles on Friday and 2.4 miles on Saturday.

Part A

How many miles did Chris walk in all?

Show your work.

Answer _____ miles

Part B

Use what you know about adding decimals to explain how you know your answer is correct. Use words, numbers, and/or pictures in your explanation.

_____

_____

13   In Narita's class, $\frac{1}{2}$ of the students are going on a school trip.

Part A

Find a fraction equivalent to $\frac{1}{2}$. You can use these models to help.

Answer _____

Part B

Use what you know about equivalent fractions to explain how you know your answer is correct. Use words and/or numbers in your explanation.

_____

_____

_____

Extended-Response Question

14   Juan kept track of the daily high temperatures for a week in March.

        Monday – 53°
        Tuesday – 49°
        Wednesday – 52°
        Thursday – 56°
        Friday – 60°
        Saturday – 55°
        Sunday – 48°

Part A

Make a line graph to show Juan's data.

Part B

How much warmer was the high temperature on the warmest day than the high temperature on the coolest day?

Answer _____

Part C

Use what you know about line graphs to explain why a line graph is the best graph to show Juan's data.

_____

_____

_____

_____

LESSON 15

Strand 1: Number Sense and Operations

Reading and Writing Numbers to 1,000,000

5.N.1 Read and write whole numbers to millions
5.N.3 Understand the place value structure of the base ten number system
　　　10 ones = 1 ten
　　　10 tens = 1 hundred
　　　10 hundreds = 1 thousand
　　　10 thousands = 1 ten thousand
　　　10 ten thousands = 1 hundred thousand
　　　10 hundred thousands = 1 million

Would you rather win $10 or $100 in a contest? You would rather win $100, of course. You know that $100 is more than $10 even though both numbers have a 1 in them. The place or position of the 1 in each number tells you its value.

This **place-value chart** shows the value of each digit in the number 824,517. The value of a digit depends on its position in a number. The 8 in this number is in the hundred thousands place, so its value is 800,000.

Hundred thousands	Ten thousands	Thousands	,	Hundreds	Tens	Ones
8	2	4	,	5	1	7

Read this number as:
eight hundred twenty-four thousand, five hundred seventeen
The comma indicates where new groupings (thousands or hundreds) start in a number.

EXAMPLE 1

The population of Rochester, New York is 219,773. What is the value of the 9 in that number?

STRATEGY **Use a place-value chart.**

STEP 1 Place the digits of 219,773 in a place-value chart.

Hundred thousands	Ten thousands	Thousands	,	Hundreds	Tens	Ones
2	1	9	,	7	7	3

STEP 2 Read the value of 9 in the chart.

The digit 9 is in the thousands place, so its value is 9 thousands.

SOLUTION **The value of the 9 is 9 thousands or 9,000.**

EXAMPLE 2

Write the number seven hundred six thousand, four hundred fifty-three in standard form.

STRATEGY **Read this number to yourself. As you read it, follow the steps below.**

STEP 1 Read the first part of the number (up to the comma).

The first part is *seven hundred six thousand,*

Write: **706,**

STEP 2 Read the second part of the number.

The second part is *four hundred fifty-three.*

Write 453 after the numbers you have already written: **706,453**

SOLUTION **The number in standard form is 706,453.**

EXAMPLE 3

How many hundred thousands are there in 1,000,000?

STRATEGY

Write 1,000,000 in a place-value chart to help you determine the answer.

STEP 1   Place the digits of 1,000,000 in a place-value chart.

Millions	,	Hundred thousands	Ten thousands	Thousands	,	Hundreds	Tens	Ones
1	,	0	0	0	,	0	0	0

STEP 2   How many hundred thousands are in 1,000,000?

Cover the chart to help you see how many hundred thousands there are.

Millions	,	Hundred thousands	
1	,	0	

Read both digits showing. (Ignore the comma.)

There are 10 hundred thousands in 1 million.

SOLUTION

There are 10 hundred thousands in 1,000,000.

CHECK IT OUT with the Coach™

What is the standard form of one hundred forty-five thousand, three hundred?

Let's check it out.

The first part of the number, before the comma is: _____.

Write the first part of the number, followed by a comma: _____

The second part of the number is: _____.

Write the second part to the number, after the comma: _____.

So, the standard form of this number is _____.

Sample Test Questions

1 What is the value of the 4 in 603,942?

A 40,000

B 4,000

C 400

D 40

2 In the number 706,423, the 0 is in which place?

F tens place

G thousands place

H ten thousands place

J hundred thousands place

3 What is another way to write the number 542,730?

A five hundred forty-two thousand, seven hundred thirty

B five hundred forty-two thousand, seven hundred three

C five hundred forty thousand, two hundred seventy-three

D fifty-four thousand, two hundred seventy-three

4 How many hundreds are there in 1,000?

F 10

G 100

H 1,000

J 10,000

5 There were nine hundred thirty-one thousand, nine hundred ten students enrolled in New York City public schools during the 1990–1991 school year. How is that number written in standard form?

A 93,191

B 930,191

C 931,901

D 931,910

6 The planet Jupiter has six moons. One of its moons, Europa, is 670,900 kilometers from Jupiter. What is the value of the 6 in that number?

F 6 millions

G 6 hundred thousands

H 6 ten thousands

J 6 hundreds

7 How many ten thousands are in 100,000?

Answer _____

8 A television show had 240,005 viewers last week. What is that number in word form?

Answer _____

Short-Response Question

9   A telethon is being held to raise money for charity. So far, $102,050 has been raised.

Part A

Express the amount that has been raised so far in words.

Answer _____

Part B

Use what you know about place value to explain how you determined your answer for Part A.

_____

_____

_____

LESSON 16

Strand 1: Number Sense and Operations

Comparing Whole Numbers

5.N.2 Compare and order numbers to millions

You can use what you know about place value to compare whole numbers. For example, you might want to compare the sizes of lakes or the distances between planets.

To compare or order large numbers, start with the greatest place value. Then compare the digits in each place until you find the greater number.

These symbols can help you compare numbers.

> means greater than

< means less than

= means equal to

EXAMPLE 1

Which of these numbers has the least value?

987,301   886,291   897,401

STRATEGY

Use place value.

STEP 1   What is the greatest place value of these numbers?

The greatest place value is the hundred thousands place.

STEP 2   Compare the digits in the hundred thousands place.

987,301   **8**86,291   **8**97,401

9 > 8, so 987,301 has the greatest value, not the least value.

STEP 3   Compare the next digit in the remaining numbers.

8**8**6,291   8**9**7,401

8 < 9, so 886,291 is less than 897,401.

SOLUTION

Of the three numbers, 886,291 has the least value.

EXAMPLE 2

This table shows the four largest natural lakes in North America.

**Largest Natural Lakes
In North America**

Lake	Area (in square Miles)
Great Bear Lake	12,275
Lake Superior	31,700
Lake Huron	23,000
Lake Michigan	22,300

Order the lakes from the lake with the smallest area to the lake with the largest area.

STRATEGY **Use place value.**

STEP 1 What is the greatest place value of these numbers?

The greatest place value is the ten thousands place.

STEP 2 Compare the digits in the ten thousands place.

1<u>2</u>,096   <u>3</u>1,700   <u>2</u>3,000   <u>2</u>2,300

1 < 2 < 3

Only the number 12,096 has a 1 in the ten thousands place, so Great Bear Lake has the smallest area.

Only the number 31,700 has a 3 in the ten thousands place, so Lake Superior has the largest area.

The other two numbers each have a 2 in the ten thousands place.

STEP 3 Compare the digits in the thousands place of the remaining numbers.

2<u>3</u>,000   2<u>2</u>,300

2 < 3, so 22,300 is less than 23,000. This means that Lake Michigan has a smaller area than Lake Huron.

SOLUTION **These lakes in order from the lake with the smallest area to the lake with the largest area are: Great Bear Lake, Lake Michigan, Lake Huron, and Lake Superior.**

Which symbol goes in the blank to make this sentence true?

618,038 _____ 599,945

Let's check it out.

Start by comparing the digits in the hundred thousands place.

The digit in the hundred thousands place of 618,038 is _____.

The digit in the hundred thousands place of 599,945 is _____

The digit _____ is greater than the digit _____.

So, 618,038 is _____ than 599,945.

The symbol that goes in the blank is _____.

Sample Test Questions

For Questions 1–3, choose the symbol that goes in the blank to make the number sentence true.

1   10,705 _____ 10,805

   A   >

   B   =

   C   <

   D   ×

2   128,729 _____ 216,290

   F   >

   G   =

   H   <

   J   ×

3   351,002 _____ 315,200

   A   >   C   <

   B   =   D   ×

4   This table shows the height of the four tallest mountains in South America.

Highest South American Mountains

Mountain	Height (in feet)
Aconcagua	22,834
Bonete	22,546
Ojos del Salado	22,572
Tupungato	22,310

Which mountain is the highest?

F   Aconcagua

G   Bonete

H   Ojos de Salado

J   Tupungato

5 An award called a Gold Record is given to a musician who sells at least 500,000 copies of a recording, such as a CD. Which of these artists would **not** receive a Gold Record?

  A   An artist whose recording sold exactly 678,060 copies.

  B   An artist whose recording sold exactly 899,999 copies.

  C   An artist whose recording sold exactly 497,129 copies.

  D   An artist whose recording sold exactly 502,023 copies.

6 Which shows the correct order?

  F $189,194 < 203,492 < 198,482$

  G $189,194 < 198,482 < 203,492$

  H $198,482 < 189,194 < 203,492$

  J $203,492 < 198,482 < 189,194$

7 What is the greatest five-digit number that can be made using each of these digits once?

  3   1   4   5   9

Answer _____

8 Katani made this table to show the four largest islands in the world.

Largest Islands In The World

Island	Area (in square Miles)
Borneo	283,400
Greenland	822,700
Madagascar	226,658
New Guinea	309,000

Which island has the second smallest area?

Answer _____

Short-Response Question

9 Antonio needs to list these numbers in order from greatest to least.

709,823   799,651   784,410   736,528

Part A

List the numbers above in order from greatest to least.

Answer _____

Part B

Use what you know about comparing whole numbers to explain why your answer is correct.

_____

LESSON 17

Strand 1: Number Sense and Operations

Equivalent Fractions and Simplifying Fractions

5.N.4 Create equivalent fractions, given a fraction
5.N.19 Simplify fractions to lowest terms

Fractions name parts of a whole or parts of a set of objects. Every fraction has a **numerator** (the number above the fraction bar) and a **denominator** (the number below the fraction bar).

When two or more fractions have the same value, they are called **equivalent fractions**.

Simplifying fractions is one way to find out if two fractions are equivalent. To simplify a fraction, find the greatest number that evenly divides both the numerator and the denominator. Then divide the numerator and the denominator by that number.

EXAMPLE 1

Is $\frac{15}{25}$ equivalent to $\frac{3}{5}$?

STRATEGY

Divide the numerator and the denominator by the same number.

STEP 1   Find a number that evenly divides both the numerator and the denominator.

> 15 can be evenly divided by 1, 3, 5, and 15. These are also the factors of 15.
>
> 25 can be evenly divided by 1, 5, and 25.
>
> Both numbers can be divided by 1 and 5. Since dividing by 1 will not change the fraction, divide by 5.

STEP 2   Divide both the numerator and denominator by 5.

$$\frac{15}{25} = \frac{15 \div 5}{25 \div 5} = \frac{3}{5}$$

SOLUTION

$\frac{15}{25}$ is equivalent to $\frac{3}{5}$.

If you divide the numerator and the denominator of a fraction by any whole number other than 1, you are simplifying the fraction. If you divide by the greatest possible number, you are writing the fraction in lowest terms.

In Example 1, $\frac{3}{5}$ is the simplified fraction in lowest term of $\frac{15}{25}$.

Simplifying fractions is one way to find equivalent fractions. Another way is to multiply the numerator and denominator by the same number.

EXAMPLE 2

Write two fractions that are equivalent to $\frac{3}{12}$.

STRATEGY

Multiply or divide the numerator and denominator by the same number to find equivalent fractions.

STEP 1   Simplify $\frac{3}{12}$ to find the first equivalent fraction.

3 can be divided by 1 and 3.

12 can be divided by 1, 2, 3, 4, 6, or 12.

The greatest number that divides 3 and 12 is 3.

$$\frac{3}{12} = \frac{3 \div 3}{12 \div 3} = \frac{1}{4}$$

STEP 2   Multiply to find a second equivalent fraction.

Multiply the numerator and the denominator by the same number. Use 2.

$$\frac{3}{12} = \frac{3 \times 2}{12 \times 2} = \frac{6}{24}$$

SOLUTION

$\frac{3}{12}$ is equivalent to $\frac{1}{4}$ and $\frac{6}{24}$.

Is $\frac{9}{54}$ equivalent to $\frac{1}{6}$?

Let's check it out.

Simplify $\frac{9}{54}$ to lowest terms.

The numbers that evenly divide 9 are _____.

Of the numbers listed above, the greatest number that also divides 54 is

_____.

Divide the numerator and the denominator by _____ to simplify the fraction.

$\frac{9}{54}$ = _____

Are $\frac{9}{54}$ and $\frac{1}{6}$ equivalent fractions? _____

Sample Test Questions

1 How would $\frac{15}{50}$ be written in lowest terms?

   A $\frac{3}{10}$

   B $\frac{5}{10}$

   C $\frac{3}{5}$

   D $\frac{1}{15}$

2 Which fraction is equivalent to $\frac{4}{5}$?

   F $\frac{6}{8}$

   G $\frac{8}{10}$

   H $\frac{10}{20}$

   J $\frac{12}{16}$

3 Which fraction is equivalent to $\frac{14}{16}$?

   A $\frac{8}{9}$

   B $\frac{7}{8}$

   C $\frac{7}{9}$

   D $\frac{2}{3}$

4 Which shows how to write $\frac{18}{24}$ in lowest terms?

   F $\frac{6}{8}$

   G $\frac{3}{5}$

   H $\frac{3}{4}$

   J $\frac{1}{2}$

5 Which fraction is **not** equivalent to $\frac{8}{12}$?

   A $\frac{16}{24}$

   B $\frac{4}{6}$

   C $\frac{2}{4}$

   D $\frac{2}{3}$

6 Which of the following is a set of equivalent fractions?

   F $\left\{\frac{1}{2}, \frac{2}{4}, \frac{6}{10}\right\}$

   G $\left\{\frac{1}{4}, \frac{5}{20}, \frac{15}{25}\right\}$

   H $\left\{\frac{1}{5}, \frac{2}{10}, \frac{4}{20}\right\}$

   J $\left\{\frac{5}{10}, \frac{15}{20}, \frac{45}{50}\right\}$

7 Camille has four pieces of ribbon, each a different color. This table shows the lengths of the four pieces of ribbon.

Color of Ribbon	Length
Blue	$\frac{1}{2}$ Foot
Yellow	$\frac{5}{6}$ Foot
Green	$\frac{10}{12}$ Foot
Red	$\frac{3}{4}$ Foot

Which two pieces of ribbon are the same length?

Answer _____

8 Keitaro has been writing a book for $\frac{6}{12}$ year. What is $\frac{6}{12}$ in lowest terms?

Answer _____

Short-Response Question

9 Maura's class is playing a math game. They need to list as many equivalent fractions for $\frac{16}{24}$ as they can.

Part A

Write three fractions that are equivalent to $\frac{16}{24}$.

Answer _____

Part B

Explain how you found your answer for Part A and why you took the steps that you did.

_____

_____

_____

LESSON 18

Strand 1: Number Sense and Operations

Comparing Fractions

5.N.5 Compare and order fractions including unlike denominators (with and without the use of a number line)

5.N.9 Compare fractions using <, >, or =

One way to compare and order fractions is to use a number line. Look at this number line.

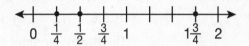

This number line also shows a **mixed number**, $1\frac{3}{4}$. A mixed number is a whole number and a fraction. From the number line, you can see that $1\frac{3}{4}$ is greater than 1 but less than 2.

EXAMPLE 1

Which symbol makes the sentence true?

$$\frac{1}{4} \underline{\hspace{2cm}} \frac{2}{3}$$

STRATEGY **Use a number line to help you compare the fractions.**

STEP 1 Draw a number line and divide it into thirds.

Plot $\frac{2}{3}$ on the number line.

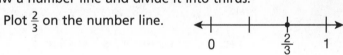

STEP 2 Where would $\frac{1}{2}$ fall on your number line?

Plot a point halfway between 0 and 1 and label it $\frac{1}{2}$.

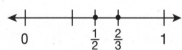

So, $\frac{2}{3}$ is greater than $\frac{1}{2}$.

STEP 3 Where would $\frac{1}{4}$ fall on your number line?

$\frac{1}{4}$ is less than $\frac{1}{2}$, so it falls halfway between 0 and $\frac{1}{2}$ on the number line.

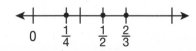

Since $\frac{1}{4}$ is to the left of $\frac{2}{3}$ on the number line, $\frac{1}{4}$ is less than $\frac{2}{3}$.

SOLUTION

So, $\frac{1}{4} < \frac{2}{3}$

Another way to compare or order fractions is to rewrite the fractions so each one has the same denominator, called a **common denominator**. If you use the least number that could be a denominator of both fractions, then you are using the **least common denominator (LCD)**.

Is $\frac{1}{4} < \frac{2}{3}$?

STRATEGY

Find the least common denominator for both fractions and then compare.

STEP 1   Skip count to find the numbers that 4 and 3 divide evenly,

4: 4, 8, 12, 16, 20, and so on. (These are also the multiples of 4.)

3: 3, 6, 9, 12, 15, and so on.

The lowest number that 4 and 3 have in common is 12.

12 is the LCD.

STEP 2   Change $\frac{1}{4}$ and $\frac{2}{3}$ to their equivalent fractions with 12 as the denominator.

Multiply the numerator and the denominator by the same number.

$$\frac{1}{4} = \frac{1 \times 3}{4 \times 3} = \frac{3}{12}$$

$$\frac{2}{3} = \frac{2 \times 4}{3 \times 4} = \frac{8}{12}$$

STEP 3   Compare $\frac{3}{12}$ and $\frac{8}{12}$.

The denominators are the same, so compare the numerators.

$3 < 8$, so $\frac{3}{12} < \frac{8}{12}$

SOLUTION

Yes, $\frac{1}{4} < \frac{2}{3}$ because $\frac{3}{12}$ is less than $\frac{8}{12}$.

EXAMPLE 3

Order these fractions from least to greatest.

$$\frac{1}{4} \qquad \frac{1}{2} \qquad \frac{3}{8}$$

STRATEGY

Find the least common denominator of the three fractions and then compare.

STEP 1   Find the least common denominator of the three fractions.

Multiples of 4: 4, 8, 12, and so on.

Multiples of 2: 2, 4, 6, 8, and so on.

Multiples of 8: 8, 16, 24, and so on.

The least common denominator of the three fractions is 8.

STEP 2   Change the fractions so each has the same denominator.

Change $\frac{1}{4}$ and $\frac{1}{2}$ to fractions with denominators of 8.

$$\frac{1}{4} = \frac{1 \times 2}{4 \times 2} = \frac{2}{8}$$

$$\frac{1}{2} = \frac{1 \times 4}{2 \times 4} = \frac{4}{8}$$

$\frac{3}{8}$ already has a denominator of 8, so leave it as is.

STEP 3   Compare the fractions with denominators of 8.

Compare the numerators: $2 < 3 < 4$, so $\frac{2}{8} < \frac{3}{8} < \frac{4}{8}$.

SOLUTION

Ordered from least to greatest, the fractions are: $\frac{1}{4}$, $\frac{3}{8}$, and $\frac{1}{2}$.

CHECK IT OUT with the Coach™

How do you find the least common denominator of $\frac{3}{10}$ and $\frac{1}{4}$?

Let's check it out.

Find a common denominator.

The multiples of 10: _____ , _____ , _____ ,

_____ , and _____ .

The multiples of 4: _____ , _____ , _____ ,

_____ , and _____ .

The least number that both 10 and 4 evenly divide is _____ .

So, the least common denominator is _____ .

Sample Test Questions

1 Which point shows $\frac{3}{4}$ on the number line?

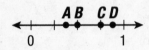

A   point *A*

B   point *B*

C   point *C*

D   point *D*

2 Which of the following shows a point at $3\frac{1}{3}$?

F

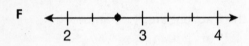

G

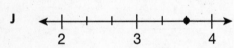

H

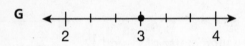

J

3 Which symbol makes the sentence true?

$$\frac{3}{4} \underline{\hspace{1cm}} \frac{7}{8}$$

A   >

B   =

C   <

D   ×

4 Which symbol makes the sentence true?

$$\frac{4}{8} \underline{\hspace{1cm}} \frac{1}{2}$$

F   >

G   =

H   <

J   ×

5 Which symbol makes the sentence true?

$$\frac{3}{10} \underline{\hspace{1cm}} \frac{2}{5}$$

A   >

B   =

C   <

D   ×

6 Which shows three fractions ordered from least to greatest?

F $\frac{1}{2}, \frac{3}{4}, \frac{1}{3}$

G $\frac{1}{2}, \frac{1}{3}, \frac{3}{4}$

H $\frac{1}{3}, \frac{1}{2}, \frac{3}{4}$

J $\frac{1}{3}, \frac{3}{4}, \frac{1}{2}$

7 Which number is represented by point *X* on the number line?

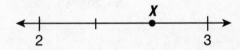

A $2\frac{1}{3}$

B $2\frac{1}{2}$

C $2\frac{2}{3}$

D $2\frac{3}{4}$

8 Which set of numbers is represented by the points on the number line?

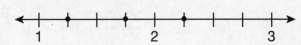

F $1\frac{1}{3}$, $1\frac{2}{3}$, $2\frac{1}{2}$

G $1\frac{1}{4}$, $1\frac{3}{4}$, $2\frac{1}{4}$

H $1\frac{1}{4}$, $1\frac{3}{4}$, $2\frac{1}{2}$

J $1\frac{1}{3}$, $1\frac{2}{3}$, $2\frac{1}{3}$

9 Write these fractions in order from greatest to least.

$\frac{3}{5}$, $\frac{7}{10}$, $\frac{1}{2}$

Answer _____

10 Write these fractions in order from least to greatest.

$\frac{3}{8}$, $\frac{1}{4}$, $\frac{3}{4}$

Answer _____

Short-Response Question

11 Below are the weights of three packages to be shipped.

$\frac{5}{8}$ pound, $\frac{1}{2}$ pound, $\frac{3}{4}$ pound

Part A

Order these weights from least to greatest.

Answer _____

Part B

Use what you know about comparing fractions to explain how you found your answer for Part A.

_____

_____

_____

LESSON

19

Strand 1: Number Sense and Operations

Ratios

5.N.6 Understand the concept of ratio
5.N.7 Express ratios in different forms

A **ratio** is a comparison of numbers. The numbers in a ratio are sometimes called terms.

A ratio is often expressed as a fraction, but may also be expressed using a colon or using words. Below are three ways to write the same ratio:

$$\frac{3}{7} \qquad 3:7 \qquad 3 \text{ to } 7$$

EXAMPLE 1

An equipment box at a school gymnasium contains 18 volleyballs and 12 basketballs. What is the ratio of volleyballs to basketballs?

STRATEGY

Write a ratio that compares the number of volleyballs to the number of basketballs.

STEP 1   Identify the number of each type of ball.

There are 18 volleyballs and 12 basketballs.

STEP 2   Write the ratio as a fraction in lowest terms.

$$\frac{\text{number of volleyballs}}{\text{number of basketballs}} = \frac{18}{12} = \frac{18 \div 6}{12 \div 6} = \frac{3}{2}$$

SOLUTION

The ratio of volleyballs to basketballs is $\frac{3}{2}$. This ratio can also be written as 3 : 2 or 3 to 2.

Even though a ratio can be written as a fraction, it is not the same as a fraction. You could rewrite the fraction $\frac{3}{2}$ as a mixed number (as $1\frac{1}{2}$), but the ratio $\frac{3}{2}$ cannot be written as a mixed number.

EXAMPLE 2

Linda's soccer team won 20 games and lost 15 games. There were no ties. What is the ratio of games won to total games played?

STRATEGY

Find the total number of games played. Then write a ratio that compares a part to a total.

STEP 1   What is the total number of games played?

20 + 15 = 35

STEP 2   Write the ratio as a fraction in lowest terms.

$$\frac{\text{number of games won}}{\text{total number of games}} = \frac{20}{35} = \frac{20 \div 5}{35 \div 5} = \frac{4}{7}$$

SOLUTION   **The ratio of games won to total games played is $\frac{4}{7}$.**

EXAMPLE 3   Frank and Elena spent a total of 15 hours working on a social studies project. The ratio of the number of hours Frank spent on the project to the number of hours Elena spent was 2 : 3. How many hours did each student spend on the project?

STRATEGY   **Find a ratio that is equivalent to 2 : 3 and whose terms add up to 15.**

STEP 1   Write the ratio as a fraction.

2 : 3 can be rewritten as $\frac{2}{3}$.

STEP 2   Write a ratio that is equivalent to $\frac{2}{3}$ and see if the terms add up to 15.

You find equivalent ratios just like you find equivalent fractions.

$$\frac{2}{3} = \frac{2 \times 3}{3 \times 3} = \frac{6}{9}$$

6 + 9 = 15, so this is the correct ratio.

STEP 3   How many hours did each student spend on the project?

The ratio $\frac{6}{9}$ compares the number of hours Frank spent to the number of hours Elena spent.

So, Frank spent 6 hours and Elena spent 9 hours.

SOLUTION   **Frank spent 6 hours on the project, and Elena spent 9 hours on the project.**

CHECK
IT OUT
with the
Coach™

A bag contains 15 red tiles and 12 blue tiles. What is the ratio of red tiles to blue tiles in the bag?

Let's check it out.

Write the ratio as a fraction:

$\dfrac{\text{number of red tiles}}{\text{number of blue tiles}} =$ _____

Simplify the fraction to lowest terms.

In lowest terms, the fraction is _____.

The ratio of red tiles to blue tiles is _____.

Sample Test Questions

1   A bag contains only blue and gray marbles. If there are 18 blue marbles and 20 gray marbles in the bag, what is the ratio of blue marbles to gray marbles?

   A $\frac{1}{10}$

   B $\frac{9}{10}$

   C $\frac{10}{9}$

   D $\frac{9}{8}$

2   A fruit punch is made with 4 liters of cranberry juice and 6 liters of grape juice. What is the ratio of liters of cranberry juice to liters of grape juice in the punch?

   F   1 to 4

   G   2 to 5

   H   2 to 3

   J   1 to 2

3   A fifth-grade class has 13 boys and 17 girls. What is the ratio of girls to all students in the class?

   A   17 : 13

   B   13 : 17

   C   17 : 30

   D   13 : 30

4   The only animals at a veterinarian's office are cats and dogs. If there are 8 cats and 10 dogs at the office, what is the ratio of cats to total animals at the office?

   F $\frac{4}{9}$

   G $\frac{5}{9}$

   H $\frac{4}{5}$

   J $\frac{5}{4}$

5   There are only blue and red pens in a box. The ratio of blue pens to red pens is 3 : 5. If there are a total of 40 pens in the box, how many blue pens and red pens are in the box?

   A   15 blue pens and 25 red pens

   B   20 blue pens and 20 red pens

   C   18 blue pens and 22 red pens

   D   25 blue pens and 15 red pens

6   There are 400 part-time employees and 1,600 full-time employees at a company. What is the ratio of part-time employees to full-time employees?

   F $\frac{1}{6}$

   G $\frac{1}{5}$

   H $\frac{1}{4}$

   J $\frac{4}{1}$

7 In a voting district, 500 voters are registered as Democrats and 550 voters are registered as Republicans. What is the ratio of Republicans to Democrats?

Answer _____

8 There are 24 students in Juan's class. The ratio of girls to boys is 1 : 2. How many girls and how many boys are in Juan's class?

Answer _____

Short-Response Question

9 There are only red and yellow counters in a box. The ratio of red to yellow counters in the box is 3 to 8.

Part A

If there are a total of 33 counters in the box, how many red counters are in the box? How many yellow counters are in the box?

Answer _____ red counters

Answer _____ yellow counters

Part B

Use words and/or numbers to explain how you determined the number of red counters and the number of yellow counters in the box.

_____

_____

LESSON 20

Strand 1: Number Sense and Operations

Reading and Writing Decimals

5.N.8 Read, write, and order decimals to thousandths

Like fractions, **decimals** are used to represent numbers that are less than one. They are parts of a whole. You read decimals all the time, like when you read a price tag that shows dollars and cents.

This place-value chart shows the value of each digit in the number 65.934.

Tens	Ones	•	Tenths	Hundredths	Thousandths
6	5	•	9	3	4

Read this number as:

> sixty-five and nine hundred thirty-four thousandths.

The word *and* takes the place of the decimal point. It separates the whole number part from the decimal part.

EXAMPLE 1

Write the number 11.289 in word form.

STRATEGY

Read the whole number part and then read the decimal part separately.

STEP 1   Write the whole number part in words.

       11 is the whole number part, so write 11 in words:

       eleven

STEP 2   How do you separate the decimal part from the whole number part?

       Write the word *and* in place of the decimal point.

       eleven **and**

STEP 3   Write the decimal part in words.

       289 thousandths is the decimal part.

       eleven and **two hundred eighty-nine thousandths**

SOLUTION

The word form of 11.289 is eleven and two hundred eighty-nine thousandths.

EXAMPLE 2

The width of a plastic pipe is two and three hundred seventy-five thousandths inches. How can you write this number in standard form?

STRATEGY **Put a decimal point in place of the word *and* to separate the whole number part from the decimal part.**

STEP 1 What is the whole number part before the word *and*?

The whole number is two. Write 2 followed by a decimal point:

2.

STEP 2 Determine the number of places after the decimal point.

The decimal part is three hundred seventy-five *thousandths*, so there are 3 places after the decimal point.

STEP 3 the decimal point:

2.375

SOLUTION **The number in standard form is 2.375.**

How do you rewrite 5.283 in word form?

Let's check it out.

First write words to show the whole number part: _____.

What word should you add next to take the place of the decimal point?

The word _____ should be added next.

Write words to show the decimal part: _____

_____.

The number 5.283 rewritten in word form is _____

_____.

Sample Test Questions

1 What is the value of the 9 in the number 60.394?

  A 9 tenths

  B 9 hundredths

  C 9 thousandths

  D 9 hundreds

2 Which shows the word form of the number 65.067?

  F sixty-five and seven tenths

  G sixty-five and sixty-seven hundredths

  H sixty-five and sixty-seven thousandths

  J sixty-five thousand, sixty-seven

3 In the number 517.936, the 6 is in which place?

  A tens place

  B tenths place

  C hundredths place

  D thousandths place

4 What is the standard form of this number?

  seven and three hundred forty-five thousandths

  F 73.45

  G 73.045

  H 7.045

  J 7.345

5 Geraldine ran a loop around the park that was 2.35 kilometers long. What is the value of the 3 in the number 2.35?

  A 3 tens

  B 3 tenths

  C 3 hundredths

  D 3 thousandths

6 In the number 102.789, which digit is in the hundredths place?

  F 1

  G 7

  H 8

  J 9

7 A scientist measured the mass of a compound as 1.63 grams. How would that number be written in word form?

  Answer _____

8 Charles bought a package of cheese that weighed four and twenty-five thousandths kilograms. How would that number be written in standard form?

  Answer _____

Short-Response Question

9   Look at the decimal shown below.

403.907

Part A

Write the number shown above in word form.

Answer _____

Part B

Use what you know about decimals to explain why your answer is correct.

_____

_____

_____

LESSON 21

Strand 1: Number Sense and Operations

Ordering Decimals

5.N.8   Read, write, and order decimals to thousandths
5.N.10 Compare decimals using <, >, or =

Just as you can compare and order whole numbers, you can also compare and order decimals. These symbols can help you compare decimals (just as they help you compare whole numbers):

> means greater than

< means less than

= means equal to

EXAMPLE 1

Order these decimals from least to greatest.

9.42   3.218   4.08   11.262

STRATEGY

Compare the whole number parts.

STEP 1   Order the whole number parts (to the left of the decimal point).

9.42   **3**.218   **4**.08   **11**.262

Ordered from least to greatest: 3, 4, 9, 11.

STEP 2   Place the decimals in the same order as the whole number parts.

3.218, 4.08, 9.42, 11.262

SOLUTION

The decimals in order from least to greatest are 3.218, 4.08, 9.42, and 11.262.

When comparing decimals, do not assume that the decimal with the most digits has the greatest value. For example, 3.218 is less than 4.08 even though 3.218 has four digits and 4.08 has three digits.

If it helps, write one or more zeros after the last decimal value so that all the decimals you are comparing have the same number of digits to the right of the decimal point. For example, you can write 1.2 as 1.20. The numbers 1.2 and 1.20 have the same value.

EXAMPLE 2

What symbol makes the sentence true?

0.286 _____ 0.268

STRATEGY

Compare the digits.

STEP 1   Since there is no whole number value in these decimals, compare the digits to the right of the decimal point.

Start with the tenths place.

0.<u>2</u>86   0.<u>2</u>68

The numbers have the same digit in the tenths place, so continue comparing.

STEP 2   Compare the digits in the next place value.

Compare digits in the hundredths places:

0.2<u>8</u>6   0.2<u>6</u>8

8 > 6, so 0.286 > 0.268

SOLUTION

0.286 > 0.268

Which number is greater—0.209 or 0.309?

Let's check it out.

These numbers do not have whole number parts.

So, compare the digits in the _____ places.

The digit _____ is greater than the digit _____.

So the greater number is _____.

Sample Test Questions

For Questions 1–3, choose the symbol that makes the sentence true.

1 3.209 _____ 4.005

    A   >

    B   =

    C   <

    D   ×

2 0.81 _____ 0.395

    F   >

    G   =

    H   <

    J   ×

3 1.28 _____ 1.280

    A   >

    B   =

    C   <

    D   ×

4 Which shows the correct order?

    F $2.109 < 1.472 < 3.285$

    G $1.472 < 2.109 < 3.285$

    H $3.285 < 2.109 < 1.472$

    J $1.472 < 3.285 < 2.109$

5 These are the distances of four different driving routes from Kurt's house to his school: 1.327 km, 1.301 km, 1.299 km, and 1.455 km. Which represents the shortest distance?

    A   1.327 km

    B   1.301 km

    C   1.299 km

    D   1.455 km

6 This table shows the capacities of three containers.

Container	Capacity (in liters)
Container A	1.555
Container B	2.061
Container C	0.982

Which shows these containers ordered from the container with the greatest capacity to the container with the least capacity?

    F   Container A, Container B, Container C

    G   Container B, Container C, Container A

    H   Container C, Container B, Container A

    J   Container B, Container A, Container C

7 Which number has a value between 4.01 and 4.03?

A 4.2

B 4.006

C 4.034

D 4.017

8 Use > to show 9.271, 9.184, and 9.93 from greatest to least.

Answer _____

9 Chandra weighed a compound four times and got four different measurements. These were her four measurements: 1.541 g, 1.543 g, 1.54 g, and 1.539 g. Which measurement is the smallest?

Answer _____

Short-Response Question

10 Look at the decimals shown below.

1.698   0.897   1.367   1.7

Part A

Order these decimals from least to greatest.

Answer _____

Part B

Use words and/or numbers to explain how you ordered the decimals and why you took the steps that you did.

_____

_____

_____

LESSON

22

Strand 1: Number Sense and Operations

Percents

5.N.11 Understand that percent means part of 100, and write percents as fractions and decimals

A **percent** is a ratio of a number to 100. Percents can be written as fractions with denominators of 100.

For example, 91 of the 100 squares shown below are shaded. You could also say that 91% or $\frac{91}{100}$ of the squares are shaded.

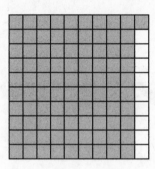

EXAMPLE 1

One hundred people saw a movie and were asked whether they liked it or not. If 33 of the 100 people said they liked the movie, what percent of the people liked the movie? What fraction of the people liked the movie?

STRATEGY

Find the percent of people who liked the movie. Then convert the percent to a fraction.

STEP 1   Find the percent.

A percent is a number out of 100.

So, if 33 out of 100 people liked the movie, then 33% of the people liked the movie.

STEP 2   Write 33% as a fraction with a denominator of 100.

Write the number of the percent in the numerator.

Write 100 in the denominator.

$33\% = \frac{33}{100}$

SOLUTION

33%, or $\frac{33}{100}$, of the people liked the movie.

If a fraction has a denominator of 100, you can convert it to a percent by writing the numerator of the fraction with a percent (%) symbol after it.

The fraction $\frac{33}{100}$ is read 33 hundredths, which is the same as 0.33. So, you can write the percent 33% as the decimal 0.33.

EXAMPLE 2

Marisol received 0.65 of the votes in the election for class president. What percent of the votes did she receive?

STRATEGY

Write the decimal as a fraction. Then convert the fraction to a percent.

STEP 1   Write the decimal as a fraction.

0.65 is 65 hundredths.

65 hundredths is $\frac{65}{100}$.

STEP 2   Convert the fraction to a percent.

Write the numerator with the percent symbol after it.

$\frac{65}{100} = 65\%$

SOLUTION

Marisol received 65% of the votes.

CHECK IT OUT *with the* **Coach**™

What decimal is the same as 19%?

Let's check it out.

The percent 19% can be written as the fraction _____.

This fraction can be read as _____ hundredths, which is the same

as the decimal _____.

So, 19% is the same as the decimal _____.

Sample Test Questions

1 What percent of the squares is shaded?

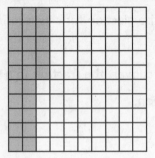

A 25%

B 26%

C 30%

D 35%

2 Which fraction is the same as 13%?

F $\frac{1}{13}$

G $\frac{13}{100}$

H $\frac{1}{3}$

J $\frac{13}{10}$

3 Which percent is the same as $\frac{27}{100}$?

A 2%

B 7%

C 20%

D 27%

4 If Darius answered 90 of the 100 questions on a test correctly, what percent of the questions did he answer correctly?

F 9%

G 19%

H 90%

J 109%

5 Which percent is the same as 0.34?

A 3%

B 4%

C 34%

D 43%

6 Which decimal is the same as 88%?

F 0.88

G 0.188

H 0.8

J 8.8

7 If $\frac{63}{100}$ of the tiles in a bag are gray, what percent of the tiles in the bag are gray?

A 6%

B 36%

C 63%

D 163%

8 A softball team won 75% of its games this year. What decimal shows the portion of this year's games that the team won?

Answer _____

9 If 83% of the students in a spelling bee made it to the second round, what fraction of the students in the spelling bee made it to the second round?

Answer _____

Short-Response Question

10 Ms. Vega teaches piano lessons.

Part A

If 0.54 of Ms. Vega's students will perform in a piano recital, what percent of her students will perform in the recital?

Answer _____

Part B

Use words and/or numbers to explain how you found the answer for Part A and why you took the steps that you did.

_____

_____

_____

LESSON 23

Strand 1: Number Sense and Operations

Prime and Composite Numbers

5.N.12 Recognize that some numbers are only divisible by one and themselves (prime) and others have multiple divisors (composite)

When we say that a number is divisible by 2, we mean that the number can be evenly divided by 2, or that 2 is one of the factors of the number. For more information on factors, take a look at Lesson 10.

A **prime number** is a counting number that is divisible by only two numbers: 1 and itself. For example, 2 is a prime number because it is divisible by only 1 and 2.

Any counting number that is divisible by more than two numbers is a **composite number**. For example, 8 is a composite number because it is divisible by four numbers: 1, 2, 4, and 8.

The number 1 is a special number. It is neither a prime number nor a composite number because it is only divisible by one number: 1.

EXAMPLE 1

Which of the following is a composite number?

A   13

B   15

C   17

D   29

STRATEGY

Find the answer choice that is divisible by more than two numbers.

13 is divisible by only two numbers: 1 and 13. So, it is prime.

15 can be evenly divided by four numbers : 1, 3, 5, and 15. So, it is composite.

17 is divisible by only two numbers: 1 and 17. So, it is prime.

29 is divisible by only two numbers: 1 and 29. So, it is also prime.

SOLUTION

The answer is B. 15 is a composite number.

EXAMPLE 2   How many prime numbers are there between 40 and 50?

STRATEGY   **List the numbers between 40 and 50. Identify the numbers that are prime.**

STEP 1   List the numbers between 40 and 50. This does not include 40 or 50.

41, 42, 43, 44, 45, 46, 47, 48, 49

STEP 2   Test each number.

All even numbers greater than 2 are divisible by at least three numbers: 1, 2, and themselves.

So, 42, 44, 46, and 48 must all be composite numbers.

41 is divisible by only two numbers: 1 and 41. So, it is prime.

43 is divisible by only two numbers: 1 and 43. So, it is prime.

45 is divisible by six numbers: 1, 3, 5, 9, 15, and 45. So, it is composite.

47 is divisible by only two numbers: 1 and 47. So, it is prime.

49 is divisible by three numbers: 1, 7, and 49. So, it is composite.

STEP 3   List the prime numbers.

41, 43, 47

SOLUTION   **Three numbers between 40 and 50 are prime: 41, 43, and 47.**

CHECK IT OUT with the Coach

Is 3 a prime number or a composite number?

Let's check it out.

The numbers that evenly divide 3 are _____.

Since 3 is divisible by _____ numbers, it is a

_____ number.

Sample Test Questions

1 Which of the following is a prime number?

A 9

B 10

C 11

D 12

2 Which of these numbers is a composite number?

F 2

G 4

H 7

J 13

3 Which of the following is a prime number?

A 22

B 21

C 20

D 19

4 Which of these numbers is prime?

F 16

G 21

H 33

J 47

5 Look at each pair of numbers below. Which pair contains two prime numbers?

A 5, 46

B 15, 25

C 21, 27

D 41, 43

6 Which of the following is true about the number 1?

F It is a prime number.

G It is a composite number.

H It is neither a prime number nor a composite number.

J It is an even number.

7 How many prime numbers are there between 60 and 70?

A 0

B 1

C 2

D 3

8 List all the prime numbers between 30 and 40.

Answer _____

9 Pedro is thinking of an even number that is also prime. What number is Pedro thinking of?

Answer _____

Short-Response Question

10 Look at the numbers shown below.

20   21   22   23   24   25   26   27   28   29   30

Part A

Which of the numbers shown above are prime numbers?

Answer _____

Part B

Explain how you found your answer for Part A and why the numbers you listed are prime numbers.

_____

_____

_____

LESSON 24

Strand 1: Number Sense and Operations

Greatest Common Factor (GCF) and Least Common Multiple (LCM)

5.N.13 Calculate multiples of a whole number and the least common multiple of two numbers
5.N.14 Identify the factors of a given number
5.N.15 Find the common factors and the greatest common factor of two numbers

FACTORS

The **factors of a number** are the counting numbers that evenly divide that number. Counting numbers are 1, 2, 3, 4, and so on.

For example, to find the factors of 6, think about the counting numbers you can multiply to get a product of 6.

$1 \times 6 = 6$, so 1 and 6 are factors of 6.

$2 \times 3 = 6$, so 2 and 3 are also factors of 6.

This means that the factors of 6 are 1, 2, 3, and 6.

GREATEST COMMON FACTOR

The **greatest common factor (GCF)** of two numbers is the greatest number that is a factor of both numbers.

EXAMPLE 1

Find the GCF of 27 and 45.

STRATEGY

Find the factors of each number first.

STEP 1   Find the factors of 27.

       The factors of 27 are 1, 3, 9, and 27.

STEP 2   Find the factors of 45.

       The factors of 45 are 1, 3, 5, 9, 15, and 45.

STEP 3   What is the greatest factor that both numbers have in common?

       Common factors of 27 and 45 are 1, 3, and 9.

       The greatest number that is a factor of both 27 and 45 is 9.

SOLUTION

The GCF of 27 and 45 is 9.

LEAST COMMON MULTIPLE (LCM)

The **multiples** of a number are the numbers you get when you multiply that number by the counting numbers.

The **least common multiple (LCM)** of two numbers is the least number that is a multiple of both.

EXAMPLE 2

Find the LCM of 6 and 9.

STRATEGY **Find the first few multiples of both numbers.**

STEP 1   Find the first six multiples of 6.

6, 12, 18, 24, 30, 36

STEP 2   Find the first six multiples of 9.

9, 18, 27, 36, 45, 54

STEP 3   Find the smallest number that is a multiple of both 6 and 9.

Common multiples of 6 and 9 are 18 and 36.

18 is the smallest multiple that is common to both 6 and 9.

SOLUTION   **The least common multiple, or LCM, of 6 and 9 is 18.**

What is the greatest common factor of 6 and 8?

Let's check it out.

The factors of 6 are _____.

The factors of 8 are _____.

The greatest number that is a factor of both 6 and 8 is _____.

So, the greatest common factor of 6 and 8 is _____.

Sample Test Questions

1 What are all the factors of 49?

A   1, 7

B   1, 2, 7

C   1, 7, 49

D   1, 6, 8, 49

2 How many factors does 72 have?

F   4

G   6

H   10

J   12

3 What is the greatest common factor of 32 and 48?

A   2

B   8

C   12

D   16

4 What is the least common multiple of 3 and 11?

F   11

G   30

H   33

J   66

5 What is the GCF of 27 and 63?

A   3

B   6

C   9

D   27

6 Anoki has a collection of toy cars. He can divide his cars into equal groups of 3 or into equal groups of 8 with no cars left over. What is the smallest possible number of cars that Anoki could have in his collection?

F   12

G   24

H   30

J   32

7 What number is the GCF of 18 and 24?

A   4

B   6

C   9

D   12

8 Hans is in a class of 21 students. Which shows equal groups into which his class can be divided, with no students left over?

F   groups of 3 students each

G   groups of 4 students each

H   groups of 5 students each

J   groups of 6 students each

9 Farzie waters one of her plants every 3 days. She waters her second plant once every 2 days. If she waters both plants today, how many days will pass before she waters them on the same day again?

Answer _____

124

10 What number is the LCM of 4 and 6?

Answer _____

Short-Response Question

11 The music teacher, Mrs. Logan, can divide the members of the chorus into equal groups of 8 or into equal groups of 10 with no students left over.

Part A

What is the smallest possible number of students who could be in the chorus?

Answer _____

Part B

Use words and/or numbers to explain how you found the answer for Part A and why you took the steps that you did.

_____

_____

_____

Progress Check for Lessons 15–24

1 Mr. Smith sold his house for two hundred ninety thousand, five hundred dollars. What is another way to write this amount?

A $295,000

B $290,500

C $290,050

D $209,500

2 Which shows all the factors of 20?

F 1, 2, 10

G 1, 2, 10, 20

H 1, 2, 4, 5, 10, 20

J 1, 2, 3, 4, 5, 6, 10, 20

3 Which of these statements is true?

A There are 10 ones in 100.

B There are 10 tens in 100.

C There are 10 thousands in 100,000.

D There are 10 ten thousands in 1,000,000.

4 Which of the following shows the greatest length?

F $\frac{7}{10}$ meter

G $\frac{4}{5}$ meter

H $\frac{1}{2}$ meter

J $\frac{3}{4}$ meter

5 A box has only green and yellow crayons in it. There are 14 green crayons and 17 yellow crayons in the box. What is the ratio of green crayons to all crayons in the box?

A 14 : 17

B 17 : 14

C 14 : 31

D 17 : 31

6 Which statement is true?

F $0.071 > 0.7$

G $0.153 > 0.591$

H $0.640 > 0.64$

J $0.763 > 0.673$

7 Of the students Paul surveyed, 25% chose science as their favorite subject. Which decimal shows the portion of students who chose science as their favorite subject?

A 0.025

B 0.205

C 0.25

D 2.5

8 Which shows how to write 253.047 in word form?

F two hundred fifty-three and forty-seven hundredths

G two hundred fifty-three and four hundred seven thousandths

H two hundred fifty-three and forty-seven thousandths

J two hundred fifty-three thousand, forty-seven

9 Which is a prime number?

A 50   **C** 52

B 51   **D** 53

10 Which symbol makes this number sentence true?

492,705 _____ 492,075

F $>$

G $=$

H $<$

J $\times$

11 Which symbol makes this sentence true?

$\frac{2}{3}$ _____ $\frac{6}{9}$

A $>$

B $=$

C $<$

D $\times$

12 Which number is the least common multiple of 6 and 15?

F 60

G 30

H 15

J 3

13 Which fraction is equivalent to $\frac{3}{7}$?

A $\frac{21}{49}$

B $\frac{12}{21}$

C $\frac{6}{10}$

D $\frac{21}{28}$

14 Which of the following shows these decimals ordered correctly?

5.094   4.99   5.084   5.1

F $4.99 > 5.084 > 5.094 > 5.1$

G $5.094 > 5.084 > 4.99 > 5.1$

H $4.99 > 5.1 > 5.084 > 5.094$

J $5.1 > 5.094 > 5.084 > 4.99$

15 Last Sunday, a movie theater sold a total of 4,800 adult tickets and a total of 1,200 children's tickets. What is the ratio of adult tickets to children's tickets sold that day?

A 4 to 1

B 1 to 4

C 8 to 1

D 1 to 8

16 Which number is the greatest common factor of 24 and 28?

F 2

G 4

H 7

J 8

Open-Ended Questions

Short-Response Question

17 Mr. Drake does his laundry every 4 days. He washes his car every 6 days.

Part A

Mr. Drake did his laundry and washed his car today. What is the least number of days that will pass before he will do his laundry and wash his car on the same day again?

Show your work.

Answer _____

Part B

Use words and/or numbers to explain how you found the answer for Part A and why you took the steps that you did.

_____

_____

_____

Extended-Response Questions

18   Use this grid to solve the problem.

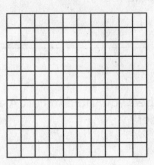

Part A

Shade the grid above so that 23% of the squares are shaded.

Part B

Write a fraction and a decimal to show the portion of the grid that you shaded.

Answer _____

Part C

Explain how you decided how many squares to shade for Part A and how you know that the fraction and decimal you wrote for Part B are correct.

_____

_____

_____

_____

_____

19 Julio is making lists of prime numbers in math class.

Part A

Julio lists all the prime numbers that are greater than 1 but less than 20.
Write all the numbers he should list.

Answer _____

Part B

Choose any two of the numbers you listed in Part A and multiply them.
Is the product a prime number?

Answer _____

Part C

Will the product of any two of the numbers you listed in Part A ever be prime?
Explain why or why not.

_____

_____

_____

_____

_____

Strand 1: Number Sense and Operations

Multiplying by Three-Digit Numbers

5.N.16 Use a variety of strategies to multiply three-digit by three-digit numbers

This lesson shows you a standard procedure for multiplying two three-digit numbers.

EXAMPLE

Multiply: $359 \times 427 =$ _____

STRATEGY

Multiply and regroup.

STEP 1   Rewrite the problem vertically and multiply the digits in the ones places.

$9 \times 7 = 63$ Think of 63 as 6 tens 3 ones.

Write the 3 in the ones place of the answer and write the 6 in the tens column.

$$\begin{array}{r} \overset{6}{3}59 \\ \times\ 427 \\ \hline 3 \end{array}$$

STEP 2   Multiply 7 by the digit in the tens place of the top factor.

7×5 (tens) $= 35$ (tens)

Add 35 to the 6 (tens) written above the 5.

$35 + 6 = 41$ (tens) $= 4$ (hundreds) $+ 1$ (ten)

Write the 1 in the tens place of the answer and write the 4 in the hundreds column.

$$\begin{array}{r} \overset{46}{3}59 \\ \times\ 427 \\ \hline 13 \end{array}$$

STEP 3   Multiply 7 by the digit in the hundreds place of the top factor.

$7 \times 3 = 21$ (hundreds)

Add 21 to 4 (hundreds) shown above the 3.

$21 + 4 = 25$ (hundreds)

Write 25 (hundreds) in the answer.

$$\begin{array}{r} \overset{46}{3}59 \\ \times\ 427 \\ \hline 2513 \end{array}$$

STEP 4   Multiply 2 by the digit in the ones place of the top factor.

2 (tens) $\times$ 9 = 18 (tens)

Think of this number as 18 tens, which is the same as 180 or 1 hundred 8 tens.

Write the 8 in the answer below the tens column. Write the 1 (hundred) above the 5 in 359. Cross out the 6 that was there.

$$
\begin{array}{r}
\overset{1}{\cancel{6}} \\
35\mathbf{9} \\
\times\ 427 \\
\hline
2513 \\
\mathbf{8}
\end{array}
$$

STEP 5   Continue multiplying 2 by the digits in the top factor.

$$
\begin{array}{r}
\overset{11}{}\ \\
4\cancel{6} \\
\mathbf{3}59 \\
\times\ 427 \\
\hline
2513 \\
\mathbf{7}18
\end{array}
$$

STEP 6   Multiply 4 by the digit (9) in the ones place of the top factor.

9 $\times$ 4 (hundreds) = 36 (hundreds)

Write the 6 in the answer below the hundreds column.

Write the 3 (thousands) above the 5 in 359. Cross out the 1 that was there.

$$
\begin{array}{r}
3 \\
\cancel{1}\cancel{1} \\
4\cancel{6} \\
35\mathbf{9} \\
\times\ 427 \\
\hline
2513 \\
718 \\
\mathbf{6}
\end{array}
$$

STEP 7   Continue multiplying 4 by the digits in the top factor.

$$
\begin{array}{r}
23 \\
\cancel{1}\cancel{1} \\
4\cancel{6} \\
3\mathbf{5}9 \\
\times\ 427 \\
\hline
2513 \\
718 \\
\mathbf{1436}
\end{array}
$$

STEP 8   Add to find the product.

$$
\begin{array}{r}
2513 \\
718 \\
+\ 1436 \\
\hline
153{,}293
\end{array}
$$

SOLUTION   **The product is 153,293.**

You can use this procedure when you multiply any two whole numbers.

**Suppose you are multiplying these numbers: 367 × 127.
What is the product of the 6 and the 1?**

Let's check it out.

What does the 6 of 367 stand for?

It stands for _____.

What does the 1 of 127 stand for?

It stands for _____.

So, what is the product of the 6 and the 1?

The product is _____.

Sample Test Questions

1

$$
\begin{array}{r}
258 \\
\times\,313 \\
\end{array}
$$

A   4,695

B   70,634

C   79,534

D   80,754

2

$$
\begin{array}{r}
205 \\
\times\,133 \\
\end{array}
$$

F   1,435

G   27,155

H   27,265

J   27,725

3   516 × 228 = _____

A   6,192   C   117,748

B   117,648   D   118,648

4   126 × 475 = _____

F   2,016

G   14,490

H   58,850

J   59,850

5   139 × 683 = _____

A   2,363

B   90,937

C   94,937

D   95,937

6   894 × 531 = _____

F   474,714

G   470,614

H   463,614

J   8,046

7 716 × 120 = _____

    A 86,636

    B 85,920

    C 8,592

    D 2,148

8 984 × 409 = _____

Answer _____

9 A large company bought 108 packs of paper. Each pack contained 250 sheets of paper. How many sheets of paper did the company buy in all?

Answer _____

Short-Response Question

10 Elsa solved a multiplication problem. Her work is shown below.

$$
\begin{array}{r}
121 \\
\times 324 \\
\hline
484 \\
242 \\
+363 \\
\hline
1{,}089
\end{array}
$$

Part A

Is Elsa's answer correct or incorrect?

Answer _____

Part B

Use what you know about multiplying to explain how you determined your answer for Part A. Use words and/or numbers in your explanation.

_____

_____

_____

LESSON 26

Strand 1: Number Sense and Operations

Division with Two-Digit Divisors

5.N.17 Use a variety of strategies to divide three-digit numbers by one- and two-digit numbers

These are the names given to the numbers used in division.

$$\text{Divisor} \overline{)\,\text{Dividend}}^{\text{Quotient}}$$

This means that the **dividend** divided by the divisor equals the quotient.

EXAMPLE 1

Divide: $9\overline{)824}$ This means 824 divided by 9.

STRATEGY

Use the steps of long division to find the answer: divide, multiply, subtract and bring down.

STEP 1   Divide.

Since dividing 8 by 9 results in a number less than 1, divide 82 by 9.

How many 9's are there in 82?

The answer is 9. Write a 9 above the 2 in 82.

$$9\overline{)824}^{\,9}$$

9 is the first digit of the quotient.

STEP 2   Multiply and subtract.

$9 \times 9 = 81$
Write the product 81 underneath the 82.

Then subtract 81 from 82.

$$\begin{array}{r} 9 \\ 9\overline{)824} \\ -81 \\ \hline 1 \end{array}$$

STEP 3   Bring down the next digit of the dividend.

$$\begin{array}{r} 91 \\ 9\overline{)824} \\ -81 \\ \hline 14 \end{array}$$

14 is the next number you will divide by 9.

STEP 4   Repeat the steps of long division until there are no more digits to bring down.

How many 9's are there in 14?

The answer is 1. Write a 1 in the quotient.

$9 \times 1 = 9$, so write 9 below the 14. Subtract 9 from 14 to get 5.

$$\begin{array}{r} 91 \\ 9\overline{)824} \\ -81 \\ \hline 14 \\ -9 \\ \hline 5 \end{array} \longleftarrow \textbf{remainder}$$

There are no more digits to bring down. So, 91 is the quotient and 5 is the remainder.

SOLUTION | **The quotient is 91 with a remainder of 5, which can be also be written 91 R5. (The R stands for the remainder.)**

The answer to Example 1 can also be written as a mixed number. The whole number part of the quotient will be the whole number part of the mixed number. The fractional part of the mixed number will have the remainder as its numerator and the divisor as its denominator.

So, the answer for Example 1, 81 R5, can also be written as $81\frac{5}{9}$.

You can also use long division to divide three-digit numbers by two-digit numbers. Since you have not memorized multiplication facts for two-digit numbers, you will need to estimate to figure out what numbers to divide by.

EXAMPLE 2

Find the quotient.

$$76\overline{)639}$$

STRATEGY | **Estimate to find the quotient.**

STEP 1   How many times does 76 divide 639?

Estimate by looking at the first digit in 76 (the 7) and the first two digits in 639 (63). Then ask yourself, how many 7's are there in 63?

The answer is 9.

$76 \times 9 = 684$, which is greater than 639. So, 9 is too big.

STEP 2   Try 8.

$76 \times 8 = 608$, which is less than 639. So 8 works.

Write 8 above the 9 in the quotient. Then write 608 beneath 639.

$$\begin{array}{r} 8 \\ 76\overline{)639} \\ 608 \end{array}$$

STEP 3   Subtract.

$$\begin{array}{r} 8 \\ 76\overline{)639} \\ -608 \\ \hline 31 \end{array} \longleftarrow \textbf{remainder}$$

There are no more digits to bring down. So, 8 is the quotient and the remainder is 31.

SOLUTION | **The quotient is 8 R31, or $8\frac{31}{76}$.**

CHECK IT OUT with the **Coach**™

What is 138 divided by 46?

Let's check it out.

Estimate to find the quotient.

Look at the first digit of 46, the 4.

Look at the first two digits of 138, the 13.

How many 4's are there in 13?

The answer is _____.

So, try multiplying that number by 46.

46 × _____ = _____

Does that number work? _____

I estimated the quotient and found that 138 ÷ 46 = _____.

Sample Test Questions

Find each quotient.

1 7)296

A   41 R2   C   42 R2

B   41 R3   D   42 R3

2 2)829

F   41 R1   H   414

G   41 R4   J   414 R1

3 Divide: 317 ÷ 8 = _____

A $39\frac{3}{8}$

B $39\frac{5}{8}$

C $40\frac{3}{8}$

D $40\frac{5}{8}$

4 Divide: 104 ÷ 4 = _____

F   26

G   26 R1

H   26 R2

J   26 R3

5 22)154

A   6

B   6 R2

C   7

D   7 R2

6 17)495

F   29 R1

G   29 R2

H   39 R1

J 39 R2

7 Divide: 668 ÷ 35. Show the quotient as a mixed number.

Answer _____

8 Divide: 373 ÷ 54. Show the answer as a whole number with a remainder.

Answer _____

Short-Response Question

9 Macon and Olivia both found this quotient: $875 \div 19 =$ _____.

Macon says that $875 \div 19 = 46$ R1.

Olivia says that Macon is wrong. She says that $875 \div 19 = 46\frac{1}{19}$.

Part A

Who is correct—Macon, Olivia, both of them, or neither of them?

Show your work.

Answer _____

Part B

Explain how you determined your answer for Part A. Show any work that you did to find your answer.

_____

_____

_____

LESSON

27

Strand 1: Number Sense and Operations

Order of Operations

5.N.18 Evaluate an arithmetic expression using order of operations including multiplication, division, addition, subtraction, and parentheses

Addition, subtraction, multiplication, and division are the **operations** that we perform on numbers or **expressions**. An expression includes numbers and one or more operation $(+, -, \times, \div)$ signs.

If an expression has several operations, you need to know the order in which you should add, subtract, multiply, and divide. Use these rules.

RULES FOR ORDER OF OPERATIONS

Rule 1:   Do what is inside the parentheses first.

Rule 2:   Multiply and divide before you add and subtract.

Rule 3:   Multiply and divide in order from left to right.

Rule 4:   Add and subtract in order from left to right.

EXAMPLE 1

What is the value of this expression?

$$12 \div 2 \times 3$$

STRATEGY

Apply the rules for the Order of Operations.

STEP 1   Check to see which rule applies first.

Rules 1 and 2 do not apply, but Rule 3 does.

STEP 2   Use Rule 3: multiply and divide in order from left to right.

Since division is on the left, divide first.

$$12 \div 2 = 6$$

STEP 3   Next, multiply.

$$6 \times 3 = 18$$

SOLUTION

The value of the expression is 18.

EXAMPLE 2

What is the value of this expression?

$$84 + 6 \times (6 - 3)$$

STRATEGY

Apply the rules for the Order of Operations.

STEP 1   Apply Rule 1: Do what is inside the parentheses first.

$$6 - 3 = 3$$

STEP 2   Figure out which rule applies next.

The expression is now: $84 + 6 \times 3$.

So use Rule 2: Multiply and divide before you add and subtract.

STEP 3   Multiply.

$$6 \times 3 = 18$$

STEP 4   Add to complete the computation.

$$84 + 18 = 102$$

SOLUTION

The value of the expression is 102.

CHECK IT OUT with the Coach™

What should you do first to find the value of $7 \times (3 + 8)$?

Let's check it out.

Apply the rules for the Order of Operations.

Which rule applies first?

Rule _____ applies first.

That rule says to _____.

Do the first step in the computation: _____

Sample Test Questions

For Questions 1–6, find the value of each expression.

1 $72 \div 9 - 5 + 7$

A   25

B   20

C   11

D   10

2 $3 \times 15 \div 5$

F   8

G   9

H   10

J   11

3 $(67 - 43) \div (64 \div 8)$

A   3

B   4

C   8

D   35

4 $7 \times (7 - 7)$

F   49

G   42

H   7

J   0

5 $20 - 5 + 10$

A   5

B   10

C   15

D   25

6 $7 \times 6 - 10 \div 2 + 18$

F   16

G   34

H   55

J   65

7 Evaluate: $50 \times (10 + 20) = $ _____

A   350

B   450

C   1,500

D   1,550

8 Evaluate: $50 \times (80 + 7) = $ _____

F   4,350

G   4,550

H   4,850

J   4,950

9 What is the value of this expression?

$$4 + 8 \div (4 \div 2)$$

A 6

B 8

C 10

D 12

10 What is the value of this expression?

$$100 \div 25 \times (6 + 4) \times 4$$

Answer _____

11 According to the Order of Operations, which operation should you do first to evaluate the expression below?

$$10 - 9 \div 3 + 4 \times 7 = \underline{\quad\quad}$$

Answer _____

Short-Response Question

12 Ms. Burrell has written this expression on the board.

$$100 - (40 + 10) \div 2$$

Part A

What is the value of this expression?

Show your work.

Answer _____

Part B

Use what you know about order of operations to explain why your answer is correct. Use words and/or numbers to support your explanation.

_____

_____

_____

LESSON

28

Strand 1: Number Sense and Operations

Converting Mixed Numbers

5.N.20 Convert improper fractions to mixed numbers, and mixed numbers to improper fractions

Recall that a mixed number is a whole number and a fraction. For example, $1\frac{1}{4}$ is a mixed number.

A mixed number can be written as an **improper fraction**. An improper fraction has a numerator that is greater than or equal to its denominator. For example, $\frac{5}{4}$ is an improper fraction.

These diagrams show that $1\frac{1}{4}$ (one and one-fourth) is equivalent to $\frac{5}{4}$ (five fourths).

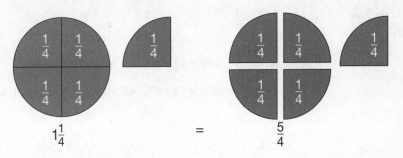

EXAMPLE 1	Convert $4\frac{2}{5}$ to an improper fraction.

STRATEGY

Multiply the whole number part by the denominator. Then add the numerator.

Multiply the whole number part by the denominator: $4 \times 5 = 20$

Add the numerator to 20: $20 + 2 = 22$

Write 22 as the new numerator and keep the denominator the same: $\frac{22}{5}$

SOLUTION

$4\frac{2}{5}$ **is the same as** $\frac{22}{5}$**.**

You can also convert an improper fraction to a mixed number.

EXAMPLE 2

Convert $\frac{13}{6}$ to a mixed number.

STRATEGY

Find the whole number first.

Divide 13 by 6.

$\frac{13}{6} = 13 \div 6 = 2$ R1

Write the remainder, 1, as a fraction over the original denominator: $\frac{1}{6}$.

$\frac{13}{6} = 2\frac{1}{6}$

SOLUTION

$\frac{13}{6}$ **is equivalent to the mixed number** $2\frac{1}{6}$**.**

CHECK IT OUT with the Coach™

What mixed number is equivalent to $\frac{31}{10}$?

Let's check it out.

Divide the numerator by the denominator: $31 \div 10 =$ _____

The whole number part of the mixed number is _____.

Write the remainder as a fraction over the original denominator:

_____

The mixed number that is equivalent to $\frac{31}{10}$ is _____.

Sample Test Questions

1 Which mixed number is equivalent to $\frac{13}{3}$?

A $1\frac{3}{10}$

B $3\frac{1}{10}$

C $4\frac{1}{3}$

D $4\frac{2}{3}$

2 Which mixed number is equivalent to $\frac{15}{4}$?

F $3\frac{3}{4}$

G $3\frac{3}{5}$

H $3\frac{1}{3}$

J $2\frac{3}{4}$

3 Which of the following is equivalent to $1\frac{1}{5}$?

A $\frac{4}{5}$

B $\frac{6}{5}$

C $\frac{7}{5}$

D $\frac{11}{5}$

4 Which improper fraction is equivalent to $1\frac{3}{8}$?

F $\frac{9}{8}$

G $\frac{11}{8}$

H $\frac{13}{8}$

J $\frac{25}{8}$

5 Which statement below is true?

A $1\frac{1}{4} = \frac{3}{4}$

B $1\frac{1}{3} = \frac{4}{3}$

C $1\frac{1}{2} = \frac{4}{2}$

D $1\frac{1}{2} = \frac{5}{2}$

6 Which statement below is true?

F $3\frac{2}{7} = \frac{12}{7}$

G $3\frac{2}{7} = \frac{24}{7}$

H $3\frac{3}{7} = \frac{12}{7}$

J $3\frac{3}{7} = \frac{24}{7}$

7 At a party, $4\frac{1}{8}$ of the pizzas were eaten. What improper fraction shows the portion of the pizzas that were eaten?

Answer _____

8 Samantha babysat for $\frac{7}{2}$ hours on Sunday. What mixed number shows how many hours she babysat on Sunday?

Answer _____

Short-Response Question

9 Enrique baked $5\frac{1}{2}$ batches of muffins for a bake sale.

Part A

Which improper fraction is equivalent to $5\frac{1}{2}$?

Answer _____

Part B

Use words and/or numbers to explain the steps you took to convert $5\frac{1}{2}$ to an improper fraction.

_____

_____

_____

LESSON 29

Strand 1: Number Sense and Operations

Adding and Subtracting Fractions and Mixed Numbers with Like Denominators

5.N.21 Use a variety of strategies to add and subtract fractions with like denominators
5.N.22 Add and subtract mixed numbers with like denominators

To add fractions with like denominators, just add the numerators. Keep the denominators the same.

To subtract fractions with like denominators, just subtract the numerators. Keep the denominators the same.

EXAMPLE 1

On Sunday, Suzanne had $5\frac{5}{8}$ cans of dog food. On Monday, her dog ate $2\frac{3}{8}$ cans. How many cans of dog food did Suzanne have left?

STRATEGY **Decide whether to add or subtract. Then solve the problem.**

STEP 1 Should you add or subtract to solve this problem?

The question asks how many cans are *left*. So you need to subtract.

So, you need to subtract $2\frac{3}{8}$ from $5\frac{5}{8}$.

STEP 2 Do the mixed numbers have like denominators?

Yes, each mixed number has a denominator of 8.

STEP 3 Rewrite the problem vertically and subtract the fractions.

$$\begin{array}{r} 5\frac{5}{8} \\ -\ 2\frac{3}{8} \\ \hline \frac{2}{8} \end{array}$$

STEP 4 Then subtract the whole numbers.

$$\begin{array}{r} 5\frac{5}{8} \\ -\ 2\frac{3}{8} \\ \hline 3\frac{2}{8} \end{array}$$

The fractional part of $3\frac{2}{8}$ can be simplified.

$$\frac{2}{8} = \frac{2 \div 2}{8 \div 2} = \frac{1}{4}$$

$$3\frac{2}{8} = 3\frac{1}{4}$$

SOLUTION **Suzanne had $3\frac{1}{4}$ cans of dog food left.**

EXAMPLE 2

Add: $1\frac{2}{3} + 6\frac{2}{3} =$ _____

STRATEGY

Add the fractions. Then add the whole numbers.

STEP 1   Rewrite the problem vertically and add the fractions.

$$\begin{array}{r} 1\frac{2}{3} \\ + 6\frac{2}{3} \\ \hline \frac{4}{3} \end{array}$$

STEP 2   Then add the whole numbers.

$$\begin{array}{r} 1\frac{2}{3} \\ + 6\frac{2}{3} \\ \hline 7\frac{4}{3} \end{array}$$

STEP 3   Rename the answer.

$\frac{4}{3}$ is an improper fraction, so rename $7\frac{4}{3}$.

$\frac{4}{3} = 4 \div 3 = 1\frac{1}{3}$

$7\frac{4}{3} = 7 + \frac{4}{3} = 7 + 1\frac{1}{3} = 8\frac{1}{3}$

SOLUTION

The sum is $8\frac{1}{3}$.

CHECK IT OUT with the Coach™

What is the sum of $1\frac{1}{5}$ and $2\frac{3}{5}$?

Let's check it out.

The mixed numbers have like denominators because each has a denominator

of _____.

To solve the problem, first add the fractions.

$\frac{1}{5} + \frac{3}{5} =$ _____

Then add the whole numbers.

$1 + 2 =$ _____

The sum of $1\frac{1}{5}$ and $2\frac{3}{5}$ is _____.

Sample Test Questions

1 $\frac{3}{10} - \frac{2}{10} =$ _____

    A $\frac{1}{10}$

    B $\frac{2}{10}$

    C $\frac{5}{10}$

    D $1\frac{1}{10}$

2 $\frac{3}{5} - \frac{3}{5} =$ _____

    F $1\frac{1}{5}$

    G $\frac{3}{5}$

    H $\frac{1}{5}$

    J   0

3 $5\frac{7}{10} - 3\frac{4}{10} =$ _____

    A $2\frac{1}{10}$

    B $2\frac{1}{5}$

    C $2\frac{3}{10}$

    D $8\frac{3}{10}$

4 $1\frac{5}{8} + 5\frac{4}{8} =$ _____

    F $7\frac{1}{8}$

    G $7\frac{1}{4}$

    H $7\frac{3}{8}$

    J $7\frac{5}{8}$

5 $7\frac{9}{10} - 1\frac{1}{10} =$ _____

    A $6\frac{4}{5}$

    B $6\frac{7}{10}$

    C $6\frac{3}{5}$

    D $6\frac{3}{10}$

6   Joanna ate $\frac{2}{8}$ of a pizza and her brother Jorge ate $\frac{3}{8}$ of the same pizza. What fraction of the pizza did they eat together?

    F $\frac{1}{8}$

    G $\frac{5}{8}$

    H $\frac{7}{8}$

    J   1

7   Alicia filled a glass of water so it was $\frac{3}{4}$ full. She drank some water until the glass was $\frac{1}{4}$ full. How much water did she drink?

    Answer _____

8 Three-fifths of the students at Hamilton Elementary School walk to school. One-fifth of the students travel by bus. What fraction of the students walk or come to school by bus?

Answer _____

Short-Response Question

9 Courtney needs to figure out how many cantaloupes she and her friends ate. At breakfast, they ate $1\frac{3}{4}$ cantaloupes. At lunch, they ate $1\frac{1}{4}$ more cantaloupes.

Part A

How many cantaloupes did Courtney and her friends eat all together?

Answer _____ cantaloupes

Part B

Use words and/or numbers to explain how you found your answer.

_____

_____

_____

LESSON 30

Strand 1: Number Sense and Operations

Adding and Subtracting Decimals

5.N.23 Use a variety of strategies to add, subtract, multiply, and divide decimals to thousandths

Knowing how to add and subtract decimals can help you solve a variety of problems, including problems involving money. Use these steps to add or subtract two decimals.

How to Add or Subtract Decimals

1. Write the problem vertically, with the decimal points lined up.

2. Add or subtract.

3. Place the decimal point in the answer, lined up under the other decimal points.

EXAMPLE 1

Tripp walked 2.75 miles on Wednesday and 4.25 miles on Thursday. How far did he walk on those two days all together?

STRATEGY **Determine whether you should add or subtract. Then solve the problem.**

STEP 1 Which operation should you use?

The question asks how far he walked on Wednesday and Thursday.

So, use addition. Add 4.25 miles to 2.75 miles.

STEP 2 Set up the addition. Line up the decimal points.

$$\begin{array}{r} 2.75 \\ + 4.25 \\ \hline \end{array}$$

STEP 3 Add the numbers. Then bring down the decimal point.

$$\begin{array}{r} 2.75 \\ + 4.25 \\ \hline 7.00 \end{array}$$

7.00 miles is the same as 7 miles.

SOLUTION **Tripp walked 7 miles on those two days.**

EXAMPLE 2

Lorraine has a red ribbon that is 2.55 meters long and a yellow ribbon that is 1.415 meters long. How much longer is the red ribbon than the yellow ribbon?

STRATEGY

Determine whether you should add or subtract. Then solve the problem.

STEP 1   Which operation should you use?

The question asks how much longer the red ribbon is.

So, use subtraction.

Subtract the length of the yellow ribbon from the length of the red ribbon.

STEP 2   Set up the subtraction. Line up the decimal points.

$$\begin{array}{r} 2.55 \\ -\,1.415 \\ \hline \end{array}$$

STEP 3   Subtract the numbers.

Add a zero to 2.55. (Remember: 2.55 = 2.550.) Then regroup and subtract.

$$\begin{array}{r} 2.5\overset{4}{5}\overset{1}{0} \\ -\,1.415 \\ \hline 1.135 \end{array}$$

SOLUTION

The red ribbon is 1.135 meters longer than the yellow ribbon.

CHECK IT OUT with the Coach™

How much do a 3.75-gram paper clip and a 2.53-gram paper clip weigh all together?

Let's check it out.

The question asks how much two paper clips weigh all together.

So, the operation that you should use is _____.

When you set up the problem vertically, be sure to line up the

_____.

Then _____ the decimals to find the answer.

The paper clips weigh _____ grams all together.

Sample Test Questions

1 Add: 0.272 + 1.498 = _____

A 0.177

B 0.187

C 1.77

D 1.87

2 Add: 8.083 + 0.95 = _____

F 8.898

G 9.033

H 88.98

J 90.33

3 Subtract: 0.821 − 0.578 = _____

A 0.243

B 0.253

C 0.359

D 0.369

4 Subtract: 5.86 − 3.318 = _____

F 3.171

G 2.552

H 2.542

J 2.458

5 Tom has 6.895 meters of string. If he cuts off a piece that is 4.99 meters long and uses it for a project, how much string will he have left?

A 1.095 meters

B 1.905 meters

C 2.095 meters

D 2.905 meters

6 Carolyn practiced her flute for 1.5 hours on Saturday. She practiced for 0.75 hour on Sunday. How many hours did she practice in total on those two days?

F 0.76 hour

G 0.9 hour

H 2.25 hours

J 2.5 hours

7 Tyrone and Jacey measured their classroom. Tyrone measured the width of the classroom as 5.53 meters. Jacey measured the width of the classroom as 5.525 meters. By how much do their measurements differ?

Answer _____

8 Richard spent $2.57 on snacks at the beach. He spent $3.25 on a sandwich later on. He spent $2.94 on flowers on the way home. How much money did Richard spend all together?

Answer _____

Short-Response Question

9 Yoko buys two kinds of nuts. She buys 1.125 kilograms (kg) of almonds and 3.9 kilograms of cashews.

Part A

How many kilograms of nuts does she buy in all?

Show your work.

Answer _____

Part B

Use words and/or numbers to explain how you solved the problem.

_____

_____

_____

LESSON 31

Strand 1: Number Sense and Operations

Multiplying and Dividing Decimals

5.N.23 Use a variety of strategies to add, subtract, multiply, and divide decimals to thousandths

To multiply two decimals, you need to remember some steps.

How to Multiply Decimals

1. Multiply the numbers without their decimal points.

2. Count the number of decimal places in each factor and add those numbers.

3. Place the decimal point in the product. Give the answer the sum of the decimal places found in Step 2.

EXAMPLE 1

Find the product.

$$\begin{array}{r} 4.13 \\ \times\,8.6 \\ \hline \end{array}$$

STRATEGY

Multiply the decimals using the steps above.

STEP 1   Multiply without the decimal points.

$$\begin{array}{r} 4.13 \\ \times\,8.6 \\ \hline 2478 \\ 3304 \\ \hline 35518 \end{array}$$

STEP 2   Add the number of decimal places in the two factors.

There are 2 decimal places in 4.13.

There is 1 decimal place in 8.6.

The sum of the decimal places is 3.

STEP 3   Place the decimal point in the product 3 places from the right.

35.518

SOLUTION

The product of the decimals is 35.518.

You can divide a decimal *by a whole number*. Doing this is similar to dividing whole numbers using long division.

EXAMPLE 2

Find the quotient.

$$9 \overline{)\, 64.8}$$

STRATEGY

First, set the decimal point in the quotient. Then divide.

STEP 1   Place the decimal point for the quotient directly above the decimal point of the dividend.

$$9 \overline{)\, 6\overset{.}{4}.8}$$

STEP 2   Find the first digit of the quotient.

How many 9's are in 64?

The answer is 7.

Write 7 above the 4.

$$9 \overline{)\, \overset{7.}{64.8}}$$

STEP 3   Multiply and subtract.

$7 \times 9 = 63$ Subtract from 64.

$$
\begin{array}{r}
7. \\
9 \overline{)\, 64.8} \\
-63 \\
\hline
1
\end{array}
$$

STEP 4   Bring down the next digit of the dividend and continue using the steps of long division until you find the quotient.

$$
\begin{array}{r}
7.2 \\
9 \overline{)\, 64.8} \\
-63 \\
\hline
18 \\
-18 \\
\hline
0
\end{array}
$$

SOLUTION

The quotient is 7.2.

You can also divide a number *by a decimal*. To do this, remember these steps.

How to Divide by a Decimal

1. Change the divisor to a whole number by moving the decimal point as many places as necessary to the right.

2. Move the decimal point in the dividend the same number of places to the right.

3. Place the decimal point in the quotient.

4. Divide as you would divide whole numbers.

EXAMPLE 3

Find the quotient.

$$3.3\overline{)\,8.25}$$

STRATEGY

Follow the steps for dividing by a decimal.

STEP 1 Change the divisor to a whole number by moving the decimal point to the right.

Move the decimal point 1 place to the right: $3.3 \rightarrow 33$.

STEP 2 Move the decimal point in the dividend the same number of places to the right.

Move the decimal point 1 place to the right. $8.25 \rightarrow 82.5$

STEP 3 Rewrite the problem and place the decimal point in the quotient.

$$33\overline{)\,82.5}$$

STEP 4 Divide as you would divide whole numbers.

```
        2.5
  33) 82.5
     - 66
      165
    - 165
        0
```

SOLUTION

8.25 divided by 3.3 is 2.5.

CHECK IT OUT with the **Coach**™

How many decimal places should the product of 1.4 × 0.36 have?

Let's check it out.

How many decimal places does each of the original factors have?

1.4 has _____ decimal place(s).

0.36 has _____ decimal place(s).

Add those numbers to find how many decimal places the product should have.

The product should have _____ decimal places.

Sample Test Questions

Find each product or quotient.

1 38.27 × 1.5 = _____

- A 5,740.5
- B 574.05
- C 57.405
- D 5.7405

2 45.8 × 7.9 = _____

- F 3.6182
- G 36.182
- H 361.82
- J 3,618.2

3 2.43 × 45.1 = _____

- A 10.9593
- B 109.593
- C 1,095.93
- D 10,959.3

4 5$\overline{)34.5}$

- F 6.9
- G 7.0
- H 7.1
- J 7.2

5 8$\overline{)27.6}$

- A 3.45
- B 3.54
- C 34.5
- D 35.4

6 3.2$\overline{)76.8}$

- F 28
- G 26
- H 24
- J 23

7   2.8)‾8.68‾

   A   3.4

   B   3.3

   C   3.2

   D   3.1

8   Mr. Wilson has 1.6 kilograms of sunflower seeds. He divides the seeds into 4 bags so that each has the same weight. How much does each bag weigh?

   Answer _____

9   Dominique paid $5.25 for 3.5 pounds of green peppers. What was the cost per pound of green peppers?

   Answer _____

Short-Response Question

10   Martha paid $4.20 for 1.5 pounds of chicken at a supermarket.

Part A

What was the price per pound for chicken?

Show your work.

   Answer _____

Part B

Use words and/or numbers to explain how you found your answer and why you took the steps you did.

_____

_____

_____

LESSON 32

Strand 1: Number Sense and Operations

Rounding to the Nearest 100, 1,000 and 10,000

5.N.24 Round numbers to the nearest hundredth and up to 10,000

Rounding is one way of approximating numbers. Knowing how to round numbers is a useful skill. For example, you can round the cost of items you want to buy and add them to help you figure out the total cost.

USING A NUMBER LINE TO ROUND NUMBERS

You can use a number line to help you round numbers. Plot the number you are rounding between the two nearest hundreds, thousands, or ten thousands—whichever value you are rounding to. Round the number to the closest of those values. If a number is halfway between two values on a number line, round the number up.

EXAMPLE 1

Ping has $5,230 in a savings account. What is this amount rounded to the nearest thousand?

STRATEGY

Plot 5,230 on a number line to decide whether to round up or down.

STEP 1   5,230 is between which two thousands?

5,230 is between 5,000 and 6,000.

STEP 2   Is 5,230 closer to 5,000 or to 6,000?

This number line shows that 5,230 is closer to 5,000.

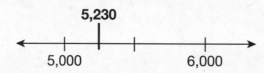

SOLUTION

$5,230 rounded to the nearest thousand is $5,000.

EXAMPLE 2

What is 67,350 rounded to the nearest hundred?

STRATEGY

Focus on the hundreds in 67,350 to determine which way to round.

STEP 1   What digit is in the hundreds place?

The digit 3 is in the hundreds place in 67,<u>3</u>50.

STEP 2   350 is between which two hundreds?

350 is between 300 and 400.

STEP 3   Is 350 closer to 300 or to 400?

350 is exactly halfway between 300 and 400.

So 67,350 rounds up to 67,400.

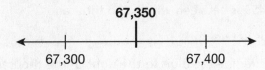

67,350

67,300   67,400

SOLUTION   **67,350 rounded to the nearest hundred is 67,400.**

USING RULES TO ROUND NUMBERS

Another way to round numbers is to look at the digits. Find the digit to the right of the place you are rounding to. Then follow these rules.

Rule 1:   If the digit to the right of the place you are rounding to is 4 or less, round down.

Rule 2:   If the digit to the right of the place you are rounding to is 5 or greater, round up.

EXAMPLE 3   The population of Middletown, New York, is 25,388. What is this number rounded to the nearest ten thousand?

STRATEGY   **Find the digit to the right of the ten thousands place. Then use the rules for rounding up or down.**

STEP 1   25,388 is between which two ten thousands?

25,388 is between 20,000 and 30,000.

STEP 2   What digit is to the right of the ten thousands place?

Underline the digit in the thousands place.

2<u>5</u>,388

STEP 3   Which rule applies?

Rule 2 applies. If the digit to the right of the place you are rounding to is 5 or greater, round up.

So, round 25,388 up to 30,000.

SOLUTION   **25,388 rounds up to 30,000.**

CHECK IT OUT *with the* **Coach**™

What is 3,459 rounded to the nearest thousand?

Let's check it out.

3,459 is between which two thousands?

It is between _____ and _____.

Underline the digit to the right of the thousands place in 3,459.

The digit _____ should be underlined.

Rule _____ applies because the digit to the right of the

thousands place is _____.

Should 3,459 be rounded up or down? It should be rounded _____.

So, 3,459 rounded to the nearest thousand is _____.

Sample Test Questions

1 What is 6,702 rounded to the nearest thousand?

A 6,000
B 6,500
C 6,700
D 7,000

2 What is 60,500 rounded to the nearest thousand?

F 60,000
G 61,000
H 61,500
J 70,000

3 What is 1,296 rounded to the nearest hundred?

A 200   C 1,200
B 300   D 1,300

4 What is 14,703 rounded to the nearest ten thousand?

F 10,000
G 14,000
H 14,700
J 15,000

5 What is 775,203 rounded to the nearest ten thousand?

A 700,000
B 770,000
C 780,000
D 800,000

6 The Mississippi River is 2,340 miles long. What is 2,340 rounded to the nearest hundred?

F 2,000   H 2,400
G 2,300   J 3,000

7 Which of these numbers does **not** round to 700 when it is rounded to the nearest hundred?

A 649

B 749

C 709

D 679

8 Which of these numbers does **not** round to 30,000 when it is rounded to the nearest ten thousand?

F 31,299

G 25,004

H 35,100

J 27,839

9 The distance between the moon and Earth is about 384,401 kilometers. What is this distance rounded to the nearest ten thousand?

Answer _____

10 A carnival was held to raise money for the local hospital. The carnival raised $11,692 for the hospital. What is that amount rounded to the nearest thousand?

Answer _____

Short-Response Question

11 Chantell is flying from New York City to Los Angeles, California, which is a distance of 2,462 miles.

Part A

What is 2,462 rounded to the nearest thousand?

Answer _____

Part B

Use words, numbers, and/or drawings to explain how you determined your answer for Part A.

_____

_____

_____

LESSON 33

Strand 1: Number Sense and Operations

Rounding Decimals

5.N.24 Round numbers to the nearest hundredth and up to 10,000

USING A NUMBER LINE TO ROUND DECIMALS

Just as you can use a number line to round whole numbers, you can also use number lines to round decimals.

EXAMPLE 1

A living room is 4.75 meters long. Round 4.75 to the nearest whole number.

STRATEGY

Use a number line to round 4.75.

STEP 1   4.75 is between which two whole numbers?

           4.75 is between 4 and 5.

STEP 2   Place 4.75 on a number line.

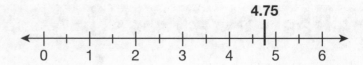

STEP 3   Is 4.75 closer to 4 or to 5?

           4.75 is closer to 5.

SOLUTION

4.75 rounded to the nearest whole number is 5. The living room is about 5 meters long.

USING RULES TO ROUND DECIMALS

You can use the same rules to round decimals that you use to round whole numbers. Find the digit to the right of the place you are rounding to.

Rule 1:   If the digit to the right of the place you are rounding to is 4 or less, round down.

Rule 2:   If the digit to the right of the place you are rounding to is 5 or greater, round up.

EXAMPLE 2

Round 23.68 to the nearest tenth.

STRATEGY

Use the rules for rounding decimals.

STEP 1   23.68 is between which two tenths?

23.68 is between 23.6 and 23.7.

STEP 2   Underline the digit to the right of the tenths place.

In other words, underline the digit in the hundredths place: 23.6<u>8</u>.

STEP 3   Use the rules for rounding decimals.

The digit to the right of the tenths place is 8.

Rule 2 applies. Round 23.68 up to 23.7.

SOLUTION

23.68 rounded to the nearest tenth is 23.7.

CHECK IT OUT *with the* **Coach**™

To round $16.72 to the nearest dollar, should you round up or down?

Let's check it out.

$16.72 is between which two whole dollar amounts?

It is between _____ and _____.

Underline the digit to the right of the ones place in $16.72.

The digit _____ should be underlined.

Which rule applies? _____

Should $16.72 be rounded up or down?

It should be rounded _____.

Sample Test Questions

1 What is 23.72 rounded to the nearest whole number?

  A 20

  B 23

  C 24

  D 30

2 What is 34.81 rounded to the nearest tenth?

  F 34.9

  G 34.8

  H 34.7

  J 34.1

3 What is 9.485 rounded to the nearest hundredth?

  A 9.4

  B 9.48

  C 9.49

  D 9.5

4 Dennis said that 10,000 meters is about 6.2 miles. Which of the following numbers rounds to 6.2 when rounded to the nearest tenth?

  F 6.21

  G 6.25

  H 6.27

  J 6.14

5 Ms. Wu spent $97.43 on groceries. What is $97.43 rounded to the nearest dollar?

  A $95

  B $97

  C $98

  D $100

6 Anna rounded the amount of money in her wallet to the nearest dollar and decided she had $80. Which of these amounts could be in her wallet?

  F $80.50

  G $79.48

  H $79.75

  J $83.12

7 Which of these amounts rounds to $40 when rounded to the nearest dollar?

  A $39.49

  B $39.45

  C $40.50

  D $40.49

8 What is 0.955 rounded to the nearest hundredth?

  F 0.95

  G 0.96

  H 0.97

  J 0.98

9 What is 67.205 rounded to the nearest hundredth?

Answer _____

10 A box weighs 4.53 kilograms. What is this number rounded to the nearest tenth?

Answer _____

Short-Response Question

11 Tanya spent $8.49 on dinner.

Part A

What is this amount rounded to the nearest dollar?

Answer _____

Part B

Use words, numbers, and/or drawings to explain how you determined your answer for Part A.

_____

_____

_____

LESSON 34

Strand 1: Number Sense and Operations

Estimating Sums and Differences of Fractions with Like Denominators

5.N.25 Estimate sums and differences of fractions with like denominators

It is not always necessary to find an exact answer to a problem. Sometimes finding an **estimate**, a number that is close to the exact answer, is good enough. We make estimates of distances, weights, and many other things in real life.

EXAMPLE 1

Estimate the sum: $\frac{2}{5} + \frac{2}{5}$

STRATEGY **Use a number line to round the fractions to the nearest half. Then add.**

STEP 1   Round the fractions.

$\frac{2}{5}$ is between 0 and $\frac{1}{2}$ on the number line, but it is closer to $\frac{1}{2}$.

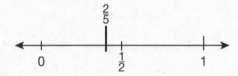

So, round $\frac{2}{5}$ up to $\frac{1}{2}$.

STEP 2   Add the rounded fractions.

$\frac{1}{2} + \frac{1}{2} = \frac{2}{2}$, which is equal to 1 whole.

So, the estimated sum is 1.

Because you rounded $\frac{2}{5}$ up to $\frac{1}{2}$, the actual answer will be a little less than 1.

SOLUTION **The estimated sum is 1. The actual answer will be a little less than 1.**

EXAMPLE 2

Five years ago, Anajilena was $4\frac{1}{6}$ feet tall. Now, she is $5\frac{2}{6}$ feet tall. Anajilena says she grew about one foot during that time. Is that a good estimate?

STRATEGY

Use a number line to round the fractions to the nearest whole number. Then subtract them.

STEP 1   Round each mixed number to the nearest whole number.

Plot $4\frac{1}{6}$ and $5\frac{2}{6}$ on a number line.

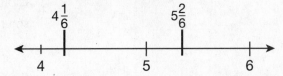

$4\frac{1}{6}$ is closer to 4 than to 5, so round $4\frac{1}{6}$ down to 4.

$5\frac{2}{6}$ is closer to 5 than to 6, so round $5\frac{2}{6}$ down to 5.

STEP 2   Subtract the rounded numbers.

$5 - 4 = 1$

Both numbers were rounded down, so Anajilena did grow about 1 foot during that time.

SOLUTION

Yes, one foot is a good estimate of how much Anajilena grew during those five years.

CHECK IT OUT with the Coach™

How would you estimate $\frac{7}{10} + \frac{1}{10}$?

Let's check it out.

Round each fraction to the nearest whole number.

$\frac{7}{10}$ rounds to _____.

$\frac{1}{10}$ rounds to _____.

So, a good way to estimate this sum would be to add

_____ + _____.

Sample Test Questions

1 Which is the best estimate of $\frac{9}{10} + \frac{5}{10}$?

A $\frac{1}{2}$

B $1\frac{1}{2}$

C 2

D $2\frac{1}{2}$

2 Which is the best estimate of $2\frac{2}{5} - 1\frac{1}{5}$?

F 0

G 1

H 2

J 3

3 Which of the following is the best way to estimate this difference?

$$7\frac{5}{6} - 3\frac{4}{6}$$

A $7 - 4$

B $7 - 5$

C $8 - 3$

D $8 - 4$

4 Which of the following is the best way to estimate this sum?

$$\frac{5}{12} + \frac{4}{12}$$

F $\frac{1}{2} + \frac{1}{2}$

G $1 + 1$

H $1\frac{1}{2} + 1\frac{1}{2}$

J $1 + 2$

5 Nadia spent $\frac{3}{4}$ of an hour reading a novel and $\frac{2}{4}$ of an hour watching television. Which of these gives the best estimate of the total amount of time she spent doing these two activities?

A $\frac{1}{2}$ hour

B $1\frac{1}{2}$ hours

C 2 hours

D $2\frac{1}{2}$ hours

6 Cedric bought two types of cheese. He bought $1\frac{2}{8}$ pounds of pepperjack cheese and $1\frac{7}{8}$ pounds of cheddar cheese. Which is the best estimate of how many pounds of cheese he bought in all?

F 1

G 2

H 3

J 4

7 Archana jogged $4\frac{2}{5}$ miles on Saturday and $2\frac{1}{5}$ miles on Monday. Estimate how many more miles she jogged on Saturday than on Sunday.

Answer _____

8   A rope is $5\frac{7}{10}$ meters long and a piece of string is $\frac{9}{10}$ meters long. Estimate how much longer the rope is than the string.

Answer _____

Short-Response Question

9   Jean-Marc bought two kinds of fruit at the supermarket. He bought $4\frac{1}{8}$ pounds of bananas and $4\frac{6}{8}$ pounds of oranges.

Part A

Estimate the total number of pounds of fruit that Jean-Marc bought.

Estimate _____ pounds

Part B

Explain how you estimated your answer for Part A and why you took the steps that you did.

_____

_____

_____

LESSON 35

Strand 1: Number Sense and Operations

Estimating Sums, Differences, Products, and Quotients of Decimals

5.N.26   Estimate sums, differences, products, and quotients of decimals

In real life, knowing how to estimate answers involving decimals is a useful skill. It is particularly useful when you need to estimate how much money you need to buy several items or how much change you should get back.

EXAMPLE 1

Nick earns $203.80 each day he works. About how much does he earn in a 5-day week?

STRATEGY

Decide which operation to use. Then estimate the answer.

STEP 1   Which operation should you use?

The question asks how much he earns in 5 days.

Since he earns the same amount each day, you can multiply to solve the problem.

STEP 2   Round $203.80 to the nearest ten dollars.

The digit to the right of the tens place is 3: $203.80.

Round the amount down to $200.

STEP 3   Multiply the rounded amount by the number of days.

$5 \times 200 = 1,000$

SOLUTION

Nick earns about $1,000 in a 5-day week.

EXAMPLE 2

Kayleigh had two bags of potatoes. The first bag weighed 8.25 kilograms. The second bag weighed 7.73 kilograms. Estimate, to the nearest whole number, the total weight of the two bags of potatoes.

STRATEGY

Decide which operation to use. Then estimate the answer.

STEP 1   Which operation should you use?

The question asks for the total weight of the two bags.

Since each bag weighs a different amount, you should add the amounts to find the total.

STEP 2   Round the decimals.

8.25 rounded to the nearest whole number is 8.

7.73 rounded to the nearest whole number is 8.

STEP 3   Add the rounded numbers.

$$8 + 8 = 16$$

SOLUTION   **A good estimate of the total weight of the two bags is 16 kilograms.**

When you need to estimate a quotient, using rounded numbers is not always the best idea. Instead, choose **compatible numbers**. Compatible numbers are numbers that are close to the given numbers, and are easy to divide mentally.

EXAMPLE 3   Eleven people had lunch in a restaurant. With tax and tip, the total came to $95.60. If they divide the check evenly, about how much will each person pay?

STRATEGY   **Decide which operation to use. Then estimate the answer.**

STEP 1   Which operation should you use?

Since the total cost is being divided evenly among 11 people, division should be used.

STEP 2   Choose compatible numbers that are easy to divide.

$95.60 is close in value to $96.

11 will not divide $96 evenly, but 11 will divide $99 evenly.

So, divide 99 by 11 to estimate the quotient.

STEP 3   Divide the compatible numbers.

$$99 \div 11 = 9$$

SOLUTION   **Each person will pay about $9.**

CHECK IT OUT with the **Coach**™

What is a good estimate of 14.4 ÷ 3.05?

Let's check it out.

Choose compatible numbers.

What two numbers are close in value to the given numbers and easy to divide?

The number _____ is close to 14.4 and the number _____ is close to 3.05.

Those numbers are also easy to divide.

Divide the compatible numbers.

_____ ÷ _____ = _____

So, a good estimate is _____.

Sample Test Questions

1 Which of the following is the best estimate of 25.9 + 16.2?

A 32

B 35

C 42

D 52

2 Which is the best estimate of 31.8 × 21?

F 50

G 60

H 500

J 600

3 Which of the following would **not** give a good estimate of 387.16 − 192.58?

A 387 − 193

B 400 − 200

C 390 − 190

D 300 − 200

4 Which of the following is the best estimate of 24.8 ÷ 7.9?

F 3

G 4

H 5

J 17

5 Sonia finds a red shirt and a black shirt that she likes. The red shirt costs $14.95. The black shirt costs $20.10. About how much more does the black shirt cost than the red shirt?

A $1.33

B $5.00

C $7.00

D $10.00

6 Tom saves $48.50 each month. Which is the best estimate of how much he will save at the end of one year?

F $300

G $350

H $400

J $600

7 Melissa's tomato plant grew 59.13 centimeters in 4 weeks. What is a good estimate of the average number of centimeters the plant grew each week?

Answer _____

8 Abdul buys three items for lunch: a sandwich for $3.35, a bottle of water for $1.05, and a salad for $2.89. If those prices include tax, about how much does he pay for lunch?

Answer _____

Short-Response Question

9 Hank wants to cut a 55.24-inch board into 9 pieces, each the same length.

Part A

Estimate the length of each piece.

Estimate _____ inches

Part B

Explain how you estimated this answer and why you took the steps that you did.

_____

_____

_____

LESSON 36

Strand 1: Number Sense and Operations

Justifying the Reasonableness of Answers by Using Estimations

5.N.27 Justify the reasonableness of answers using estimation

EXAMPLE 1

Anton is one of four workers who will help carry boxes into the school. There are 63 boxes, each with 37 paperback books in them. Anton and the others will carry about the same number of books into the school. He estimates that if he carries about 400 books, he will have done his fair share. Is his estimate reasonable?

STRATEGY **Estimate how many books each worker should carry. Compare Anton's estimate to your estimate.**

STEP 1 Which operation or operations should you use to estimate the answer?

Since each box contains the same number of books, multiply to estimate the total number of books. Then divide to find how many books each person should carry.

STEP 2 Estimate the total number of books.

There are 63 boxes with 37 books in each.

63 rounds to 60 and 37 rounds to 40.

$60 \times 40 = 2,400$

So there are about 2,400 books in total.

STEP 3 Divide to estimate the number of books each worker should carry.

There are 4 workers.

Since 2,400 and 4 are compatible numbers, divide.

$2,400 \div 4 = 600$

STEP 4 Is the estimate Anton made reasonable?

No, he underestimated how many books he should carry.

To be fair, each person should carry about 600 books.

SOLUTION **The estimate Anton made is not reasonable. Each worker should carry about 600 books, not 400 books, into the school.**

EXAMPLE 2

Yvette buys two items at a store: a CD for $15.79 and a DVD for $22.13. Those prices include tax, and Yvette pays the clerk $40. She estimates that she should get about $2 back in change. Is her estimate reasonable?

STRATEGY

Estimate how much change Yvette should receive. Compare Yvette's estimate to your estimate.

STEP 1 Which operation or operations should you use to estimate your answer?

Since each item costs a different amount, add to find the estimated total. Then subtract to estimate the change.

STEP 2 Estimate the total cost.

$15.79 rounded to the nearest dollar is $16.

$22.13 rounded to the nearest dollar is $22.

16 + 22 = 38, so the estimated cost is about $38.

STEP 3 Subtract the estimated cost from $40 to estimate the change.

40 − 38 = 2, so she should get back about $2 in change.

STEP 4 Compare your estimate to Yvette's estimate.

Yes, Yvette's estimate is reasonable. She should get about $2 in change.

SOLUTION

Yvette's estimate is reasonable. She should receive about $2 in change.

CHECK IT OUT with the Coach™

Caitlyn wants to buy 8 magazines, each of which costs $2.95. She has $16 and estimates that this is enough money to buy all 8 magazines. Is her estimate reasonable?

Let's check it out.

Round $2.95 to the nearest dollar.

$2.95 is about _____.

Multiply to estimate the cost of all 8 magazines.

_____ × 8 = _____

Caitlyn has $16. She needs about _____ to buy the magazines.

So, her estimate is _____.

Sample Test Questions

1 Armen needs 122 fluid ounces of cranberry juice to make fruit punch. There are 33.8 fluid ounces of juice in each bottle. Which is a good estimate of the number of bottles of juice he should buy?

A   1

B   2

C   3

D   4

2 Kaleesha bought 4.2 pounds of tuna salad. She paid a total of $16.38 for the tuna salad. Kaleesha estimates how much the tuna salad costs per pound. Which of these shows a good estimate of this cost?

F $2 per pound

G $3 per pound

H $4 per pound

J $5 per pound

3 Ms. Allen bought a pack of 107 marbles which she will divide equally among her 3 children. She estimates that she can give each child about 50 marbles. Which statement is true about her estimate?

A   Her estimate is very reasonable.

B   Her estimate is too high. She can give each child about 45 marbles.

C   Her estimate is too high. She can give each child about 35 marbles.

D   Her estimate is too low. She can give each child about 65 marbles.

4 Gillian buys 6 hair clips, each of which costs $2.09 including tax. She pays the clerk with a $20 bill and quickly estimates that her change should be $12. Which statement is true about her estimate?

F   Her estimate is very reasonable.

G   Her estimate is about $4 too low.

H   Her estimate is about $4 too high.

J   Her estimate is about $10 too high.

5 Brent has three puppies. The weights of the puppies are: $5\frac{7}{8}$ pounds, $6\frac{1}{8}$ pounds, and $5\frac{3}{4}$ pounds. He needs to take all his puppies to the vet's office in a pet carrier. He estimates that the total weight of all three puppies will be about 12 pounds. Which statement is true about his estimate?

A   His estimate is very reasonable.

B   His estimate is about 6 pounds too low.

C   His estimate is about 3 pounds too high.

D   His estimate is about 6 pounds too high.

6 Gaby is one of 4 students who is helping to photocopy 122 programs for the school play. Each program will have 6 pages in it. In order to be fair, Gaby thinks that each student should photocopy about the same number of pages. She estimates that each student should photocopy about 180 pages. Which statement is true about her estimate?

F Her estimate is very reasonable.

G Her estimate is about 50 pages too low.

H Her estimate is about 100 pages too high.

J Her estimate is about 50 pages too high.

7 Anita buys two items at the computer store: a computer program for $36.25 and a printer ribbon for $26.95. Both of those prices include tax. Anita pays the clerk $80 and quickly estimates how much change she should receive. What is a reasonable estimate of the change she should receive?

Answer _____

8 Shawn is one of 3 students helping to reshelve books in the school library. There are 5 carts of books to reshelve and each cart has 46 books on it. In order to be fair, Shawn thinks that each student should reshelve about the same number of books. What is a reasonable estimate of the number of books each student should reshelve?

Answer _____

Short-Response Question

9 Mr. Soldati buys 29 portfolios for his office. Each portfolio costs $15.10. He pays the clerk $500.

Part A

He estimates that he should receive about $20 in change. Is his estimate reasonable? If not, what would be a reasonable estimate?

Answer _____

Part B

Use words and/or numbers to explain how you determined what a reasonable estimate of the change would be.

_____

_____

Progress Check for Lessons 25–36

1 $21\overline{)842}$

    A   40 R2

    B   41

    C   41 R1

    D   41 R2

2 $284 \times 126 = \underline{\hspace{1cm}}$

    F   36,784

    G   35,784

    H   25,784

    J   2,556

3   A company manufactured 65,295 pens on Tuesday. What is this number rounded to the nearest ten thousand?

    A   60,000

    B   65,000

    C   65,300

    D   70,000

4   Which mixed number is equivalent to $\frac{13}{3}$?

    F $3\frac{1}{3}$

    G $3\frac{2}{3}$

    H $4\frac{1}{3}$

    J $4\frac{2}{3}$

5   A group of students is placing 904 pencils into boxes. Each box can hold 32 pencils, and the students are filling each box to capacity. Nari estimated that they would use about 30 boxes to complete the task. Which statement is true about Nari's estimate?

    A   His estimate is reasonable.

    B   His estimate is too low. A better estimate is 40 boxes.

    C   His estimate is too low. A better estimate is 300 boxes.

    D   His estimate is too high. A better estimate is 20 boxes.

6   Solve: $\frac{7}{10} - \frac{3}{10} = \underline{\hspace{1cm}}$

    F $\frac{1}{10}$

    G $\frac{3}{10}$

    H $\frac{2}{5}$

    J $\frac{4}{5}$

7   Ms. Martinez spent $145.79 on a new appliance. What is that amount rounded to the nearest dollar?

    A $140

    B $145

    C $146

    D $150

8 What is the value of this expression?

$$18 + (5 - 3) \times 2$$

F 17

G 22

H 34

J 40

9 Delilah saves $405.76 each year. If she continues saving at this rate, what is a reasonable estimate of how much money she will have saved in 8 years?

A $2,800

B $3,200

C $3,800

D $4,000

10 A scientist is measuring the masses of two substances. Substance A measures 1.97 grams. Substance B measures 2.675 grams. How much more is the mass of Substance B than Substance A?

F 0.705 gram

G 1.525 grams

H 2.478 grams

J 4.645 grams

11 $2.6\overline{)9.36}$

A 0.36

B 3.6

C 36

D 360

12 Add: $4\frac{1}{8} + 1\frac{5}{8} = $ _____

F $3\frac{1}{2}$

G $5\frac{1}{4}$

H $5\frac{1}{2}$

J $5\frac{3}{4}$

13 Curtis buys 3.8 pounds of egg salad at a cost of $2.05 per pound. About how much does he pay for the egg salad?

A $2

B $5

C $6

D $8

14 Leonard is $5\frac{2}{12}$ feet tall. His younger brother Terrence is $4\frac{1}{12}$ feet tall. Which is the best estimate of how much taller Leonard is than Terrence?

F $\frac{1}{2}$ foot

G 1 foot

H 2 feet

J $2\frac{1}{2}$ feet

Open-Ended Questions

Short-Response Question

15 Beth has $2\frac{2}{3}$ yards of trim to make costumes for the class play. She needs another $3\frac{2}{3}$ yards of trim to complete the costumes.

Part A

How many yards of trim will she use in all to make the costumes?
Write your answer as a mixed number.

Show your work.

Answer _____ yards

Part B

Use words and/or numbers to explain how you found your answer for Part A.

_____

_____

_____

Extended-Response Questions

16 Ms. Warner is buying furniture. She wants to spend $67.75 on a coffee table, $703.12 on a sofa, and $93.12 on a chair.

Part A

She estimates that the total cost of these items will be about $810. Is her estimate reasonable? If it is not reasonable, what would be a reasonable estimate?

Answer _____

Part B

Use words and/or numbers to explain how you determined your estimate for Part B.

_____

_____

Part C

Ms. Warner pays for the furniture with nine $100 bills. Estimate the amount of change she should expect to receive.

Estimate _____

Part D

Use words and/or numbers to explain how you determined what a reasonable estimate of the change would be.

_____

_____

17 Look at the problem below.

$$9\frac{9}{10} - 3\frac{7}{10} = \underline{\hspace{2cm}}$$

Part A

Estimate the solution to this problem.

Estimate _____

Part B

Use words and/or numbers to explain how you determined your estimate for Part A.

_____

_____

Part C

Now subtract the mixed numbers to find the exact solution. Simplify your answer.

Show your work.

Answer _____

Part D

Was the estimate you found in Part A close to the actual sum you found in Part C? Use words and/or numbers to explain.

_____

_____

_____

LESSON 37

Strand 2: Algebra

Algebraic Terminology

5.A.1 Define and use appropriate algebraic terminology when referring to constants, variables, and algebraic expressions

An expression includes numbers and operation signs $(+, -, \times, \div)$.

They do not include equals signs, or inequality symbols $(<, >, \text{ or } \neq)$.

Some expressions are **algebraic expressions**.

An algebraic expression has one or more **variables**. Variables are letters or symbols that stand for unknown numbers. These expressions all include variables:

$$3 + x \qquad b - a \qquad 5 \times \square \qquad 14 \div a$$

The expression $3 + x$ includes the variable x. It also includes a **constant**, 3. A constant in an expression is a value that does not change. So, while x can stand for any value, the constant 3 always has a value of 3.

EXAMPLE 1

Which is an algebraic expression?

  A $8 - 5$

  B $9 + 3 = 12$

  C $18 \div n$

  D $14 \times d > 186$

STRATEGY

Consider each answer. Eliminate those that are not expressions.

STEP 1   Look at Choice A.

      This is an expression, but there are no variables.

STEP 2   Look at Choice B.

      This is not an expression. It has an equals sign.

STEP 3   Look at Choice C.

      This is an expression, and it has a variable.

STEP 4   Look at Choice D.

      This is not an expression. It has a greater than sign $(>)$.

SOLUTION

Choice C is an algebraic expression.

EXAMPLE 2

What is the constant in this expression?

$$m \div 9$$

STRATEGY

Find the value that does not change.

The variable *m* can be any number, so its value can change.

The symbol / is an operation sign meaning division.

Only the 9 does not change, so 9 is the constant.

SOLUTION

The constant in the expression is 9.

CHECK IT OUT with the **Coach**™

What is the variable and what is the constant in the algebraic expression below?

186 − *j*

Let's check it out.

Which letter represents an unknown number? _____

Which value does not change? _____

So, _____ is the variable and _____ is the constant.

Sample Test Questions

1 What is the variable in this algebraic expression?

$$8x + 19$$

A 8

B *x*

C +

D 19

2 Which is an algebraic expression?

F 8*y*

G 9*y* = 72

H 17 + 9 > 12

J 22 < *x* + 3

3 What is the constant in the algebraic expression?

$$16t + g$$

A 16

B t

C +

D g

5 What is the constant in this algebraic expression?

$$6 + a \times b$$

A 6

B ×

C a

D b

4 Which is **not** an algebraic expression?

F $94w$

G $100 \div g$

H $15 + 81$

J $h - 37$

Short-Response Question

6 Julia picked from cards below while playing a game called "Make an Expression."

3 + < x = 8

Part A

Write an algebraic expression using three of the cards.

Answer _____

Part B

Which card used in Part A is the variable? Which card used in Part A is the constant?

_____

_____

_____

LESSON 38

Strand 2: Algebra

Using Formulas to Find Perimeter

5.A.6 Evaluate the perimeter formula for given input values
5.G.1 Calculate the perimeter of regular and irregular polygons

Formulas are useful in mathematics. A formula is an equation that shows a specific mathematical relationship. For example, you can use a formula to find the **perimeter** of a figure, such as a **polygon**. A polygon is a closed figure made up of **line segments** that meet at their endpoints. The perimeter of a polygon is the distance around it.

You can find the perimeter of a polygon by adding the lengths of all the sides. These formulas show how to add the lengths of the sides of triangles, quadrilaterals, and pentagons.

A **triangle** has three sides.

A **quadrilateral** has four sides.

A **pentagon** has five sides.

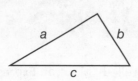

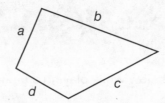

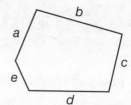

$$P = a + b + c \qquad P = a + b + c + d \qquad P = a + b + c + d + e$$

EXAMPLE 1

Find the perimeter of this triangle. Use the formula $P = a + b + c$, where a, b, and c are the lengths of the sides of a triangle.

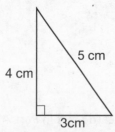

5 cm

4 cm

3cm

STRATEGY

Use the formula for the perimeter of a triangle.

The lengths of the sides are 3 cm, 4 cm, and 5 cm.

$P = a + b + c = 3 + 4 + 5 = 12$

SOLUTION

The perimeter of the triangle is 12 cm.

There are formulas for finding the perimeters of special quadrilaterals, such as parallelograms, rectangles, and squares.

A **parallelogram** is a quadrilateral with opposite sides that have the same length and are parallel.

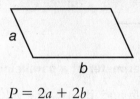

$$P = 2a + 2b$$

where b is the length of the base
and a is the length of the side next to the base

A **rectangle** is a parallelogram with four right angles (square corners) and with opposite sides the same length.

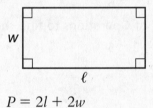

$$P = 2l + 2w$$

where l is the length and w is the width

A **square** is a rectangle with four sides that are all the same length.

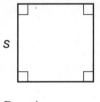

$$P = 4s$$

where s is the length of each side

EXAMPLE 2

What is the perimeter of this parallelogram? Use the formula $P = 2a + 2b$, where b is the base length and a is the length of the side next to the base.

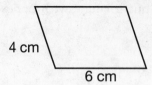

4 cm

6 cm

STRATEGY

Use the formula for the perimeter of a parallelogram.

STEP 1   Write the formula and identify the values of a and b.

$P = 2a + 2b$

The base is 6 cm long, so $b = 6$.

The other side is 4 cm long, so $a = 4$.

STEP 2   Substitute those values into the formula.

$P = 2a + 2b$

$P = 2 \times 4 + 2 \times 6$

STEP 3   Use the Order of Operations to find the perimeter.

$P = 2 \times 4 + 2 \times 6$

$= 8 + 12$

$= 20$

SOLUTION

The perimeter is 20 cm.

EXAMPLE 3

Mr. Palmer is building a fence around this yard. His yard is in the shape of a square. How many feet of fencing does he need to completely surround the yard? Use the formula $P = 4s$, where s is the length of a side.

20 ft | **Yard**

STRATEGY | **Use the formula for the perimeter of a square.**

STEP 1   Write the formula and identify the value of s.

$P = 4s$

Each side of the yard is 20 feet, so $s = 20$.

STEP 2   Substitute that value into the formula.

$P = 4s$

$P = 4 \times 20$

STEP 3   Find the perimeter.

$P = 4 \times 20 = 80$

The perimeter of the yard is 80 feet.

SOLUTION | **To surround the yard, Mr. Palmer needs 80 feet of fencing.**

CHECK IT OUT with the Coach™

What is the perimeter of a rectangle with a length of 8 cm and width of 3 cm?

Let's check it out.

What is the formula for the perimeter of a rectangle?

The formula is $P = 2l + 2w$, where l stands for the _____ and

w stands for the _____.

Substitute _____ for the length in the formula

and _____ for the width in the formula.

Then solve.

$P = 2 \times$ _____ $+ 2 \times$ _____ $=$ _____

The perimeter is _____ cm.

Sample Test Questions

1 What is the perimeter of this pentagon? (Use the formula $P = a + b + c + d + e$, where a, b, c, d, and e are the lengths of the sides.)

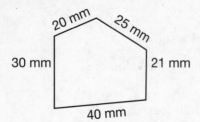

A 96 cm   **C** 137 cm

B 136 cm   **D** 140 cm

2 What is the perimeter of this quadrilateral? (Use the formula $P = a + b + c + d$, where a, b, c, and d are the lengths of the sides.)

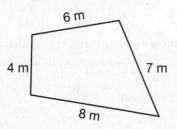

F 19 m

G 24 m

H 25 m

J 30 m

3 Use the formula $P = 2\ell + 2w$ to find the perimeter of a rectangle with $\ell = 4$ cm and $w = 3$ cm.

A 7 cm

B 6 cm

C 14 cm

D 30 cm

4 Use the formula $P = 4s$ to find the perimeter of a square with $s = 9$ meters.

F 13 meters

G 14 meters

H 32 meters

J 36 meters

5 Use the formula $P = 2a + 2b$ to find the perimeter of a parallelogram with $a = 5$ ft and $b = 7$ ft.

A 12 feet

B 16 feet

C 24 feet

D 84 feet

6 Cassie wants to put fencing around this triangular flower bed. How many yards of fencing will she need to surround the entire flower bed? (Use the formula $P = a + b + c$, where a, b, and c are the lengths of the sides.)

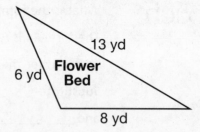

F 14 yd

G 27 yd

H 28 yd

J 36 yd

7 Shakir wants to put a border around this rectangular bulletin board.

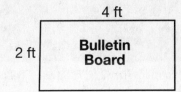

How many feet of border does he need? (Use the formula $P = 2\ell + 2w$, where ℓ is the length and w is the width.)

Answer _____

8 What is the perimeter of this square classroom? (Use $P = 4s$, where s is the length of each side.)

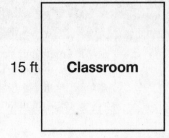

Answer _____

Short-Response Question

9 Rita used a computer program to draw this parallelogram. She labeled the lengths of two sides of her parallelogram.

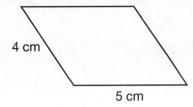

What is the perimeter of Rita's parallelogram? To find the perimeter of a parallelogram, use the formula $P = 2a + 2b$ where b is the length of the base and a is the length of the side next to the base.

Show your work.

Answer _____ cm

LESSON 39

Strand 2: Algebra

Algebraic and Geometric Patterns

5.A.7 Create and explain patterns and algebraic relationships (i.e., 2, 4, 6, 8, . . .) algebraically: 2*n* (doubling)

5.A.8 Create algebraic or geometric patterns using concrete objects or visual drawings (e.g., rotate and shade geometric shapes)

A **pattern** is a predictable arrangement of numbers or shapes. Patterns are everywhere. You encounter them in everyday life. For example, you may see patterns on wallpaper or on quilts. You may see patterns in nature.

There are many different kinds of patterns. Some patterns are number patterns, like this one:

2, 4, 6, 8, 10, . . .

Other patterns are **geometric patterns**, like this one:

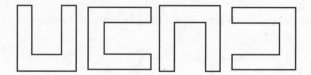

Geometric patterns are made with shapes.

RULES FOR NUMBER PATTERNS

All patterns follow rules. Sometimes, it helps to represent these rules with an algebraic expression.

Think back to the pattern 2, 4, 6, 8, 10 . . . This pattern can be represented by the rule 2*n*, where *n* stands for the position of the number in the pattern. Look at this table.

Position in Pattern (*n*)	Number (2*n*)
$n = 1$	$2n = 2 \times 1 = 2$
$n = 2$	$2n = 2 \times 2 = 4$
$n = 3$	$2n = 2 \times 3 = 6$
$n = 4$	$2n = 2 \times 4 = 8$
$n = 5$	$2n = 2 \times 5 = 10$

You could use the rule 2*n* to find the 100th number in the pattern.

When $n = 100$, $2n = 2 \times 100 = 200$. So, the 100th number in the pattern is 200.

EXAMPLE 1

Create a pattern that follows the rule 4*n*, where *n* represents the position of the number in the pattern. List the first five numbers in the pattern.

STRATEGY

Create a table to find the first five numbers in the pattern.

Make a table like this one.

Fill in the table.

Position in Pattern (*n*)	Number (4*n*)
n = 1	4*n* = 4 x 1 = **4**
n = 2	4*n* = 4 x 2 = **8**
n = 3	4*n* = 4 x 3 = **12**
n = 4	4*n* = 4 x 4 = **16**
n = 5	4*n* = 4 x 5 = **20**

So, the 1st number in the pattern is 4, the 2nd number is 8, and so on.

SOLUTION

The first five numbers in a 4*n* pattern are 4, 8, 12, 16, and 20.

RULES FOR GEOMETRIC PATTERNS

Geometric patterns follow rules, also. If you can determine the rule, you can create or add to geometric patterns.

EXAMPLE 2

Ahmad made a pattern by shading the squares in the first four figures below.

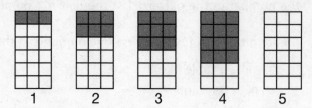

1   2   3   4   5

To continue this pattern, how should he shade Figure 5?

STRATEGY   **Find the rule. Use the rule to determine how many squares will be shaded in Figure 5.**

STEP 1   How does the shading of the shapes change?

The first row of Figure 1 is shaded.

The first 2 rows of Figure 2 are shaded.

The first 3 rows of Figure 3 are shaded.

The first 4 rows of Figure 4 are shaded.

So, the number of the figure tells how many rows should be shaded.

STEP 2   How many rows should be shaded in Figure 5?

The first 5 rows of Figure 5 should be shaded.

SOLUTION

CHECK IT OUT *with the* **Coach**™

A pattern follows the rule 8n, where n represents the position of a number in the pattern. What will the 20th number in this pattern be?

Let's check it out.

The 20th number is represented by $n =$ _____.

So, to find the number, multiply: $8n = 8 \times$ _____ $=$ _____.

The 20th number in the 8n pattern is _____.

Sample Test Questions

For Questions 1–5, *n* represents the position of a number in a pattern.

1 Which of the following patterns follows the rule 3*n*?

   A 1, 3, 5, 7, . . .

   B 3, 9, 27, 81, . . .

   C 2, 5, 8, 11, . . .

   D 3, 6, 9, 12, . . .

2 Which of the following patterns follows the rule 9*n*?

   F 1, 10, 19, 28, . . .

   G 9, 10, 11, 12, . . .

   H 6, 9, 12, 15, . . .

   J 9, 18, 27, 36, . . .

3 Marlena is writing a 5*n* pattern. What number should she write next to continue her pattern?

   5, 10, _____

   A 3

   B 15

   C 20

   D 50

4 Which rule fits this pattern?

   0.5, 1.0, 1.5, 2.0, . . .

   F $0.5 \times n$

   G $1 \times n$

   H $5 \times n$

   J $10 \times n$

5 A pattern follows the rule 8*n*. What is the 30th number in that pattern?

A	B	C	D
24	38	240	380

6 Jasper is creating a pattern by shading triangles.

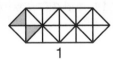 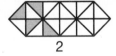 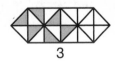

       1   2   3

If he continues his pattern, what should the 4th figure in the pattern look like?

     F   **G**   **H**   **J**

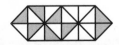   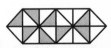

7 Emma drew an arrow on a computer screen. She copied and turned the arrows to make the first eight figures in this pattern.

If she continues this pattern, what will the 10th arrow in the pattern look like?

A

B

C

D

8 If the 1st, 2nd, and 4th numbers in a pattern are 7, 14, and 28, what is the 3rd number?

Answer _____

9 If the 2nd, 3rd, and 4th numbers in a pattern are 13, 19, and 25, what is the 1st number?

Answer _____

Short-Response Questions

 10   The figures below were shaded to form a pattern.

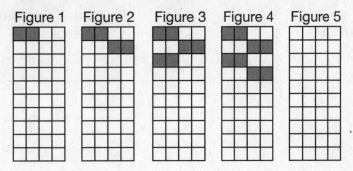

Part A

Draw and shade to show what Figure 5 would look like if the pattern were continued.

Part B

Describe the rule that this pattern follows and explain why you shaded Figure 5 as you did.

_____

_____

11   Tobe is creating a number pattern that follows the rule $6n$, where n represents the position of the number in the pattern.

Part A

What are the first five numbers in a $6n$ pattern?

Answer _____

Part B

Use words, tables, and/or numbers to explain how you used the rule $6n$ to determine the first five numbers in a pattern.

_____

_____

Progress Check for Lessons 37–39

1 What is the variable in this algebraic expression?

$$16 + k + 9$$

A 16

B +

C k

D 9

2 What is the value of the constant in the expression $a + 7 \times y$?

F a

G +

H 7

J y

3 Simone is creating a pattern by shading triangles.

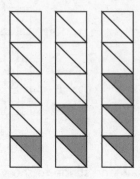

If she continues this pattern, what should the next figure in the pattern look like?

    A   B   C   D

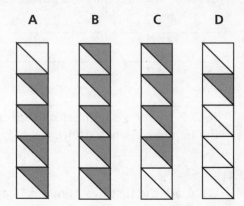

4 The formula for finding the perimeter of a triangle is $P = a + b + c$, where a, b, and c stand for the lengths of the sides. What is the perimeter of this triangle?

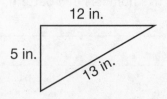

F 20 in.   H 29 in.

G 25 in.   J 30 in.

5 If *n* stands for the position of a number in a pattern, what would be the 10th number in a pattern that follows the rule 4*n*?

A   14

B   36

C   40

D   44

6 What is the perimeter of this rectangular sandbox? (Use the formula $P = 2\ell + 2w$ where ℓ stands for the length and *w* stands for the width.)

4 meters

| Sandbox | 3 meters |

F   16 meters

G   14 meters

H   12 meters

J   5 meters

Open-Ended Questions

Short-Response Question

7 Fernando is creating a number pattern that follows the rule 10*n*, where *n* represents the position of the number in the pattern.

Part A

What are the first five numbers in Fernando's pattern?

Answer _____

Part B

Use words, tables, and/or numbers to explain how you used the rule 10*n* to determine the first five numbers in the pattern.

_____

_____

_____

Extended-Response Question

8   Traci wrote the expression below. She wants to know the names of the parts of her expression.

$$4 + 2z$$

Part A

What is the variable of this expression?

Answer _____

Part B

What is the value of the constants in this expression?

Answer _____

Part C

Write another algebraic expression using the same variables and constants. Explain what must be included in an algebraic expression. Explain what may or may not be included.

_____

_____

_____

_____

_____

         Duplicating any part of this book is forbidden by law.

LESSON 40

Strand 3: Geometry

Perimeter of Polygons

5.A.6 Evaluate the perimeter formula for given input values
5.G.1 Calculate the perimeter of regular and irregular polygons

A **regular polygon** has all sides the same length and all **angles** the same measure. Here are some regular polygons. The tick marks show that the angles are equal in measure.

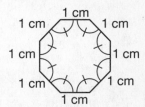

An **irregular polygon** is any polygon that is not regular. The polygons below are all irregular. Notice in each polygon that not all the side lengths and not all the angle measures are the same.

You can find the perimeter of regular and irregular polygons the same way you find the perimeter, *P*, of any polygon—by adding the lengths of the sides.

EXAMPLE 1

What is the perimeter of this irregular hexagon?

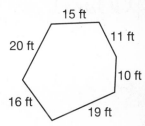

STRATEGY

Add the lengths of the sides.

This hexagon has 6 sides, so add all 6 lengths.

$P = 20 + 15 + 11 + 10 + 19 + 16 = 91$

SOLUTION

The perimeter of this hexagon is 91 feet.

EXAMPLE 2   What is the perimeter of this regular hexagon?

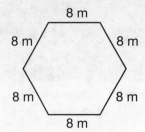

8 m
8 m   8 m
8 m   8 m
8 m

STRATEGY   **Add the lengths of the sides.**

This hexagon has 6 sides, so add all 6 lengths.

$P = 8 + 8 + 8 + 8 + 8 + 8 = 48$

Since six 8's is the same as 6×8, there is another way you could have found the perimeter.

P = (number of sides) $\times$ (length of side)

$P = 6 \times 8 = 48$

SOLUTION   **Whether you add or multiply, the perimeter of this figure is 48 m.**

In Lesson 38, you learned some formulas for finding perimeter. Example 2 introduced you to a formula that you can use to find the perimeter of a regular polygon. You can use this formula to find the perimeter of any regular polygon.

P = (number of sides) $\times$ (length of side)

CHECK IT OUT *with the* **Coach**™

If a regular polygon has 7 sides that are each 2 feet in length, how would you find its perimeter?

Let's check it out.

Since the polygon is regular, all the sides have the same _____.

The number of sides of the polygon is _____.

The length of each side is _____.

So, the formula for finding the perimeter of a regular polygon could be used.

P = (number of sides) $\times$ (length of each side)

$P =$ _____ $\times$ _____

$P =$ _____ feet

Sample Test Questions

1 What is the perimeter of this irregular pentagon?

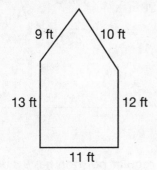

A 45 feet

B 50 feet

C 55 feet

D 56 feet

2 What is the perimeter of this irregular polygon?

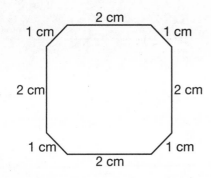

F 8 cm

G 12 cm

H 13 cm

J 16 cm

3 What is the perimeter of this regular pentagon?

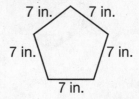

A 28 in.

B 35 in.

C 36 in.

D 42 in.

4 What is the perimeter of this irregular polygon?

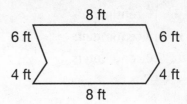

F 20 ft

G 28 ft

H 36 ft

J 48 ft

5 This tile is shaped like a regular hexagon. What is the perimeter of this tile?

9 mm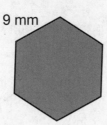

A   9 mm

B   36 mm

C   45 mm

D   54 mm

6 A regular polygon has 5 sides, each 4 centimeters in length. What is the perimeter of the polygon?

F   9 centimeters

G   16 centimeters

H   18 centimeters

J   20 centimeters

7 This irregular polygon shows a field. What is the perimeter of this field?

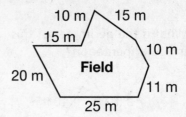

Answer _____

8 This regular polygon has 9 sides. What is the perimeter of this polygon?

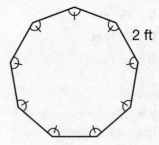

Answer _____

Short-Response Question

9 This diagram shows the plans for a deck that is shaped like a regular polygon.

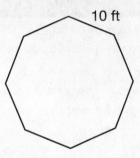

10 ft

Find the perimeter of the deck.

Show your work.

Answer _____ feet

LESSON 41

Strand 3: Geometry

Congruent Triangles

5.G.9 Identify pairs of congruent triangles
5.G.10 Identify corresponding parts of congruent triangles

Congruent figures have the same size and shape. Below are some examples of congruent triangles. Notice that two figures can be congruent even if they face different directions.

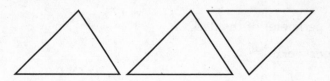

EXAMPLE 1

Which triangles are congruent?

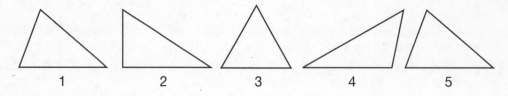

| 1 | 2 | 3 | 4 | 5 |

STRATEGY   **Find the two triangles that have the same size and shape.**

STEP 1   Which triangles have the same shape?

Triangles 1 and 5 have the same shape.

STEP 2   Do those triangles also have the same size?

Imagine placing one exactly on top of the other.

Yes, they look the same size.

SOLUTION   **Triangles 1 and 5 are congruent because they have the same size and shape.**

If two triangles are congruent, then

- corresponding sides of the triangles are congruent (have the same length), and

- corresponding angles of the triangles are congruent (have the same measure).

Look at these congruent triangles.

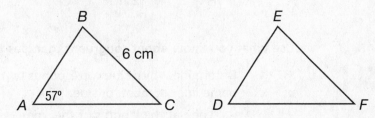

Triangle *ABC* is congruent to triangle *DEF*. So, corresponding sides such as side *AB* and side *DE* have the same length. Corresponding angles, such as angles *A* and *D*, have the same measure.

EXAMPLE 2

Triangle *JKL* is congruent to triangle *PQR*. What is the measure of angle *R*?

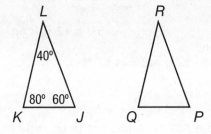

STRATEGY   **Use what you know about congruent triangles to determine the answer.**

STEP 1   Determine which angles are corresponding angles.

Look at the order of the letters in the triangles' names.

Since *J* is listed first in triangle *JKL* and *P* is listed first in triangle *PQR*, angles *J* and *P* are corresponding angles.

Angles *K* and *Q* are also corresponding angles, and angles *L* and *R* are corresponding angles.

STEP 2   Find the measure of ∠*R*. (Note that ∠*R* is another way to write angle *R*.)

Corresponding angles in congruent triangles have the same measure.

So, if ∠*L* measures 40°, ∠*R* measures 40°.

SOLUTION   **Angle *R* measures 40°.**

EXAMPLE 3

Triangle *FGH* is congruent to triangle *XYZ*. What is the length of side *YZ*?

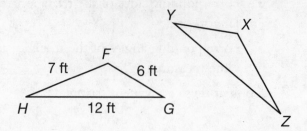

STRATEGY

Use what you know about congruent triangles to determine the answer.

STEP 1   Determine which side corresponds to $\overline{YZ}$. ($\overline{YZ}$ is another way to name line segment, or side, *YZ*.)

Look at the lengths of the sides.

$\overline{YZ}$ is the longest side of triangle *XYZ*.

$\overline{GH}$ is the longest side of triangle *FGH*.

So, $\overline{YZ}$ and $\overline{GH}$ are corresponding sides.

STEP 2   Find the length of $\overline{YZ}$.

Corresponding sides of congruent triangles have the same length.

So, if $\overline{GH}$ is 12 ft long, then $\overline{YZ}$ is 12 ft long.

SOLUTION

Side *YZ* measures 12 ft.

Triangle *ABC* is congruent to triangle *KLM*. Which angle in triangle *KLM* is congruent to angle *A*?

Let's check it out.

Use the order of the letters in the triangles' names to find corresponding angles.

Since *A* is listed first in triangle *ABC* and _____ is listed first in triangle *KLM*, angles *A* and _____ are corresponding angles.

Since corresponding angles of congruent triangles have the same

_____, angle *A* must be congruent to angle _____.

Sample Test Questions

1 Which triangles are congruent?

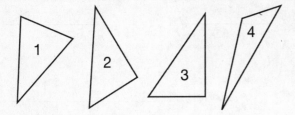

A Triangles 1 and 2

B Triangles 1 and 3

C Triangles 2 and 3

D Triangles 2 and 4

2 Which triangle is **not** congruent to the others?

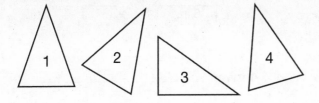

F Triangle 1

G Triangle 2

H Triangle 3

J Triangle 4

3 Triangle *PQR* is congruent to triangle *XYZ*. Which two angles are corresponding angles?

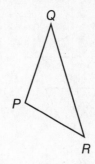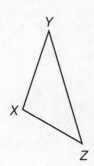

A ∠*P* and ∠*Y*

B ∠*Q* and ∠*Z*

C ∠*R* and ∠*Z*

D ∠*R* and ∠*X*

4 Triangle *DEF* is congruent to triangle *GHJ*. Which two sides are corresponding sides?

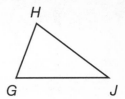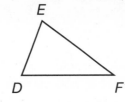

F $\overline{DF}$ and $\overline{HJ}$

G $\overline{DE}$ and $\overline{GH}$

H $\overline{EF}$ and $\overline{GH}$

J $\overline{DF}$ and $\overline{GH}$

5 Which pair of triangles shown below is congruent?

A

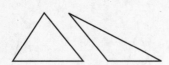

B

C

D

6 Triangle *BCD* is congruent to triangle *MNP*. What is the measure of ∠*P*?

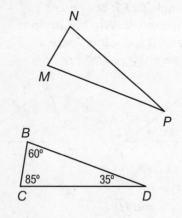

F   35°

G   60°

H   85°

J   90°

7 If triangle *FGH* is congruent to triangle *JKL*, what is the length of *KL*?

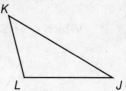

Answer _____

8 Triangle *RST* is congruent to triangle *VWX*. What is the length of *VW*?

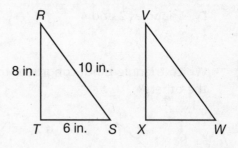

Answer _____

Short-Response Question

 9   Triangle *RST* is congruent to triangle *UVW*.

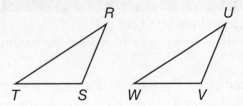

Part A

Identify three pairs of angles that are congruent in these triangles.

Answer _____

Part B

Explain how you know that the angles you named in Part A are congruent angles.

_____

_____

_____

LESSON 42

Strand 3: Geometry

Corresponding Sides of Similar Triangles

5.G.2 Identify pairs of similar triangles
5.G.3 Identify the ratio of corresponding sides of similar triangles

Similar figures have the same shape, but not necessarily the same size. Look at this set of triangles.

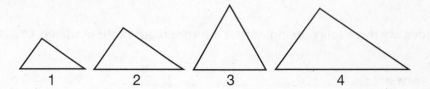

Triangles 1, 2, and 4 are similar triangles because they have the same shape. Like congruent triangles, the corresponding angles of similar figures are congruent (equal in measure).

EXAMPLE 1

Is triangle *XYZ* similar to triangle *ABC*?

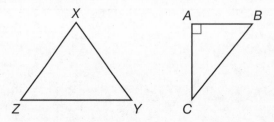

STRATEGY **Determine if the two triangles have the same shape.**

STEP 1 Look at the triangles to compare their shapes.

You may be able to tell, just by looking, that the shapes are different.

STEP 2 Check your answer by comparing the angles of the triangles.

If these triangles were similar, angles *X* and *A* would be congruent.

∠*A* is a right angle, and ∠*X* is smaller than a right angle.

Since those angles are not congruent, the triangles are not similar.

SOLUTION **Triangle *XYZ* is not similar to triangle *ABC*.**

The lengths of the corresponding sides of similar triangles are the same ratio. For example, triangle *MNP* is similar to triangle *STV* below.

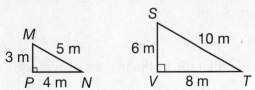

$\overline{MP}$ and $\overline{SV}$ are corresponding sides. The ratio of their lengths is $\frac{3}{6}$.

$\overline{PN}$ and $\overline{VT}$ are corresponding sides. The ratio of their lengths is $\frac{4}{8}$.

$\overline{MN}$ and $\overline{ST}$ are corresponding sides. The ratio of their lengths is $\frac{5}{10}$.

All of the ratios are equivalent because they all simplify to $\frac{1}{2}$.

$$\frac{3}{6} = \frac{1}{2} \qquad \frac{4}{8} = \frac{1}{2} \qquad \frac{5}{10} = \frac{1}{2}$$

For more information about ratios, see Lesson 19.

EXAMPLE 2

Triangle *DEF* is similar to triangle *GHJ*. What is the ratio of the lengths of the corresponding sides of these triangles?

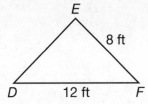
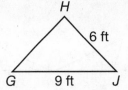

STRATEGY **Find two corresponding sides. Then find their ratios.**

STEP 1   Find two corresponding sides.

Sides *EF* and *HJ* are corresponding sides.

Sides *DF* and *GJ* are also corresponding sides.

STEP 2   Write a ratio of the lengths of the sides in simplest form.

Either pair of corresponding sides may be used.

$\overline{EF}$ is 8 ft long. $\overline{HJ}$ is 6 ft long.

The ratio of their lengths is: $\frac{8}{6} = \frac{8 \div 2}{6 \div 2} = \frac{4}{3}$.

STEP 3   Check your answer using another pair of corresponding sides.

$\overline{DF}$ is 12 ft long. $\overline{GJ}$ is 9 ft long.

The ratio of their lengths is: $\frac{12}{9} = \frac{12 \div 3}{9 \div 3} = \frac{4}{3}$.

So the ratio found in Step 2 checks.

SOLUTION **The ratio of the lengths of the corresponding sides of these triangles is $\frac{4}{3}$.**

The ratio of the lengths of the corresponding sides of two similar triangles is $\frac{2}{7}$. Could two corresponding sides of these triangles have lengths of 4 cm and 14 cm?

Let's check it out.

Write the ratio of the lengths of two corresponding sides that have lengths of 4 cm and 14 cm: _____.

Simplify the ratio: _____.

Does the ratio simplify to $\frac{2}{7}$? _____

Are 4 cm and 14 cm possible lengths of the sides of the two similar triangles?

_____

Sample Test Questions

1 Which two triangles appear to be similar?

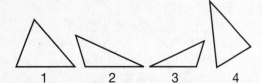

1   2   3   4

A Triangles 1 and 4

B Triangles 1 and 3

C Triangles 2 and 3

D Triangles 2 and 4

2 Which two triangles appear to be similar?

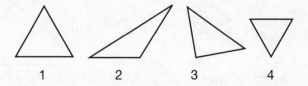

1   2   3   4

F Triangles 1 and 2

G Triangles 2 and 3

H Triangles 2 and 4

J Triangles 1 and 4

3 Which pair of triangles appears to be similar?

A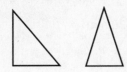

B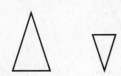

C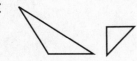

D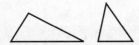

4 Triangle *ABC* is similar to triangle *XYZ*. What is the ratio of the lengths of the corresponding sides?

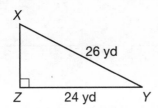

F $\frac{1}{12}$

G $\frac{1}{3}$

H $\frac{1}{2}$

J $\frac{2}{3}$

5 The triangles below are similar.

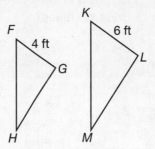

If $\overline{FG}$ and $\overline{KL}$ are corresponding sides of these triangles, which of these shows the ratio of the lengths of the corresponding sides?

A	B	C	D
$\frac{1}{3}$	$\frac{1}{2}$	$\frac{2}{3}$	$\frac{3}{5}$

6 Which of these triangles appear to be similar?

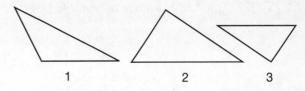

F Triangles 1 and 2

G Triangles 2 and 3

H Triangles 1 and 3

J Triangles 1, 2, and 3

7 Triangle *XYZ* is similar to triangle *TUV*. What is the ratio of the lengths of the corresponding sides?

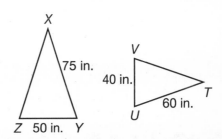

Answer _____

8 Triangle *JKL* is similar to triangle *PQR*.
What is the ratio of the corresponding
sides of these triangles?

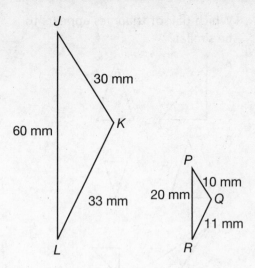

Answer _____

Short-Response Question

9 Triangle *ABC* is similar to triangle *DEF*.

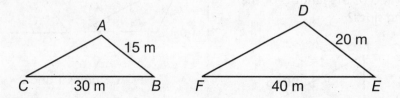

What is the ratio of the lengths of the corresponding sides of these triangles?
Express the ratio in simplest form.

Show your work.

Answer _____

LESSON 43

Strand 3: Geometry

Special Triangles and Quadrilaterals

5.G.4 Classify quadrilaterals by properties of their angles and sides
5.G.6 Classify triangles by properties of their angles and sides

Take a moment to review the different kinds of angles.

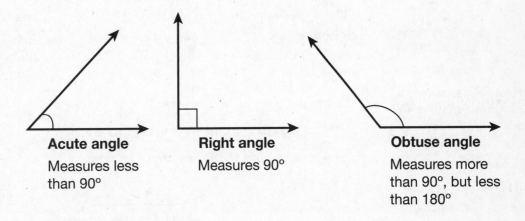

Acute angle
Measures less than 90°

Right angle
Measures 90°

Obtuse angle
Measures more than 90°, but less than 180°

SPECIAL TRIANGLES

Triangles are polygons with 3 sides, 3 angles, and 3 **vertices** (plural of **vertex**). The vertices of a polygon are the points where the sides of the polygon meet.

Triangles can be classified in a number of ways.

They can be classified according to the measures of their angles.

Acute triangle   **Right triangle**   **Obtuse triangle**

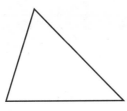   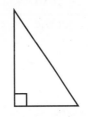   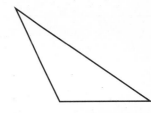

has 3 acute angles   has a right angle   has an obtuse angle

Triangles can also be classified according to the lengths of their sides.

Isosceles triangle	**Equilateral triangle**	**Scalene triangle**

 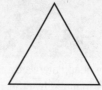 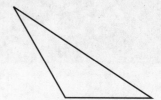

has at least two congruent sides (The angles opposite those sides are also congruent.)

has three congruent sides (and three congruent angles)

has three sides, each with a different length (Each of the three angles is a different measure.)

EXAMPLE 1

Classify the triangle in two ways:

a) according to the measures of its angles

b) according to the lengths of its sides

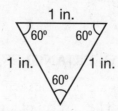

STRATEGY

Look at the angle measures and side lengths. Then classify the triangle.

STEP 1   Look at the angles.

Each angle measures less than 90°, so each angle is acute.

This triangle has 3 acute angles, so it is an acute triangle.

STEP 2   Look at the lengths of the sides.

All the sides measure 1 in., so this triangle has 3 congruent sides.

That means this triangle is an equilateral triangle.

SOLUTION

This triangle can be classified as (a) an acute triangle and (b) an equilateral triangle.

SPECIAL QUADRILATERALS

Quadrilaterals are polygons with 4 sides, 4 angles, and 4 vertices. Like triangles, quadrilaterals can be classified according to the measures of their angles and the lengths of their sides.

Parallelogram

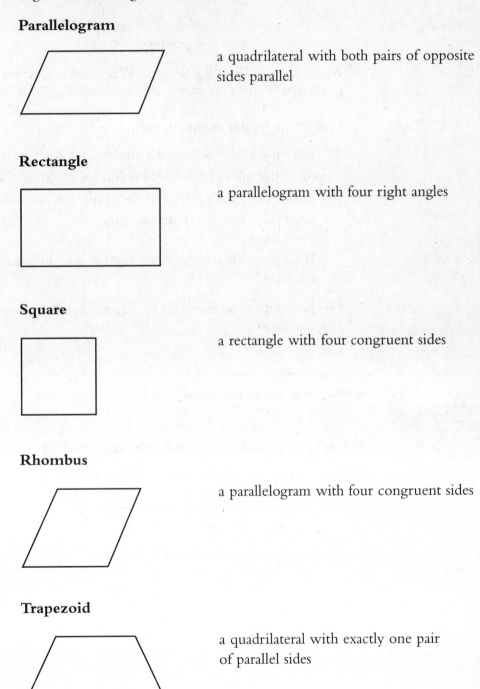

a quadrilateral with both pairs of opposite sides parallel

Rectangle

a parallelogram with four right angles

Square

a rectangle with four congruent sides

Rhombus

a parallelogram with four congruent sides

Trapezoid

a quadrilateral with exactly one pair of parallel sides

EXAMPLE 2

Look at the polygon shown below.

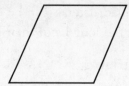

Which of the following names could be used to describe this figure: quadrilateral, parallelogram, rectangle, square, rhombus, or trapezoid?

STRATEGY

Look at the figures and definitions.

This figure has 4 sides and 4 angles, so it is a quadrilateral.

All of the sides of the quadrilateral are congruent, so it is a rhombus.

Since a rhombus is a type of parallelogram, it is also a parallelogram.

Since parallelograms have more than one pair of parallel sides, it is *not* a trapezoid.

This figure does not have any right angles, so it is *not* a square or a rectangle.

SOLUTION

This polygon can be classified as a quadrilateral, a parallelogram, and a rhombus.

Is every square also a rhombus?

Let's check it out.

A rhombus is a parallelogram with four sides that are _____.

A square is a parallelogram with four sides that are _____.

Is every square also a rhombus? _____

Sample Test Questions

1 Which of these does **not** describe a square?

    A parallelogram

    B rhombus

    C trapezoid

    D rectangle

2 Which of the following describes this triangle?

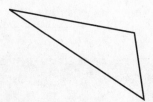

    F equilateral triangle

    G isosceles triangle

    H scalene triangle

    J right triangle

3 A triangle has two congruent sides. Which of the following **must** be true?

    A It is an equilateral triangle.

    B It is an isosceles triangle.

    C It is a scalene triangle.

    D It is an obtuse triangle.

4 In the figure below, $\overline{WX}$ is parallel to $\overline{ZY}$. Which of the following best names figure *WXYZ*?

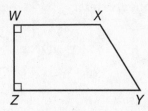

    F parallelogram

    G rectangle

    H right triangle

    J trapezoid

5 Which of the following shows an obtuse triangle?

    A

    B

    C

    D

6 Which of these statements is **not** true?

F Any square must also be a rectangle.

G Any rhombus must also be a square.

H Any rectangle must also be a parallelogram.

J Any trapezoid must also be a quadrilateral.

7 Which type of triangle can never have three acute angles?

Answer _____

8 Arnob is thinking of a quadrilateral. He says that it has two pairs of parallel sides. Two of its angles are acute and the other two angles are obtuse. Not all of its sides are congruent. What kind of quadrilateral is Arnob thinking of?

Answer _____

Short-Response Question

9 Natasha and Cecily are looking at this triangle. Natasha says that the triangle is a right triangle. Cecily says that the triangle is an isosceles triangle.

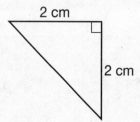

2 cm

2 cm

Part A

Who is correct—Natasha, Cecily, both of them, or neither of them?

Answer _____

Part B

Explain how you determined what type of triangle is shown and how you know that your answer for Part A is correct.

_____

_____

LESSON 44

Strand 3: Geometry

Sum of Angles of Triangles and Quadrilaterals

5.G.5 Know that the sum of the interior angles of a quadrilateral is 360 degrees
5.G.7 Know that the sum of the interior angles of a triangle is 180 degrees
5.G.8 Find a missing angle when given two angles of a triangle

SUM OF THE ANGLES OF A TRIANGLE

The sum of the angles of any triangle is 180°.

EXAMPLE 1

What is the missing angle measure in this triangle?

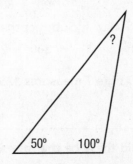

STRATEGY

Use the fact that the sum of the three angles is 180°.

STEP 1   Add the angle measures that you know.
100° + 50° = 150°

STEP 2   Subtract that sum from 180°.
180° − 150° = 30°, so the missing angle measures 30°.

SOLUTION

The missing angle measure is 30°.

SUM OF THE ANGLES OF A QUADRILATERAL

You can use what you know about the sum of the angle measures of a triangle to figure out the sum of the angle measures of a quadrilateral.

Look at quadrilateral *ABCD*. A line segment can be drawn to connect points *A* and *C* in this quadrilateral.

The dashed line segment divides the quadrilateral into two triangles: △*ACD* and △*ABC*.

The sum of the measures of the angles of a triangle is 180°. Since there are two triangles in the quadrilateral, the sum of the measures of the angles of any quadrilateral is 180° × 2, or 360°.

EXAMPLE 2

What is the measure of angle *T* in the quadrilateral below?

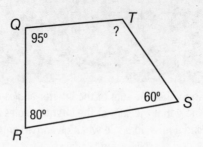

STRATEGY

Use the fact that the sum of the angles of a quadrilateral is 360°.

STEP 1   Add the three angle measures you know.

$$95° + 80° + 60° = 235°$$

STEP 2   Subtract that sum from 360°.

$$360° - 235° = 125°$$

SOLUTION

Angle *T* measures 125°.

Could these be the four angle measures of a quadrilateral: 45°, 45°, 90°, 90°?

Let's check it out.

The sum of the measures of the angles of a quadrilateral is

_____ degrees.

Add the angle measures given.

$45° + 45° + 90° + 90° =$ _____

Since the sum of those angle measures is _____, those angle

measures _____ the measures of the four angles of a quadrilateral.

Sample Test Questions

1 What is the missing angle measure in this triangle?

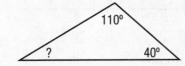

- A 30°
- B 40°
- C 60°
- D 110°

2 What is the missing angle measure in this quadrilateral?

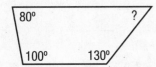

- F 60°
- G 50°
- H 40°
- J 35°

3 What is the missing angle measure in this figure?

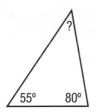

- A 35°
- B 45°
- C 55°
- D 225°

4 Two angles in an isosceles triangle each have a measure of 40°. What is the measure of the third angle?

- F 40°
- G 80°
- H 100°
- J 140°

5 What is the measure of ∠J in this parallelogram?

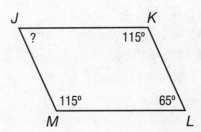

- A 15°
- B 55°
- C 65°
- D 115°

6 What is the measure of ∠Q in this triangle?

- F 30°
- G 40°
- H 60°
- J 90°

7 One of the angles in a triangle measures 50°. Which of the following are possible measures for the other two angles in this triangle?

A   50° and 40°

B   40° and 70°

C   30° and 100°

D   20° and 100°

8 One of the angles of a quadrilateral has a measure of 90°. Which of the following shows possible measures for the other three angles of the quadrilateral?

F   30°, 30°, 30°

G   90°, 80°, 110°

H   30°, 60°, 90°

J   80°, 90°, 100°

9 What is the missing angle measure in this trapezoid?

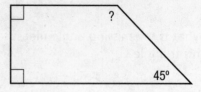

Answer _____

10 One angle of an isosceles triangle measures 20°. The other two angles are equal in measure. What is the measure of each of the other two angles?

Answer _____

Short-Response Question

11 Brendon knows the measures of three angles of this quadrilateral. There is one missing angle measure.

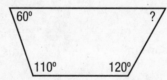

Part A

Brendon says that the missing angle measures 50°. Is he correct or incorrect?

Answer _____

Part B

Explain how you determined whether Brendon was correct or incorrect and what steps you took to arrive at your answer.

_____

_____

LESSON 45

Strand 3: Geometry

Symmetry

5.G.11 Identify and draw lines of symmetry of basic geometric shapes

The figure below is a regular hexagon. If you fold this polygon in half along the dashed line, the two halves will match exactly. The two halves are congruent.

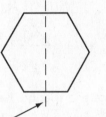 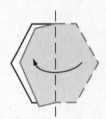

This line is called the **line of symmetry**.

If a line can be drawn that divides a figure into two congruent halves that match when the figure is folded along the line, we say that figure has **line symmetry**. A geometric figure can have one line of symmetry, two or more lines of symmetry, or no lines of symmetry.

EXAMPLE 1

Draw a line of symmetry through this polygon.

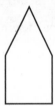

STRATEGY

Imagine folding the polygon exactly in half.

How would this polygon need to be divided so the two halves match exactly? Draw a vertical line through the middle of the polygon.

SOLUTION

The dashed line above shows the line of symmetry for this polygon.

EXAMPLE 2   How many lines of symmetry does this scalene triangle have?

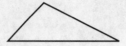

STRATEGY   **Imagine folding the triangle exactly in half as many ways as you can.**

There is no way to draw a line through a scalene triangle so that the halves match exactly. None of the lines drawn below are lines of symmetry.

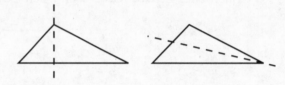

SOLUTION   **This scalene triangle has no lines of symmetry.**

Sometimes, you may need to use a ruler to help you draw lines of symmetry or to help you draw figures. Your drawings should be close, but they do not have to be perfect. To review how to use a ruler, look at Lesson 46.

CHECK IT OUT with the Coach™

How many lines of symmetry can you draw through a square?

Let's check it out.

Draw a square on scrap paper.

Draw all the lines of symmetry that you can.

How many vertical (up and down) lines of symmetry could you draw?

I drew _____ vertical line (or lines) of symmetry.

How many horizontal (left to right) lines of symmetry could you draw?

I drew _____ horizontal line (or lines) of symmetry.

How many other lines of symmetry could you draw?

I drew _____ other lines of symmetry.

How many lines of symmetry does the square have all together?

It has _____ lines of symmetry.

Sample Test Questions

1 Which of these figures has no lines of symmetry?

A

B

C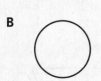

D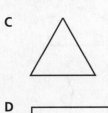

2 Which of these figures has exactly 4 lines of symmetry?

F

G

H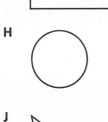

J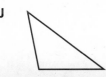

3 Which of the following shows a line of symmetry?

A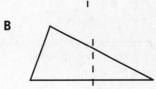

B

C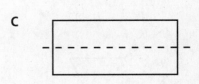

D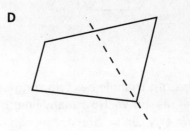

4 Which of the following shows a line of symmetry?

F

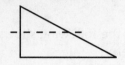

G

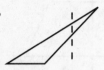

H

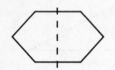

J

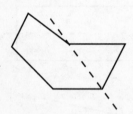

6 Which of the following shows a line of symmetry?

F

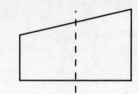

G

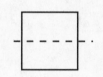

H

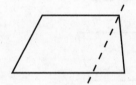

J

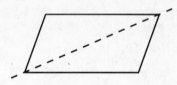

5 This right triangle has two congruent sides, as shown. How many lines of symmetry can be drawn through this right triangle?

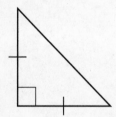

A 0

B 1

C 2

D 3

7 This trapezoid has two congruent sides. How many lines of symmetry can be drawn through this trapezoid?

Answer _____

8 How many lines of symmetry can be drawn through this regular pentagon?

Answer _____

Short-Response Question

9 Below is an isosceles triangle. This triangle has exactly two congruent sides.

Part A

How many lines of symmetry can be drawn through this triangle? Draw all the possible lines of symmetry on the triangle above.

Answer _____ lines of symmetry

Part B

Explain how you decided how many lines of symmetry the isosceles triangle had.

_____

_____

_____

Progress Check for Lessons 40–45

1 Which triangles appear to be congruent?

A Triangles 1 and 2

B Triangles 1, 2, and 3

C Triangles 1 and 3

D Triangles 2 and 4

2 Which of the following describes the triangle below?

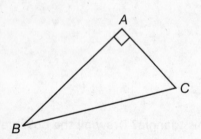

F acute triangle

G right triangle

H obtuse triangle

J isosceles triangle

3 Which of the following shows a line of symmetry?

A
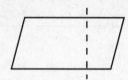

B
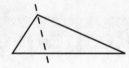

C
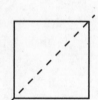

D
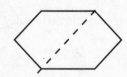

4 Triangle *KLM* is congruent to triangle *PQR*. What is the measure of ∠*Q*?

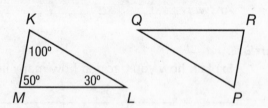

F 30°

G 50°

H 80°

J 100°

5 What is the measure of ∠C in this triangle?

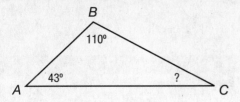

A   27°

B   37°

C   127°

D   217°

6 What is the perimeter of this regular pentagon?

F   36 m

G   45 m

H   54 m

J   90 m

7 Which triangles appear to be similar?

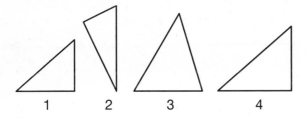

A   Triangles 1 and 2

B   Triangles 2 and 3

C   Triangles 3 and 4

D   Triangles 1 and 4

8 If you were asked to draw a quadrilateral with one pair of sides parallel and the other pair of sides not parallel, what kind of quadrilateral should you draw?

F   parallelogram

G   square

H   trapezoid

J   rhombus

9 Three angles of a quadrilateral have measures of 98°, 52°, and 100°. What is the measure of the fourth angle?

A   250°

B   120°

C   110°

D   70°

10 Triangle *ABC* is similar to triangle *DEF*. Which of the following does not represent the ratio of the lengths of the corresponding sides?

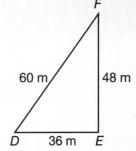

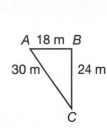

F $\frac{1}{4}$

G $\frac{18}{36}$

H $\frac{24}{48}$

J $\frac{30}{60}$

Open-Ended Questions

Short-Response Question

11   Look at the trapezoid shown below. This trapezoid has two congruent sides.

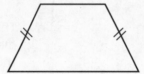

Part A

How many lines of symmetry does this trapezoid have? If it has one or more lines of symmetry, draw them.

Answer _____ lines of symmetry

Part B

Explain how you know that your answer for Part A is correct.

_____

_____

_____

Extended-Response Question

12   Calvin measures two angles of △*ABC*. He found that angle *A* measured 53° and
angle *B* measured 37°.

Part A

What is the measure of ∠*C*?

Answer _____

Part B

What kind of triangle is △*ABC*?

Answer _____

Part C

Explain how you found the measure of ∠*C* and how you used that information to determine
what kind of triangle *ABC* was?

_____

_____

_____

_____

_____

LESSON 46

Strand 4: Measurement

Measuring Length (to the Nearest $\frac{1}{8}$ of an Inch and Centimeter)

5.M.1 Use a ruler to measure to the nearest inch, $\frac{1}{2}$, $\frac{1}{4}$, and $\frac{1}{8}$ inch
5.M.3 Measure to the nearest centimeter
5.M.6 Determine the tool and technique to measure with an appropriate level of precision: lengths and angles

In real life, you often need to know the length of something. You might need to buy ribbon for an art project. You might need to measure the height of a plant you are growing for science class.

One way to measure length is to use a ruler. You can use a ruler to measure in inches or in centimeters.

MEASURING LENGTH IN INCHES

Part of a ruler is shown below. This part shows one inch. (It has been enlarged so that you can more easily focus on the markings that show fractional parts of an inch.)

This inch has been divided into 16 parts. Every two parts represent $\frac{1}{8}$ inch.

Two parts: $\frac{1}{8}$ inch

Four parts: $\frac{2}{8}$, or $\frac{1}{4}$, inch

Six parts: $\frac{3}{8}$ inch

Eight parts: $\frac{4}{8}$, or $\frac{1}{2}$, inch

Ten parts: $\frac{5}{8}$ inch

Twelve parts: $\frac{6}{8}$, or $\frac{3}{4}$, inch

Fourteen parts: $\frac{7}{8}$ inch

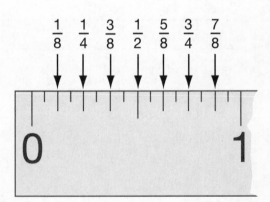

You can measure an object to the nearest inch, to the nearest $\frac{1}{2}$ inch, to the nearest $\frac{1}{4}$ inch, or to the nearest $\frac{1}{8}$ inch.

EXAMPLE 1   What is the length of the line segment shown below to the nearest $\frac{1}{8}$ inch?

STRATEGY   **Use your ruler to measure the length of the line segment to the nearest $\frac{1}{8}$ inch.**

STEP 1   Line up one end of the line segment with the zero-mark on your ruler. (If there is no zero-mark on your ruler, line up the segment with the edge of your ruler.)

STEP 2   Measure the length of the line segment.

Find the mark on your ruler that lines up with the other end of the segment.

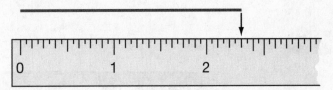

STEP 3   Determine the length of the line to the nearest $\frac{1}{8}$ inch.

The line segment is more than 2 inches, but less than 3 inches, long.

The line segment extends six marks past the 2-inch mark.

Six marks represent $\frac{3}{8}$ inch, so the line segment is $2\frac{3}{8}$ inches long.

SOLUTION   **The line segment is $2\frac{3}{8}$ inches long.**

EXAMPLE 2   Draw a line segment that is $1\frac{3}{4}$ inches long.

STRATEGY   **Use a ruler to measure and draw the line.**

STEP 1   Place your ruler on the paper and draw a line segment from the zero-mark (or edge) of the ruler to the 1-inch mark.

STEP 2   Extend the line to the $\frac{3}{4}$-inch mark between the 1-in. and 2-in. marks.

Look back to the information given at the beginning of the lesson.

Twelve marks on the ruler represent $\frac{6}{8}$, or $\frac{3}{4}$, inch.

SOLUTION   **The line segment in Step 2 is $1\frac{3}{4}$ inches.**

MEASURING LENGTH IN CENTIMETERS

You can also use a ruler to measure lengths in centimeters. This picture shows a centimeter ruler.

Each whole number on the ruler represents 1 centimeter (cm). You need to know how to measure lengths to the *nearest* centimeter. That means, if you measure an object that is between 8 and 9 centimeters long, figure out which centimeter it is closest to on the ruler.

EXAMPLE 3

What is the length of this crayon to the nearest centimeter?

STRATEGY

Use your ruler to measure the length of the crayon to the nearest centimeter.

STEP 1   Measure the length of the crayon.

Line up one end of the crayon with the zero-mark (or edge) of your ruler.

Find the mark on your ruler that lines up with the other end of the crayon.

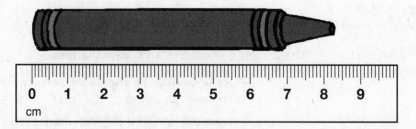

STEP 2   Determine the length of the line to the nearest centimeter.

The crayon is more than 8 centimeters, but less than 9 centimeters, long.

It is closer to the 8-cm mark.

SOLUTION

The crayon is 8 centimeters long to the nearest centimeter.

Many rulers have two sides—an inches side and a centimeters side. When you are asked to measure an object, be sure to use the correct side of your ruler.

How do you draw a line segment that is exactly 6 cm long?

Let's check it out.

Should you use the inches or centimeters side of a ruler?

The abbreviation cm stands for _____, so use the _____ side of the ruler.

Next, put the ruler on a piece of paper.

Line up the tip of a pencil with the _____ of the ruler to start.

Then draw a line segment up to the _____ mark.

That line segment will be 6 cm long.

Sample Test Questions

Use your ruler to measure the lengths of the objects in the questions.

1 What is the length of the pencil below to the nearest $\frac{1}{4}$ inch?

A   3 inches

B $3\frac{1}{2}$ inches

C $3\frac{3}{4}$ inches

D   4 inches

2 What is the length of this ribbon to the nearest centimeter?

F   4 cm

G   8 cm

H   9 cm

J   10 cm

3 What is the length of this line segment to the nearest $\frac{1}{8}$ inch?

_____

A $2\frac{1}{8}$ inches

B $2\frac{3}{8}$ inches

C $2\frac{5}{8}$ inches

D $2\frac{7}{8}$ inches

4 What is the length of this line segment to the nearest centimeter?

F   1 cm

G   2 cm

H   3 cm

J   4 cm

5 What is the length of this arrow to the nearest centimeter?

A   1 cm

B   2 cm

C   4 cm

D   5 cm

6   Which of these line segments is $\frac{3}{8}$ inch long?

F ———

G ——————

H ————

J ——————

7   Which of these line segments, when measured to the nearest centimeter, measures 2 cm long?

A ———

B —————

C ——————

D ———————

8   What is the length of this paperclip to the nearest inch?

Answer _____

Short-Response Question

9   Use a ruler to complete Part A.

Part A

Draw a line that measures $3\frac{7}{8}$ inches long.

Part B

Use what you know about measuring lengths to explain why your drawing is correct.

_____

_____

_____

LESSON 47

Strand 4: Measurement

Units of Length

5.M.2 Identify customary equivalent units of length
5.M.4 Identify equivalent metric units of length
5.M.5 Convert measurement within a given system

Suppose you need 20 yards of rope, but the store sold rope by the foot. You would need to convert from yards to feet to figure out how much rope to buy.

Take some time to study and learn the unit conversions in these tables. They will help you convert units.

Customary Units of Length
1 foot (ft) = 12 inches (in.)
1 yard (yd) = 3 feet (ft)
1 mile (mi) = 5,280 feet (ft)

Metric Units of Length
1 centimeter (cm) = 10 millimeters (mm)
1 meter (m) = 100 centimeters (cm)
1 kilometer (km) = 1,000 meters (m)

In addition to knowing these conversions, you also need to know when to multiply and when to divide.

WHEN TO MULTIPLY

If you convert from yards to feet, you use the number 3 to make the conversion because 1 yard = 3 feet.

1 yard $= 1 \times 3 = 3$ feet

2 yards $= 2 \times 3 = 6$ feet

3 yards $= 3 \times 3 = 9$ feet

. . . and so forth.

To convert from yards to feet, you *multiply by 3*. This leads to Rule 1:

RULE 1
When you go from a larger unit to a smaller unit, multiply.

WHEN TO DIVIDE

If you convert from feet to yards, you still use the number 3, but you use the opposite operation.

$$18 \text{ feet} = 18 \div 3 = 6 \text{ yards}$$
$$15 \text{ feet} = 15 \div 3 = 5 \text{ yards}$$
$$12 \text{ feet} = 12 \div 3 = 4 \text{ yards}$$

. . . and so forth.

To convert from feet to yards, you *divide by 3*. This leads to Rule 2:

RULE 2

When you go from a smaller unit to a larger unit, divide.

EXAMPLE 1

The length of José's bedroom is 6 meters 30 centimeters. What is the length of his bedroom in centimeters?

STRATEGY

Use the table and the rules for when to multiply or divide.

STEP 1 Which Rule applies?

Meters are larger than centimeters.

You are converting from a larger unit to a smaller unit.
Use Rule 1, multiply.

STEP 2 What unit conversion do you need? (Look back at the table if you need to.)

$$1 \text{ m} = 100 \text{ cm}$$

STEP 3 First, convert 6 meters to centimeters.

$$6 \text{ m} = 6 \times 100 = 600 \text{ cm}$$

STEP 4 Add 30 centimeters to 600 centimeters.

$$600 + 30 = 630$$

SOLUTION

José's room is 630 centimeters long.

Sometimes you may need to use two unit conversions to solve a problem.

EXAMPLE 2

How many meters are 6,000 millimeters?

STRATEGY

Use the table and the rules for when to multiply and divide.

STEP 1   Which Rule applies?

You are converting from a smaller unit to a larger unit.
Use Rule 2, divide.

STEP 2   What unit conversions do you need?

You will need to convert from millimeters to centimeters, and then from centimeters to meters.

1 meter = 100 centimeters

1 centimeter = 10 millimeters

STEP 3   First, convert from millimeters to centimeters.

Since 1 cm = 10 mm, divide by 10.

6000 mm = 6000 ÷ 10 = 600 cm

STEP 4   Then, convert from centimeters to meters.

Since 1 m = 100 cm, divide by 100.

600 cm = 600 ÷ 100 = 6 meters

SOLUTION

There are 6 meters in 6,000 millimeters.

Do you need to divide or multiply to convert 10 miles to feet?

Let's check it out.

Is this a conversion from a smaller unit to a larger unit, or from a larger unit to a smaller unit?

Miles are _____ than feet.

Should you multiply or divide?

Since the problem involves converting from a _____ unit to a

_____ unit, _____ to convert the units.

Sample Test Questions

For Questions 1–4, find the number that goes in the blank to make the sentence true.

1   1 meter = _____ millimeters

     A   10

     B   100

     C   1000

     D   10,000

2   24 ft = _____ yd

     F   2

     G   8

     H   12

     J   72

3   7000 m = _____ km

     A   7

     B   70

     C   700

     D   700,000

4   2 miles = _____ feet

     F   200

     G   2,000

     H   2,640

     J   10,560

5   Miguel is 60 inches tall. What is Miguel's height in feet?

     A   3 feet

     B   4 feet

     C   5 feet

     D   6 feet

6   Jennifer runs a 1-mile race. How many yards are in 1 mile?

     F   760 yd

     G   1,760 yd

     H   2,640 yd

     J   15,840 yd

7   Alexander has a pen that is 140 millimeters long. What is the length of Alexander's pen in centimeters?

     A   4,200

     B   1400

     C   42

     D   14

8   Which of these lengths is equivalent to 9 yards?

     F   3 inches

     G   27 inches

     H   108 inches

     J   324 inches

9 Don's fishing pole is 3 ft 4 in. long. What is the total length of Don's fishing pole in inches?

Answer _____

10 A piece of string is 8,000 millimeters long. What is the length of the string in meters?

Answer _____

Short-Response Question

11 Chantell builds a coat rack that is 72 inches tall.

Part A

How tall is the coat rack in yards?

Answer _____ yards

Part B

Explain how you determined your answer for Part A and why you took the steps you did.

_____

_____

_____

LESSON 48

Strand 4: Measurement

Measuring Angles to the Nearest Degree

5.M.6 Determine the tool and technique to measure with an appropriate level of precision: lengths and angles

5.M.8 Measure and draw angles using a protractor

To measure length, you use a ruler. To measure angles, you need a different tool—a **protractor**.

To measure this angle with a protractor, line up the center of the protractor with the vertex. Then line up one ray of the angle with the bottom of the protractor.

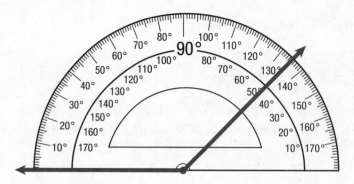

The other ray of this angle lines up with two measures on the protractor—45° and 135°. How do you know which measurement is correct?

You can determine which measurement is correct by identifying the type of angle.

• If the angle is acute, choose the number that is *less than* 90°.

• If the angle is obtuse, choose the number that is *greater than* 90°.

This angle is obtuse, so its measure is 135°.

EXAMPLE 1

What is the measure of the angle shown below?

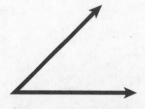

STRATEGY   **Use a protractor to measure the angle to the nearest degree.**

STEP 1   Place the center of the protractor on the vertex of the angle.

           Line up the bottom of the protractor with one ray of the angle.

STEP 2   Extend the angle to make it easier to measure.

           Use a ruler to extend the other ray of the angle like this.

STEP 3   Read the measurement.

           This angle is acute, so it measures between 40° and 50°. Count the tick marks above the 40° mark. The ray crosses at the 44° mark.

SOLUTION   **This angle measures 44°.**

EXAMPLE 2   Draw an angle that measures 150°.

STRATEGY   **Use a protractor to draw a 150° angle.**

STEP 1   With the straight edge of your protractor, draw a ray.

STEP 2   Place the center of the protractor on the endpoint of the ray.

           Find 150° on the scale of the protractor.

           Place a mark above the protractor at the 150° mark.

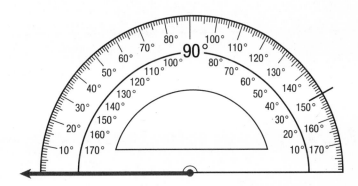

STEP 3   Draw a second ray to form a 150° angle.

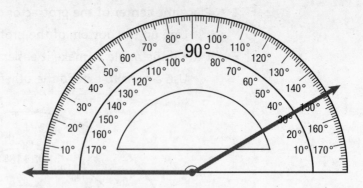

SOLUTION   **The angle below measures 150°.**

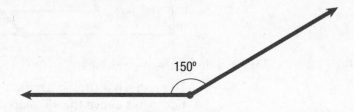

An angle measured with a protractor crosses the 10° mark and the 170° mark. If the angle is acute, which of those is the correct measure?

Let's check it out.

All acute angles measure less than _____ degrees.

So, the correct measure for this angle must be _____ degrees.

Sample Test Questions

Use a protractor for questions 1–8.

1 What is the measure of the angle shown below?

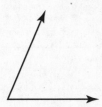

A 115°		**C** 70°	
B 110°		**D** 67°	

2 What is the measure of the angle shown below?

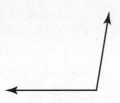

F 119°

G 100°

H 95°

J 90°

3 What is the measure of this angle?

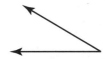

A 30°

B 35°

C 145°

D 150°

4 What is the measure of this angle?

F 18°

G 28°

H 152°

J 162°

5 Which of these angles measures 45°?

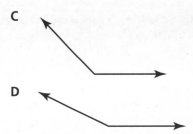

A

B

C

D

6 What is the measure of the angle shown below?

F 13°

G 17°

H 163°

J 167°

7 Which of these angles measures 57°?

A

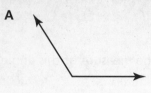

B

C

D

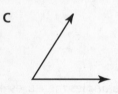

8 What is the measure of the angle shown below?

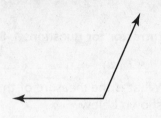

Answer _____

Short-Response Question

9 Use your protractor to solve this problem.

Part A

Draw an angle that measures 140°.

Part B

Explain how you know that the angle you drew measures 140° and not 40°.

_____

_____

Strand 4: Measurement

Elapsed Time

5.M.7 Calculate elapsed time in hours and minutes

Sometimes we need to know how much time passed between two events. This is called **elapsed time**. Knowing how to convert between seconds, minutes, and hours can help you to calculate elapsed time.

Learn these equivalent units of time.

1 minute (min) = 60 seconds (sec)

1 hour (h) = 60 minutes (min)

EXAMPLE 1

Alison worked on a poster for $2\frac{1}{2}$ hours. How many minutes did Alison work on the poster?

STRATEGY

Use equivalent units of time to convert hours to minutes.

STEP 1   Convert 2 hours to minutes.

1 hour = 60 minutes, so 2 hours = 2 × 60 = 120 minutes

STEP 2   Convert $\frac{1}{2}$ hour to minutes.

To find $\frac{1}{2}$ of a number, divide the number by 2.

$\frac{1}{2}$ hour = 60 ÷ 2 = 30 minutes

STEP 3   Add to find the total number of minutes.

120 + 30 = 150

SOLUTION

Alison worked on the poster for 150 minutes.

Sometimes we need to know when an event started or ended, or how much time it took to do something.

EXAMPLE 2

Mario has timed how long it takes him to walk from his house to school. It takes 17 minutes. If Mario needs to be at school at 8:40 A.M., what time does he need to leave his house?

STRATEGY

Subtract to find out what time Mario needs to leave his house.

STEP 1   What time does Mario need to be at school?

Mario needs to be at school at 8:40 A.M.

STEP 2   How long does it take Mario to get to school?

It takes 17 minutes for Mario to get to school.

STEP 3   Subtract 17 minutes from 8:40 A.M.

$$
\begin{array}{r}
8{:}40 \\
-\ :17 \\
\hline
8{:}23
\end{array}
$$

SOLUTION   **Mario needs to leave his house at 8:23 A.M.**

Sometimes it is easier to count up or count backward from the time given than it is to add or subtract.

EXAMPLE 3   Naomi started reading at 7:35 P.M. She stopped reading at 9:15 P.M. How much time did Naomi spend reading?

STRATEGY   **Count up from 7:35 P.M. to 9:15 P.M.**

STEP 1   Count up to find the total number of hours Naomi read.
            7:35 to 8:35 is 1 hour.

STEP 2   Count up to find the number of minutes from 8:35 P.M. to 9:15 P.M.
            From 8:35 to 9:00 is 25 minutes.
            From 9:00 to 9:15 is 15 minutes.

STEP 3   Add to find the total amount of time that passed.
            Add the minutes: 25 minutes + 15 minutes = 40 minutes
            Add the hour: 1 hour + 40 minutes = 1 hour 40 minutes

SOLUTION   **Naomi spent 1 hour 40 minutes reading.**

CHECK IT OUT *with the* **Coach**™

Menzo's guitar lesson starts at 4:15 P.M. and lasts for 40 minutes. At what time does his lesson end?

Let's check it out.

Count up from 4:15 P.M. by 10-minute intervals.

From 4:15 to _____ is 10 minutes.

From 4:25 to _____ is 10 minutes.

From 4:35 to _____ is 10 minutes.

From 4:45 to _____ is 10 minutes.

10 + 10 + 10 + 10 = 40 minutes

If his lesson lasts for 40 minutes, his lesson ends at _____.

Sample Test Questions

1 Justin spent $1\frac{1}{2}$ hours running errands. How many minutes did he spend running errands?

A   60 minutes

B   90 minutes

C   150 minutes

D   180 minutes

2 Linda's math class lasts for 50 minutes. If her class ends at 3:05 P.M., at what time does it start?

F   2:05 P.M.

G   2:15 P.M.

H   2:55 P.M.

J   3:55 P.M.

3 It took Mark 2 minutes 45 seconds to run around the school yard three times. How many seconds did it take?

A   165 seconds

B   145 seconds

C   120 seconds

D   105 seconds

4 Thalia held a headstand for 180 seconds. If she started doing the headstand at 4:08 P.M., at what time did she end the headstand?

F   4:05 P.M.

G   4:08 P.M.

H   4:11 P.M.

J   4:13 P.M.

5 Lucas went to a movie that lasted 2 hours 20 minutes. The movie ended at 4:15 P.M. At what time did it start?

A   2:15 P.M.

B   2:05 P.M.

C   1:55 P.M.

D   1:45 P.M.

6 Holly started working on her science project at 3:15 P.M. She stopped working at 5:35 P.M. How much time did Holly spend working on her science project?

F   2 hours 10 minutes

G   2 hours 15 minutes

H   2 hours 20 minutes

J   2 hours 25 minutes

7 Mrs. Kowalski likes to ride her bike for 75 minutes each day. If she wants to end her ride by 8:00 A.M., at what time should Mrs. Kowalski start riding her bike?

A   6:30 A.M.

B   6:45 A.M.

C   7:00 A.M.

D   7:15 A.M.

8 Amal wants to spend 55 minutes practicing violin today. If he begins to practice at 1:30 P.M., at what time should he finish?

F   1:55 P.M.

G   2:15 P.M.

H   2:20 P.M.

J   2:25 P.M.

9 The Rivera family will drive from Brooklyn, New York, to Albany, New York. The trip takes 2 hours 50 minutes. If they leave Brooklyn at 7:30 A.M., at what time will they arrive in Albany?

Answer _____

10 Kiri helped pick up litter in the park from 7:45 A.M. to 11:30 A.M. as part of "Clean Up the Park Day." How long did Kiri spend picking up litter?

Answer _____

Short-Response Question

11 It took Mr. Adams 45 minutes to get to work this morning.

Part A

If Mr. Adams arrived at work at 8:30 A.M., at what time did he leave for work?

Answer _____

Part B

Use words and/or numbers to explain how you determined your answer for Part A.

_____

_____

_____

LESSON 50

Strand 4: Measurement

Estimating Length

5.M.9 Determine personal references for customary units of length
(i.e., your pace is approximately 3 feet, your height is approximately 5 feet, etc.)
5.M.10 Determine personal references for metric units of length

Sometimes you do not need to find an exact length. An estimated length might be good enough.

To estimate lengths, you need to have an idea in your head of how long each unit is. You can use the following examples to help you. These examples are called referents because you can *refer* to them to help you estimate lengths.

CUSTOMARY UNITS OF LENGTH

inch (in)   This segment is 1 inch long.   ————

foot (ft)   This page, from top to bottom, is a little less than 1 foot long.

yard (yd)   A kitchen table top is about 1 yard high.

mile (mi)   You would measure the distance you travel by car, train, or plane in miles.

METRIC UNITS OF LENGTH

millimeter (mm)   This segment is 1 millimeter long.   -

centimeter (cm)   This segment is 1 centimeter long.   ——

meter (m)   A meter is as long as a meter stick. It is a little longer than 3 feet.

kilometer (km)   You would measure the distance you travel by car, train or plane in kilometers. Specifically, 1 kilometer is about $\frac{6}{10}$ mile.

EXAMPLE 1

What would be the best measure for the length of a small paper clip?

A 2 millimeters

B 2 centimeters

C 10 centimeters

D 2 meters

STRATEGY

Use referents to rule out answer choices that do not make sense.

STEP 1 Think about answer choice A.

2 millimeters is too short for the length of a paperclip—even a small one.

STEP 2 Think about answer choice B.

2 centimeters seems about right.
Check the other answer choices just to be sure.

STEP 3 Think about answer choice C.

10 centimeters is too long.

STEP 4 Think about answer choice D.

2 meters would be as long as 2 meter sticks.
That is much too long for a paperclip!

SOLUTION

The best answer is B, 2 centimeters.

Example 1 shows how to use the referents given in this lesson to estimate length. Another way to estimate length is to use referents that come from your own life.

For example, how far do you live from school? If you knew that you lived about 3 miles from school, you would have a sense of how long 3 miles is.

FINDING PERSONAL REFERENTS

You can come up with your own set of referents for customary and metric units by taking measurements like the ones below.

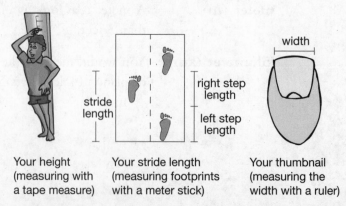

Your height
(measuring with
a tape measure)

Your stride length
(measuring footprints
with a meter stick)

Your thumbnail
(measuring the
width with a ruler)

Your referents do not need to be exact measurements. For example, if your stride length is nearly 1 meter, then think of your stride length as about 1 meter.

EXAMPLE 2

What is the most likely height for a 10-year-old child?

F   1 foot

G $2\frac{1}{2}$ feet

H $4\frac{1}{2}$ feet

J   6 feet

STRATEGY   **Use personal referents to figure out the answer.**

STEP 1   How tall are you in feet?

On average, most 10-year-olds are somewhere between 4 and 5 feet tall. Your height is probably within that range, or close.

STEP 2   Which answer choice makes sense?

See which height is closest to your height or a classmate's height. Choice C, $4\frac{1}{2}$ feet, should be closest.

SOLUTION   **Choice C, $4\frac{1}{2}$ feet, is the best answer.**

CHECK IT OUT with the Coach™

Which is a better estimate for the height of a door—3 meters or 10 meters?

Let's check it out.

About how long is 1 meter? Use the referent in this lesson or use your own referent.

1 meter is about as long as _____.

So, 3 meters would be about as long as _____.

That seems _____ to be the height of a door.

10 meters would be about as long as _____.

That seems _____ to be the height of a door.

So, _____ meters would be the better estimate for the height of the door.

Sample Test Questions

1 Which is the most likely width of a picture frame?

A 10 miles

B 10 feet

C 10 inches

D 10 yards

2 Sarah is 10 years old. She measures the length of her arm from the shoulder to the tips of her fingers. Which is probably closest to that length?

F 12 inches

G 25 inches

H 4 feet

J 6 feet

3 Chad needs to travel from his home in Islip, New York, to his grandmother's house in Montauk, New York. Which of the following is the most likely distance between those two towns?

A 113 millimeters

B 113 kilometers

C 113 meters

D 113 centimeters

4 Which is the most probable length for a soccer field?

F 12 inches

G 12 feet

H 120 inches

J 120 yards

5 Which is the most probable length for a dining room table?

A 2 meters

B 20 centimeters

C 20 meters

D 200 millimeters

6 Shayla measured the width of her thumbnail. Which is the best estimate of the width of her thumbnail?

F 4 centimeters

G 4 millimeters

H 12 centimeters

J 12 millimeters

7 Which of these is probably about 10 feet?

A the height of a drinking fountain

B the height of a fifth-grade student

C the distance from the floor of a room to its ceiling

D the height of a five-story building

8 It is too far for Winston to ride his bike to his aunt's house. He must take a bus or a car. Which could be the distance to his aunt's house?

F 18 feet

G 18 miles

H 20 yards

J 1 mile

Lesson 50: Estimating Length

9 Ciro measured the length of his bedroom and got 15 units. If he measured in customary units, what is the probable length of his bedroom?

Answer _____

10 Cindy measured the length of her pencil and got 15 units. If she measured in metric units, what is the probable length of her pencil?

Answer _____

Short-Response Question

11 Brooke bought some curtains for her living room windows.

Part A

Which is a better estimate for the length of the curtains—6 feet or 6 yards?

Answer _____

Part B

Use words and/or numbers to explain how you know that your answer for Part A is correct.

_____

_____

_____

LESSON 51

Strand 4: Measurement

Reasonable Estimates

5.M.11 Justify the reasonableness of estimates

Sometimes you may need to figure out whether someone's estimated measurement is reasonable or not. The best way to do this is to estimate the measurement yourself. Then compare your estimate with the given estimate.

EXAMPLE 1

A park ranger needs 574 feet of fencing to enclose a playground. Since fencing is sold by the yard, he estimates that he will need about 190 yards of fencing. Is his estimate reasonable?

STRATEGY

Estimate the answer. Compare the park ranger's estimate to your estimate.

STEP 1   What unit conversion do you need?

1 yard = 3 feet

STEP 2   Estimate the number of yards of fencing he needs.

Since yards are larger than feet, divide by 3.

574 rounds up to 600. 600 and 3 are compatible numbers, so estimate the answer.

600 feet = 600 ÷ 3 = 200 yards

A good estimate would be 200 yards of fencing.

STEP 3   Is the estimate the park ranger made reasonable?

Yes, 190 yards is close to 200 yards.

SOLUTION

The park ranger's estimate of 190 yards is a reasonable estimate.

In Example 1, the park ranger's estimate was not exactly the same as the estimate we found. That is okay. There is usually a range of possible estimates. Reasonable estimates will be close in value to one another.

EXAMPLE 2

Kathy ran 19 laps around the school track. Each lap around the track is 985 yards. Kathy decided that she ran about 6 miles. Is her estimate reasonable?

STRATEGY   **Estimate the answer. Compare Kathy's estimate to your estimate.**

STEP 1   First, estimate the total distance she ran in yards.

She ran 19 laps, each 985 yards in length.

19 rounds to 20, and 985 rounds to 1,000.

$1,000 \times 20 = 20,000$, so she ran about 20,000 yards in total.

STEP 2   Estimate the distance she ran in miles.

1 mile = 5,280 feet, and 1 yard = 3 feet.

So, 5,280 feet = $5,280 \div 3 = 1,760$ yd.

1,760 rounds to 2,000.

$20,000 \div 2,000 = 10$, so she ran about 10 miles.

STEP 3   Is Kathy's estimate reasonable?

No, 6 miles is not close to 10 miles.

SOLUTION   **The estimate Kathy made is not reasonable. A more reasonable estimate is 10 miles.**

Is 3 hours a reasonable estimate for the length of a play that begins at 4:05 P.M. and ends at 6:55 P.M.?

Let's check it out.

Round each time to the nearest hour.

4:05 P.M. is about _____ o'clock.

6:55 P.M. is about _____ o'clock.

Subtract the rounded times to find the number of hours the play lasts.

_____ – _____ = _____ , so the play lasted about _____ hours.

Therefore, 3 hours _____ a reasonable estimate of the length of the play.

Sample Test Questions

1 Patsy has 10 wooden boards, each 342 centimeters long. She places all 10 boards lengthwise with no gaps between them. Which is the best estimate of the total length in meters of the boards?

    A 3 meters

    B 4 meters

    C 34 meters

    D 40 meters

2 A surprise party begins at 3:55 P.M. and lasts until 8:10 P.M. Which is the best estimate of how long the party lasted?

    F 2 hours   **H** 4 hours

    G 3 hours   **J** 5 hours

3 Mr. Donavan wants to place a fence around his square yard. Each of the four sides of his yard is 179 feet long. Which is the best estimate of the amount of fencing he needs, in yards?

    A 45 yards

    B 240 yards

    C 360 yards

    D 720 yards

4 Orlando has a piece of string that is 289 inches long. If he divides the string into 5 equal-sized pieces, about how many feet long will each piece be?

    F 4 feet

    G 5 feet

    H 25 feet

    J 58 feet

5 Ms. Hanson teaches two pottery classes on Saturdays. One class starts at 9:55 A.M. and ends at 11:45 A.M. and the other class starts at 1:10 P.M. and ends at 3:15 P.M. Ms. Hanson estimates that she teaches pottery for a total of 6 hours on Saturdays. Is her estimate reasonable?

    A Yes, her estimate is very reasonable.

    B No, a better estimate would be 2 hours.

    C No, a better estimate would be 4 hours.

    D No, a better estimate would be 8 hours.

6 Luke has small rectangular blocks, each of which is 11 inches long. He places 22 blocks in a row, lengthwise, with no space between them. He estimates that his row is about 20 feet long. Which statement is true about his estimate?

    F Yes, his estimate is very reasonable.

    G No, his estimate is about 5 feet too long.

    H No, his estimate is about 5 feet too short.

    J No, his estimate is about 10 feet too short.

7 Carmen rode her bicycle around a loop in the park 12 times. One loop around the park is 1,904 meters. Which is a reasonable estimate of the total number of kilometers Carmen rode her bike?

Answer _____

8 The perimeter of Dominic's yard is 586 feet. He wants to place stones end to end around its perimeter. Each stone is 6 inches long. About how many stones will he need to completely surround the yard?

Answer _____

Short-Response Questions

9 A piece of rope is 62 feet long. Mark divides the rope into 3 equal-sized pieces. He estimates that each piece of rope will be about 250 inches long.

Part A

Is Mark's estimate reasonable? If not, what would be a reasonable estimate?

Answer _____

Part B

Use words and/or numbers to explain how you determined if Mark's estimate was reasonable.

_____

_____

10 One lap of a swimming pool is 75 feet long. Ginny swims 33 laps in the pool.

Part A

Ginny estimates that she swam 1,200 yards. Is her estimate reasonable? If not, what would be a reasonable estimate?

Answer _____

Part B

Use words and/or numbers to explain how you determined if Ginny's estimate was reasonable.

_____

_____

Progress Check for Lessons 46–51

1 What is the measure of the angle shown below?

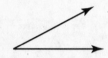

A 23°

B 27°

C 157°

D 153°

2 What is the length of the line segment shown below to the nearest $\frac{1}{8}$ inch?

_____

F $1\frac{7}{8}$ inches

G 2 inches

H $2\frac{1}{8}$ inches

J $2\frac{1}{4}$ inches

3 Margaret is 4 feet 10 inches tall. What is Margaret's total height in inches?

A 41 inches

B 50 inches

C 56 inches

D 58 inches

4 Ned spends 1 hour 55 minutes at football practice on Monday nights. If practice ends at 7:00 P.M., at what time does it begin?

F 5:00 P.M.

G 5:05 P.M.

H 6:05 P.M.

J 8:55 P.M.

5 Lauren is running a 5-kilometer race on Sunday. How many meters long is the race?

A 60

B 500

C 5,000

D 6,000

6 What is the length of this leaf to the nearest centimeter?

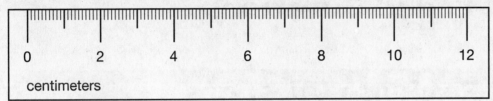

F	G	H	J
4 cm	5 cm	6 cm	7 cm

7 Gordon measured the length of his foot with a ruler. Which is the most likely length of his foot?

A 8 inches

B 4 inches

C 2 yards

D 1 yard

8 Which number makes the sentence true?

1 kilometer = _____ centimeters

F 100

G 1,000

H 10,000

J 100,000

9 Greg has a large pine tree in his backyard. Which is the most likely height of the tree?

A 20 meters

B 20 kilometers

C 200 centimeters

D 200 meters

10 Several parents are setting up for a teacher appreciation breakfast in the cafeteria. They place 11 tables together to make one long buffet table. Each of the 11 tables is 8 feet long. Mrs. Mars thinks that the buffet table they formed is about 20 yards long. Is her estimate reasonable?

F Yes, her estimate is reasonable.

G No, a better estimate would be 10 yards.

H No, a better estimate would be 30 yards.

J No, a better estimate would be 80 yards.

Open-Ended Questions

Short-Response Questions

11   Use your protractor to solve this problem.

Part A

Draw an angle that measures 70°.

Part B

Explain how you know that the angle you drew measures 70° and not 110°.

_____

_____

12   Marcella runs on a circular path that is 607 feet long. She runs around the path 18 times in one day.

Part A

Marcella thinks that she ran a total distance of about 2,000 yards. Is her estimate reasonable? If not, what would be a reasonable estimate?

Answer _____

Part B

Use words and/or numbers to explain how you determined what a reasonable estimate of the distance would be.

_____

_____

Extended-Response Question

13 Brad takes classes on Saturdays at the community center.

Part A

His art class starts at 12:30 P.M. and ends at 1:15 P.M. How many minutes does his art class last?

Answer _____ minutes

Part B

His computer class is the same length as his art class, but it ends at 3:10 P.M. At what time does his computer class begin?

Answer _____

Part C

Explain how you determined your answers for Parts A and B and why you took the steps that you did.

_____

_____

_____

_____

_____

LESSON 52

Strand 5: Statistics and Probability

Collecting and Recording Data

5.S.1 Collect and record data from a variety of sources (i.e., newspapers, magazines, polls, charts, and surveys)

A newspaper may report that 50 out of 100 students surveyed think there should be more art and music classes offered in school. How did the newspaper find that out? They had to ask 100 students and record the information, or **data**, that they collected. You can conduct your own surveys and collect data, too. A table is one way to organize the information that you collect.

TABLES

EXAMPLE 1

Zeke asked 10 students in his class this question:

Which of these colors is your favorite—red, blue, green, or yellow?

Below are his results.

Student	Favorite Color
Charlie	blue
Katrina	red
Gus	green
Taylor	blue
Jonas	blue
Mariana	yellow
Abim	red
Matt	blue
Lise	blue
Chen	green

Zeke wants to organize his data better. Make a table to show the number of students who chose each color.

STRATEGY   **Make a table based on the color choices.**

STEP 1   Make a table.

Include a title and labels for the columns.

Students' Favorite Colors

Favorite Color	Number of Students
red	
blue	
green	
yellow	

STEP 2   Count the number of students who chose each color and record those numbers in the table.

2 students chose red; 5 blue; 2 green; 1 yellow

SOLUTION   **This table better organizes Zeke's data:**

Students' Favorite Colors

Favorite Color	Number of Students
red	2
blue	5
green	2
yellow	1

A tally chart for Zeke's data would look like this:

Students' Favorite Colors

Favorite Color	Number of Students
red	||
blue	|||||
green	||
yellow		

BAR GRAPHS

Another way to record data is to create a bar graph. A bar graph uses bars to represent data. If you use a grid or graph paper, you can record each piece of data by shading one square.

EXAMPLE 2

Hal asked 10 classmates this question:

> Do you think recess is long enough, or do you think it should be longer or shorter?

Hal will make a bar graph to show his results. If 2 classmates said they think recess is long enough, 7 classmates said they think recess should be longer, and 1 classmate said it should be shorter, what should Hal's bar graph look like?

STRATEGY

Draw a bar graph to show his results.

STEP 1   Use a grid or graph paper.

Title your graph and label the horizontal and vertical axes.

STEP 2   Graph the data.

Shade 2 squares to show the 2 classmates who said recess is long enough.

Shade 7 squares to show the 7 classmates who said recess should be longer.

Shade 1 square to show the 1 classmate who said recess should be shorter.

SOLUTION

Hal's bar graph should look like this:

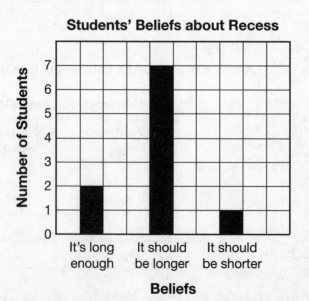

Students' Beliefs about Recess

CHECK IT OUT with the Coach

Fred is making a tally chart to show people's favorite toothpaste. If 14 of the people he surveyed like Brand A best, how many tally marks should be in the row for Brand A?

Let's check it out.

How would you draw 14 tally marks?

10 of the 14 tally marks would look like this: _____

The other 4 tally marks would look like this: _____

So, 14 tally marks would look like this: _____

Sample Test Questions

The cafeteria staff wants to know which kinds of fruit to serve at lunch, so they asked 10 students to name their favorite fruit. This chart shows the results. Use this chart for Questions 1 and 2.

Student	Favorite Fruit
Emilia	apple
Jake	apple
Charlotte	banana
Calhoun	orange
Deya	orange
Daniel	banana
Megan	apple
Nathaniel	apple
Vanessa	apple
Oliver	banana

1 Which table shows another way that the data could be organized?

A Fifth-Grade Students' Favorite Fruits

Favorite Fruit	Number of Students
apple	3
banana	2
orange	5

B Fifth-Grade Students' Favorite Fruits

Favorite Fruit	Number of Students
apple	5
banana	3
orange	2

C Fifth-Grade Students' Favorite Fruits

Favorite Fruit	Number of Students
apple	5
banana	2
orange	3

D Fifth-Grade Students' Favorite Fruits

Favorite Fruit	Number of Students
apple	2
banana	3
orange	5

2 Which bar graph shows another way that the data could be organized?

F

H

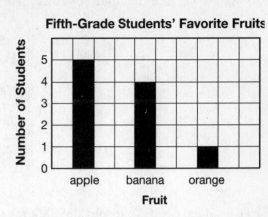

G

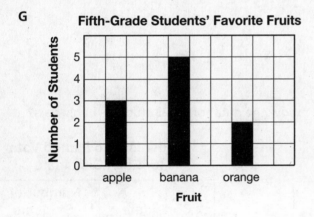

J

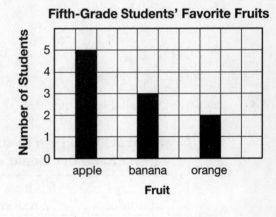

Steve is polling 23 students to find out who they plan to vote for in the election for school president. So far, he has recorded data for 20 students in this tally chart. Use this chart for Questions 3 and 4.

**Students Who Plan to
Vote For Each Candidate**

Neil	|||||
Tamera	||||| |||
Gary	||||| ||

3 Steve needs to record the data for three more students, all of whom plan to vote for Tamera. After he records these data, what will the tallies in the row for Tamera look like?

A ||||| |||

B ||||| |||||

C ||||| ||||| |

D ||||| ||||| |||

4 Which of these tables could Steve use to show the data for all 23 students in his class?

F

**Students Who Plan to Vote
for Each Candidate**

Candidate	Number of Students
Neil	5
Tamera	11
Gary	7

H

**Students Who Plan to Vote
for Each Candidate**

Candidate	Number of Students
Neil	5
Tamera	8
Gary	10

G

**Students Who Plan to Vote
for Each Candidate**

Candidate	Number of Students
Neil	10
Tamera	21
Gary	12

J

**Students Who Plan to Vote
for Each Candidate**

Candidate	Number of Students
Neil	2
Tamera	3
Gary	5

5 A tally chart shows this many votes for a field trip to a museum:

卌 卌 卌 |

How many votes is this?

Answer _____

6 A tally chart shows this many votes for a field trip to see a play:

卌 ||||

In a bar graph, how many grid boxes would be shaded to show the number of votes for the play?

Answer _____

Short-Response Questions

7 Collect data about 10 students in your class. Ask each of the 10 students this question.

How many pets do you have?

Part A

Record your results by drawing tallies in the appropriate rows of a chart.

Number of Pets Students Have

Numbet of Pets	Number of Students
0 pets	
1 pet	
2 pets	
More than 2 pets	

Part B

Use words and or numbers to explain how you collected and recorded your data. Then, write one or more sentences describing your results. (For example, you can write a sentence explaining how many students had 2 or more pets.)

_____

_____

_____

8   Collect data about 10 students in your class. Ask each of the 10 students this question.

Which of these subjects do you like best—English Language Arts, Math, Science, or Social Studies?

Part A

Record your data by making a bar graph on a grid. Be sure to title your graph and label each axis.

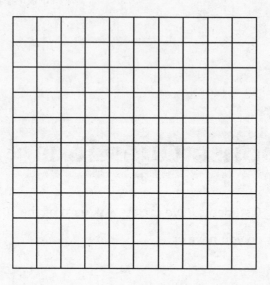

Part B

Use words and or numbers to explain how you collected and recorded your data. Then, write one or more sentences describing your results (for example, you can write a sentence explaining which subject was most popular).

_____

_____

_____

9 Ask 10 students in your class to imagine that they have this choice.

You could either have a longer school day and more days off in the summer, or you could keep the school year the way it is. Which would you prefer?

Part A

Collect data by writing the name of each student you ask in the first column of the chart and recording their choices.

Students' Choices

Student	Choice

Part B

Use words to explain how you could use a table to organize the data in Part A. Fill in a table like the one below to show how you would do this.

Students' Choices

Choice	Number of Students
Longer school day and more days off	
Keep school year the way it is	

10   Think of a survey question that you would like to ask 10 students in your class.

Part A

Write your question below.

_____

Part B

Ask your question to 10 students in your class. Record your data by drawing a table, a tally chart, or a bar graph. (If you draw a bar graph, use graph paper). Be sure to include a title and labels.

LESSON 53

Strand 5: Statistics and Probability

Line Graphs

5.S.2 Display data in a line graph to show an increase or decrease over time.

A **line graph** uses points connected by line segments to show data. It is a useful way to show how data change over time.

In a line graph, the horizontal (left to right) axis usually shows units of time, such as days, weeks, or months. The vertical (up and down) axis usually shows numbers.

EXAMPLE 1

Every week at the park, Daphne attempts 20 foul shots. This table shows the number of foul shots she made each week for the past five weeks.

Foul Shots Daphne Made

Week	1	2	3	4	5
Number of Foul Shots Made	4	8	10	14	16

Use this table to make a line graph.

STRATEGY

Give the graph a title and labels. Then plot points for the data and connect them.

STEP 1 Give the graph a title and labels.

Give the graph the same title as the table—"Foul Shots Daphne Made." Label the horizontal and vertical axes.

STEP 2 Choose a scale for the vertical axis.

The greatest number of shots she made on any day was 16.

So, a scale of 0 to 16 would work.

There are only 10 units on the vertical axis, so you cannot include every number from 0 to 16. Count by 2's instead.

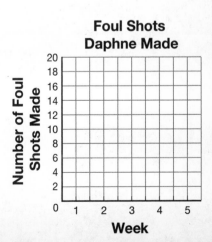

STEP 3   Plot the first piece of data in the table.

The table shows that Daphne made 4 shots in Week 1.

Find Week 1 on the horizontal axis.

Move up until you are directly across from the 4 on the vertical axis.

Plot a point there to show this piece of data.

STEP 4   Plot points for the other pieces of data just as you did in Step 3.

STEP 5   Use a ruler to connect each of the points you plotted.

SOLUTION   **The completed graph will look like this.**

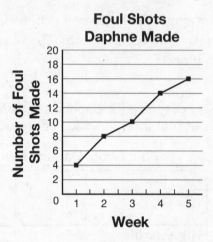

You can use line graphs to look for trends in data.

EXAMPLE 2   Look at the graph you drew for Example 1. Describe the trend you see in the data.

STRATEGY   **Look at whether the data points are increasing or decreasing.**

The line on the graph from Example 1 moves up from left to right.

So the line graph shows an increase in the number of foul shots made.

SOLUTION   **The trend is that the number of foul shots Daphne made increased each week over the five-week period.**

Some graphs use two lines to show two sets of related data. These are called **double-line** graphs. A key is usually given to show what each line on the graph represents.

EXAMPLE 3

This double-line graph compares the temperatures of the first 10 days of winter for the last two years.

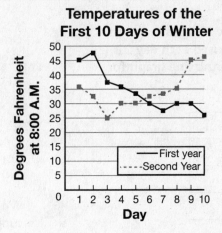

Temperatures of the First 10 Days of Winter

On which day are the two years' temperatures the farthest apart? What is the approximate difference in temperature between the years on that day?

STRATEGY   **Find the widest gap between two points on the graphs.**

STEP 1   Look at the gaps between the line graphs for all 10 days, and find the day where the gap is the widest.

The widest gap is on Day 10.

STEP 2   Use the vertical scale for these two days to find the temperature differences for Day 10.

The data points for Day 10 show 46°F and 26°F.

46 − 26 = 20, so the difference is about 20°F.

SOLUTION   **The two years' temperatures were farthest apart on Day 10. The temperature difference for Day 10 was about 20°F.**

CHECK IT OUT with the Coach™

Rory wants to create a line graph to show the number of cans he collected over the course of three weeks. If he collected 20 cans during Week 1, 34 cans during Week 2, and 28 cans during Week 3, what scale could he use for the vertical axis of his graph?

Let's check it out.

What is the greatest number of cans he collected during any one week?

The greatest number was _____ cans during Week _____.

The scale must go up to a number that is at least that high.

So, a possible scale for the vertical axis is 0 to _____.

Sample Test Questions

Giuseppe exercises every day. This graph shows the number of hours he exercised each day from Monday to Sunday. Use this line graph for Questions 1–3.

Student	Favorite Color
Charlie	blue
Katrina	red
Gus	green
Taylor	blue
Jonas	blue
Mariana	yellow
Abim	red
Matt	blue
Lise	blue
Chen	green

1 How many minutes did Giuseppe exercise in all from Monday to Sunday?

A 220

B 230

C 250

D 275

2 On how many days did Giuseppe exercise for 40 or more minutes?

F 7

G 6

H 5

J 4

3 Which of the following statements is supported by the data in the graph?

A Giuseppe exercised more on the weekend than on weekdays.

B Giuseppe exercised more on weekdays than on the weekend.

C The number of minutes Giuseppe exercised increased from Monday to Wednesday and then decreased from Wednesday to Sunday.

D The number of minutes Giuseppe exercised showed a steady decrease from Monday to Sunday.

This double-line graph compares the amount of money that Emma and Oprah have saved over the past five years. The amounts are the total savings at the end of each year. Use this double-line graph for Questions 4–6.

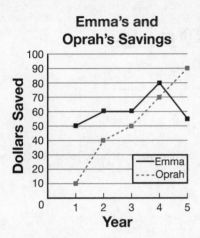

This line graph shows the attendance at a street fair over five days. Use the line graph to answer Questions 7–9.

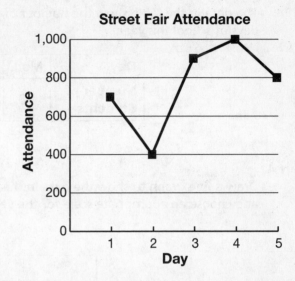

4 Approximately how much more money did Emma save than Oprah in Year 1?

   F $50   **H** $30

   G $40   **J** $20

5 Approximately how much more money did Oprah save than Emma in Year 5?

   A $15   **C** $35

   B $25   **D** $45

6 Which of the following trends does the double-line graph show for this five-year period?

   F Both Emma's and Oprah's savings increased every year.

   G Only Oprah's savings increased every year.

   H Only Emma's savings increased every year.

   J Both Emma's and Oprah's savings decreased every year.

7 On which day was attendance at the street fair the greatest?

   A Day 1

   B Day 3

   C Day 4

   D Day 5

8 About how many people attended the street fair on Day 3?

   Answer _____

9 Between which two days did the greatest increase in street fair attendance occur?

   Answer _____

Short-Response Question

10 The data in the table show the number of students who came to school late on the first five days of school this year.

Day	Mon.	Tues.	Wed.	Thurs.	Fri.
Number of Students	20	12	7	6	2

Part A

Draw a line graph to show the data in the table. Be sure to title your graph, label each axis, and choose an appropriate scale for the vertical axis.

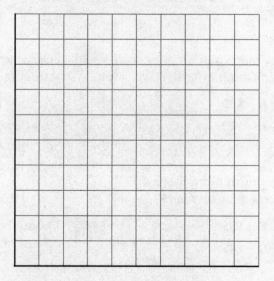

Part B

Use words and/or numbers to explain how you chose the scale for your line graph and why you knew that the scale you chose would work.

_____

_____

_____

LESSON 54

Strand 5: Statistics and Probability

Mean

5.5.3 Calculate the mean for a given set of data and use to describe a set of data

One way to describe a set of data is to find the **mean**, or the average.

To find the mean, follow these steps:

- First, add the numbers in the set of data.
- Then, divide the sum by the number of addends in the set.

EXAMPLE 1

These are the distances Tanya biked last week. What is the mean (average) distance she biked per day?

Number of Miles Biked

Day	Number of Miles
Monday	15
Tuesday	12
Wednesday	14
Thursday	12
Friday	17

STRATEGY **Use the steps for finding the mean.**

STEP 1 Add the number of miles.

$$15 + 12 + 14 + 12 + 17 = 70$$

STEP 2 Divide by the number of days.

$$70 \div 5 = 14$$

SOLUTION **The mean (average) number of miles per day is 14.**

Finding a mean can help you compare a piece of data to an entire set of data.

EXAMPLE 2

There were 10 participants in a dance contest. Their scores for the contest were:

7, 9, 5, 4, 3, 7, 9, 8, 6, 2

Maureen got a score of 7. How does her score compare to the scores of the other participants?

STRATEGY

To compare Maureen's score to the other scores, find the mean score and see if her score is below or above the average.

STEP 1   Find the mean score.

Add the scores.

7 + 9 + 5 + 4 + 3 + 7 + 9 + 8 + 6 + 2 = 60

Divide the sum by the number of scores, 10.

60 ÷ 10 = 6

STEP 2   Compare Maureen's score to the average score.

Maureen's score of 7 is higher than the mean score of 6.

SOLUTION

Maureen's score is above the average. In other words, her score was higher than the mean score of all the participants.

CHECK IT OUT *with the* **Coach**™

What is the mean of these numbers?

4, 7, 8, 9

Let's check it out.

Add the numbers: 4 + 7 + 8 + 9.

The sum is _____.

There are _____ numbers in the set,

so divide the sum by _____.

Since _____ ÷ _____ = _____,

the mean is _____.

Sample Test Questions

1   What is the mean of these numbers?

     25, 50, 75

A   25

B   50

C   75

D   100

2   Jordan spends a lot of time writing stories. He wrote stories for 3 hours on Friday, 5 hours on Saturday, 3 hours on Sunday, and 1 hour on Monday. What is the mean number of hours he spent writing stories over these 4 days?

F   12

G   5

H   4

J   3

3   What is the mean of these numbers?

     56, 60, 68, 72, 77, 87, 91

A   73

B   72

C   71

D   70

4   Nadia and four of her friends went bowling. These were their bowling scores:

     110, 108, 123, 115, 104

If Nadia's score was 108, which statement accurately compares her score to all five bowling scores?

F   Nadia's score was lower than the mean score.

G   Nadia's score was the same as the mean score.

H   Nadia's score was higher than the mean score.

J   There is no way to compare her score to all five scores.

5   Martha keeps track of the number of points she scores during each basketball game. In her last five basketball games, Martha scored 16, 20, 8, 12, and 9 points. What was the mean number of points she scored for those five games?

A   10

B   12

C   13

D   14

6 Larry recorded the temperature at noon for six days in a row. Below are the temperatures he recorded.

72°F, 68°F, 73°F, 70°F, 55°F, 58°F

What was the mean temperature for those six days?

F   63°F

G   64°F

H   66°F

J   67°F

7 Anya earned these grades on her last six math quizzes:

90, 80, 85, 88, 91, 100

What is her mean quiz score?

Answer _____

8 David read an entire book in 7 days. He recorded the number of pages he read each day.

Number of Pages Read Each Day

Day	Number Read
Monday	23
Tuesday	12
Wednesday	20
Thursday	15
Friday	10
Saturday	32
Sunday	35

What was the mean number of pages he read each day?

Answer _____

Short-Response Question

9 Below are the weights, in kilograms, of six packages that are being shipped.

8 kg, 16 kg, 12 kg, 20 kg, 18 kg, 10 kg

What is the mean weight of these six packages?

Show your work.

Answer _____

LESSON 55

Strand 5: Statistics and Probability

Making Predictions

5.S.4 Formulate conclusions and make predictions from graphs

PREDICTIONS BASED ON LINE GRAPHS

Sometimes you can use data to make **predictions**. Predictions are statements about what might happen in the future. For example, you may be able to use the trend you see on a line graph to make a prediction.

EXAMPLE 1

This line graph shows the number of cats that were adopted from the Adopt-a-Pet Foundation over a six-month period.

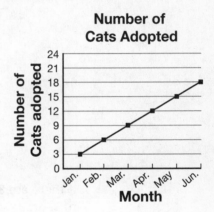

If the number of cats adopted continues to increase at this rate, predict the number of cats that will be adopted in July.

STRATEGY   **Extend the line segment on the graph.**

STEP 1   Line up a ruler with the existing line segment and extend it to include a point for July.

The dashed segment shows how the line segment has been extended.

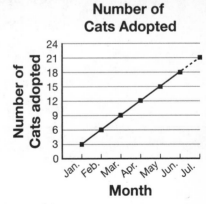

STEP 2   Use the graph to make a prediction.

The extended line on the graph shows that, in July, about 21 cats will be adopted.

SOLUTION   **If the number of cats adopted continues to increase at the same rate, about 21 cats will be adopted in July.**

You could also have found the answer for Example 1 a different way. You could have figured out that the number of cats adopted each month was increasing by 3. Since 18 cats were adopted in June, you could predict that 18 + 3, or 21, cats would be adopted in July.

PREDICTIONS BASED ON SAMPLES

Another way to make predictions is to use the results of surveys. Surveys are used to gather information about a group. If the group is large, a part of the group is randomly selected to represent the entire group. That part is called a **sample**. You can then survey the sample and use the results to make a prediction about the larger group.

EXAMPLE 2

Ruth randomly selected 40 students in the fifth grade at her school and asked them which they would prefer—a field trip to the museum, a field trip to a state park, or a field trip to see a play. This graph shows the results of her survey.

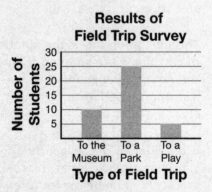

Results of Field Trip Survey

If there are 80 students in the fifth grade at Ruth's school, predict how many fifth-grade students would prefer to go the museum.

STRATEGY

Find the fraction of the sample that prefer to go to the museum and use it to make a prediction.

STEP 1 What fraction of the fifth-grade students surveyed preferred to go the museum?

10 out of 40 fifth-graders surveyed preferred to go a museum.

So, $\frac{10}{40}$, or $\frac{1}{4}$, of the students surveyed preferred to go a museum.

STEP 2 Use this fraction to make a prediction.

Predict that $\frac{1}{4}$ of the 80 fifth-grade students would prefer to go to the museum.

To find $\frac{1}{4}$ of 80, divide 80 by 4.

$80 \div 4 = 20$

SOLUTION

A good prediction for the total number of fifth-grade students who would prefer to go to the museum is 20.

EXAMPLE 3

Based on Ruth's survey from Example 2, what conclusion can you draw about which field trip would be most popular among all fifth-grade students at her school?

STRATEGY

Use the graph to predict the most popular field trip.

The tallest bar on the bar graph is labeled "To a park."

So, the most popular choice among the students surveyed was to go to a state park.

Since Ruth selected a random sample, you can conclude that the most popular choice among all fifth-graders would be to go to a state park, too.

SOLUTION

It can be concluded that going to a state park would probably be the most popular choice of all fifth-grade students at the school.

CHECK IT OUT with the **Coach**™

How could you use a line graph to make a prediction about a future event?

Let's check it out.

One way would be to look at the line graph and see if it shows a trend.

If it shows a trend, you can use a ruler to _____ the line segment on the graph.

Doing this could help you see where the future event would fall on the graph.

You could also look at the data points and see by how much they are

_____ or decreasing.

You could then _____ or subtract that amount from a known data point to predict a data point that is not on the graph.

Sample Test Questions

This line graph shows how many books were sold by a bookstore over the course of five months last year. Use this graph for Questions 1 and 2.

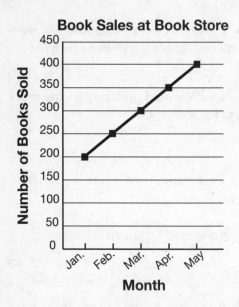

Book Sales at Book Store

Lamont randomly surveyed 50 parents of fifth graders at his school to find out whether they support the building of a new middle school. This bar graph shows the results of his survey. Use this graph for Questions 3 and 4.

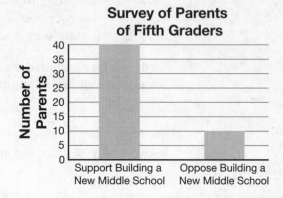

Survey of Parents of Fifth Graders

1 If the number of books sold continues to increase at the same rate, which is the best prediction of the number of books the store will sell in June?

A 50

B 450

C 500

D 550

2 If the number of books sold continues to increase at the same rate, which is the best prediction of the number of books the store will sell in July?

F 100

G 450

H 500

J 550

3 There are a total of 100 parents of fifth graders at Lamont's school. Based on the survey results, how many of those 100 parents would you expect to oppose the building of the middle school?

A 10   C 50

B 20   D 100

4 Which would be the best conclusion to draw from Lamont's survey?

F Most parents of fifth graders support the building of a new middle school.

G Most parents of fifth graders oppose the building of a new middle school.

H Most parents of fifth graders are undecided about the building of a new middle school.

J The number of parents who support the building of a new middle school is equal to the number of parents who oppose it.

Marla randomly surveyed 30 fifth-grade students at her school to find out how many of them play musical instruments. The bar graph below shows her results. Use this graph for Questions 5 and 6.

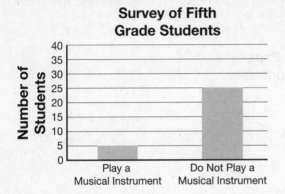

This line graph shows the monthly profits earned by a restaurant over a 5-month period. Use this graph for Questions 7 and 8.

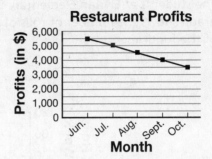

5 There are 90 fifth-grade students at Marla's school. Based on the survey results, how many of the 90 students would you expect to play a musical instrument?

A 5

B 10

C 15

D 20

6 Which would be the best conclusion to draw from Marla's survey?

F Most of the fifth-grade students at Marla's school play a musical instrument.

G Most of the fifth-grade students at Marla's school do *not* play a musical instrument.

H Most of the fifth-grade students at Marla's school play several musical instruments.

J The number of students who play a musical instrument at Marla's school is equal to the number of students who do not play a musical instrument.

7 If the restaurant's profits continue to decrease at the same rate, what would you expect the restaurant's profits to be in November?

Answer _____

8 If the restaurant's profits have been decreasing at this rate since May, what is the best estimate of the restaurant's profits in May?

Answer _____

Short-Response Question

9   The students at Elysian Elementary School are selling wrapping paper for a fundraiser. This line graph shows the number of rolls of wrapping paper that were sold during the first five weeks of the fundraiser.

Part A

If the number of rolls sold each week continues to increase at the same rate, predict the number of rolls of wrapping paper that will be sold during Week 6.

Answer _____ rolls

Part B

Use words and/or numbers to explain how you made your prediction for Part A.

_____

_____

_____

Progress Check for Lessons 52-55

Ms. Festa, the P.E. teacher, is randomly surveying 30 fifth-grade students to find out which activity they like best—kickball, frisbee, or badminton. So far, she has recorded data for 27 students in this tally chart. Use this chart for Questions 1–2.

Activity Fifth-Grade Students Like Best

Activity	Number of Students
kickball	~~HHH~~ |||
frisbee	~~HHH~~ ~~HHH~~
badminton	~~HHH~~ ||||

1 Ms. Festa needs to record the data for three more students, all of whom prefer kickball. After she records these data, what will the tallies in the row for kickball look like?

A   ~~HHH~~ ~~HHH~~

B   ~~HHH~~ ~~HHH~~ \|

C   ~~HHH~~ ~~HHH~~ \|\|\|

D   ~~HHH~~ ~~HHH~~ ~~HHH~~

2 There are 60 fifth-grade students at Ms. Festa's school. Based on the survey results, how many of those 60 students would you expect to like frisbee best?

F   10

G   15

H   20

J   30

3 Which question is best answered using information from a newspaper?

A   What is the favorite color of students in Mr. Bell's class?

B   What is the most popular cafeteria food item sold?

C   How long do students in Ms. Fry's class study each night?

D   What were the winning scores of last night's baseball game?

4 Felicia sold lemonade for five days. The table below shows how many glasses she sold each day.

Glasses of Lemonade Sold

Day	Number of Glasses Sold
Wed.	21
Thurs.	17
Fri.	14
Sat.	28
Sun.	15

What is the mean number of glasses of lemonade that Felicia sold?

F   15

G   19

H   20

J   21

This line graph shows the number of cans of food collected during the first five weeks of a food drive. Use this graph for Questions 5 and 6.

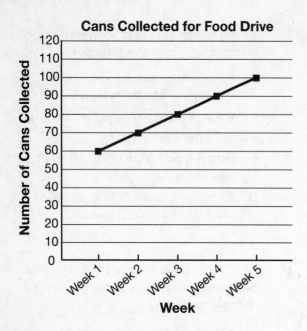

Cans Collected for Food Drive

6 If the number of cans collected continues to increase at the same rate, which is the best prediction of the number of cans that will be collected during week 6?

F   10

G   105

H   110

J   120

5 What is the total number of cans collected during the first five weeks of the food drive?

A   100

B   300

C   400

D   500

Open-Ended Questions

Short-Response Question

7 This table shows how many minutes Khalid practiced playing his trombone this week.

Khalid's Trombone Practice

Day	Number of Minutes
Mon.	35
Tues.	50
Wed.	40
Thur.	50
Fri.	35

Part A

What is the mean number of minutes that Khalid practiced this week?

Answer _____

Part B

Use words and/or numbers to explain how you found the mean for part a and why you took the steps that you did.

_____

_____

_____

Extended-Response Question

8   Celia made a table to show the number of words she misspelled in her class's monthly spelling tournament.

Words Celia Misspelled in Spelling Tournaments

Month	Jan.	Feb.	Mar.	Apr.	May
Number of Words Misspelled	18	16	12	11	8

Part A

Draw a line graph to show the data in the table. Be sure to title your graph, label each axis, and choose an appropriate scale for the vertical axis.

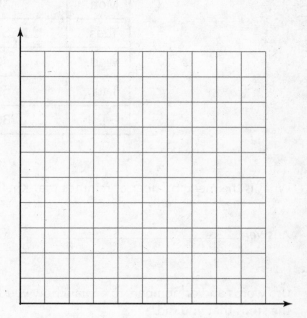

Part B

Use words and/or numbers to explain how you chose the scale for the vertical axis of your line graph in Part A.

_____

_____

Part C

Look at the line graph you drew for Part A. What trend is shown by the line graph?

Answer _____

Practice Test 2

Session 1

1   Divide: $15\overline{)259}$

   A   17 R3

   B   17 R4

   C   18 R3

   D   18 R4

2   A wooden board has a length of 5 yards 11 inches. What is the total length of this board in inches?

   F   26 inches

   G   52 inches

   H   180 inches

   J   191 inches

3   Which list shows all the prime numbers between 70 and 80?

   A   71, 73, 75, 77, 79

   B   71, 73, 77

   C   71, 73, 79

   D   71, 73

4   What two fractions name the part of the spinner that has even numbers?

   F $\frac{2}{6}$ and $\frac{1}{3}$ **H** $\frac{3}{6}$ and $\frac{1}{2}$

   G $\frac{3}{6}$ and $\frac{1}{3}$ **J** $\frac{4}{6}$ and $\frac{2}{3}$

5   What is the measure of the angle shown below?

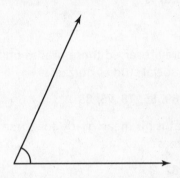

   A   65°

   B   75°

   C   115°

   D   125°

6   Which of the following shows a pair of similar triangles?

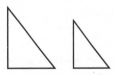

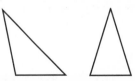

Go On

PRACTICE TEST 2

7 If Soraya answered 87 of the 100 questions on a test correctly, what percent of the questions did she answer correctly?

A 7%

B 78%

C 87%

D 187%

8 Aubrey received these grades on his last five social studies quizzes.

89, 85, 78, 75, 83

What is his mean grade for these quizzes?

F 82

G 83

H 84

J 85

9 This table shows the weights of three packages waiting to be shipped.

Package	Weight (in kg)
Package A	13.15
Package B	12.25
Package C	12.3

Which shows these packages ordered from the package with the least weight to the package with the greatest weight?

A Package A, Package B, Package C

B Package B, Package A, Package C

C Package C, Package B, Package A

D Package B, Package C, Package A

10 Jonathan is creating a pattern by shading triangles. Below are the first four figures in his pattern.

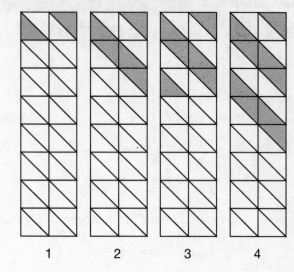

If he continues this pattern, what should Figure 5 look like?

F

H

G

J

11 A triangle has three congruent sides. Which of the following **must** be true?

A It is an equilateral triangle.

B It is a right triangle.

C It is a scalene triangle.

D It is an obtuse triangle.

Go On

Test 2: Session 1

12 The historical society sends out a newsletter each month to all of its subscribers. This graph shows the number of subscribers who received newsletters from January to May.

Newsletter Subscriptions

If the number of subscribers continues to increase at the same rate, what is the best prediction for the number of subscribers the magazine will have in June?

F 200

G 1,900

H 2,000

J 2,200

13 Which of these ribbons, when measured to the nearest centimeter, has a length of 5 centimeters?

A
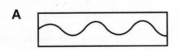

B
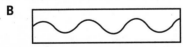

C
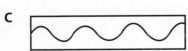

D
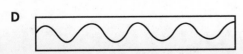

14 Which sentence is true?

F $\frac{1}{5} < \frac{1}{4}$

G $\frac{1}{3} < \frac{1}{10}$

H $\frac{1}{10} > \frac{1}{2}$

J $\frac{1}{5} > \frac{1}{3}$

15 Triangle *BCD* is congruent to triangle *TVU*. Which two sides are corresponding sides of these triangles?

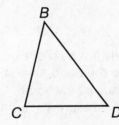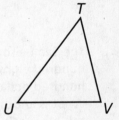

A $\overline{BC}$ and $\overline{TV}$

B $\overline{BC}$ and $\overline{TU}$

C $\overline{DC}$ and $\overline{TV}$

D $\overline{DC}$ and $\overline{TU}$

16 In the expression below, which is the variable?

$$5n = 16$$

F 5

G *n*

H =

J 16

Go On

PRACTICE TEST 2

17 Mr. Garcia worked in the garden for $1\frac{3}{4}$ hours on Saturday morning. His daughter Ria worked in the garden for $2\frac{1}{4}$ hours that same day. How much longer did Ria work in the garden than her father?

A $\frac{1}{4}$ hour

B $\frac{1}{2}$ hour

C $\frac{3}{4}$ hour

D $1\frac{1}{2}$ hours

18 The Samuelson family just paid one hundred eighty-nine thousand, five-hundred dollars to buy a new house. What is another way to express this amount?

F $18,950

G $189,005

H $189,050

J $189,500

19 Arlene drew a quadrilateral which has two pairs of parallel sides, two acute angles, and two obtuse angles. Which kind of quadrilateral did she draw?

A a square

B a trapezoid

C a parallelogram that is not a rectangle

D a rectangle that is not a square

20 Chemequa needs $\frac{3}{4}$ cup of flour for a recipe. Which of the following is an equivalent amount of flour?

F $\frac{3}{6}$ cup flour

G $\frac{5}{6}$ cup flour

H $\frac{5}{8}$ cup flour

J $\frac{6}{8}$ cup flour

21 If $a = 6$, what is the value of the expression $5 + (a - 2) \times 3$?

A 5

B 11

C 17

D 27

22 Dana spent $\frac{5}{12}$ of an hour doing homework and $\frac{11}{12}$ of an hour doing chores. Which of these gives the best estimate of how much time she spent doing these two activities?

F $\frac{1}{2}$ hour

G $1\frac{1}{2}$ hours

H 2 hours

J $2\frac{1}{2}$ hours

23 Which symbol makes this sentence true?

$$\frac{2}{5} \underline{\hspace{1cm}} \frac{3}{10}$$

A $>$

B $=$

C $<$

D $\times$

Go On

24 Demetrius has 25 baseball cards. He wants to divide his cards into equal piles, with no cards left over. Which of the following shows piles into which his cards can be divided?

F piles of 2 cards each

G piles of 3 cards each

H piles of 4 cards each

J piles of 5 cards each

25 Jayden has a backyard that is shaped like a square with sides that are 36 feet in length.

Backyard 36 ft

He wants to know how many feet of fencing are needed to surround his backyard. How many feet of fencing does he need?

A 40 feet

B 72 feet

C 108 feet

D 144 feet

26 What is the measure of ∠A in this triangle?

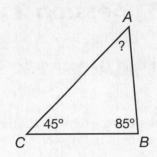

F 40°

G 50°

H 55°

J 130°

STOP

Test 2: Session 1

Session 2

27   The ratio of boys to girls in Bibi's class is 2 to 3.

Part A

If there are a total of 20 students in Bibi's class, how many boys are in the class? How many girls are in the class?

Show your work.

Number of boys _____

Number of girls _____

Part B

On the lines below, explain how you found your answer.

_____

_____

_____

28   Lloyd is creating a number pattern that follows the rule $7n$, where n represents the position of the number in the pattern.

Part A

What should be the first five numbers in Lloyd's pattern?

Answer _____

Part B

Use words, tables, and/or numbers to explain how you used the rule $7n$ to determine the first five numbers in the pattern.

_____

_____

_____

Go On

29   Look at the square shown below.

Part A

How many lines of symmetry does this square have? If it has one or more lines of symmetry, draw them above.

Answer _____ lines of symmetry

Part B

On the lines below, explain how you know that your answer for Part A is correct.

_____

_____

_____

30   Mrs. Wilkins can divide her music class into equal groups of 6 or equal groups of 9, with no students left over.

Part A

What is the least possible number of students in her class

Answer _____

Part B

On the lines below, explain how you found your answer.

_____

_____

_____

Go On

31   Emily works at a radio station on Sunday mornings.

Part A

She begins taping her first program at 8:45 A.M. and stops taping at 9:35 A.M. How many minutes does her first program last?

Answer _____

Part B

The next program she tapes lasts the same length as the first program, but it ends at 11:05 A.M. At what time does she start taping her second program?

Answer _____

Part C

On the lines below, explain how you found your answer for Parts A and B.

_____

_____

_____

_____

_____

Go On

32 A designer created a new logo for the Kennedy Highlanders. He labeled several points as shown below.

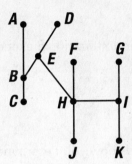

Part A

Name a pair of line segments that appear parallel.
Name a pair of line segments that appear perpendicular.

Parallel _____

Perpendicular _____

Part B

Name the line segments that form ∠EHI.

Answer _____

Part C

Name an angle that appears to be an acute angle. Name an angle that appears to be an obtuse angle. Name an angle that appears to be a right angle. Name an angle that appears to be a straight angle.

Acute _____

Obtuse _____

Right _____

Straight _____

Go On

Test 2: Session 2

33 Mr. Mason is in charge of buying potato salad for a picnic. He plans to buy 13.9 pounds of potato salad at a cost of $1.90 per pound. This price includes tax.

Part A

What is a good estimate of the amount he should expect to pay?

Estimate _____

Part B

On the lines below, explain in words how you determined your estimate for Part A.

_____

_____

_____

Part C

What will be the exact cost of the potato salad?

Show your work.

Exact Cost _____

Part D

Is the exact cost you found for Part C a reasonable answer? Use your estimate from Part A to explain.

_____

_____

_____

Go On

34 Brandon made a table to show the total number of miles he ran each week for the last five weeks.

Miles Brandon Ran Each Week

Week	1	2	3	4	5
Total Number of Miles Run	6	8	9	12	14

Part A

Draw a line graph on the grid below to show the data in the table. Be sure to title your graph, label each axis, and choose an appropriate scale for the vertical axis.

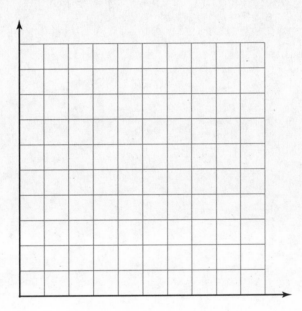

Part B

Use words and/or numbers to explain how you chose the scale for the vertical axis of your line graph in Part A.

_____

_____

_____

Part C

Look at the line graph you drew for Part A. What trend is shown by the line graph?

Answer _____

STOP

LESSON 56

Strand 2: Algebra

Using Variables to Translate Words into Expressions

5.A.2 Translate simple verbal expressions into algebraic expressions

Sometimes, it is helpful to translate a word expression into an algebraic expression. Here are some key words to help you figure out which operation to include in the expressions you write.

Phrases That Mean ADDITION

x plus 4	$x + 4$
Add y to 8	$y + 8$
2 more than z	$z + 2$
The sum of 3 and a	$3 + a$

Phrases That Mean SUBTRACTION

a minus 4	$a - 4$
Subtract 3 from b	$b - 3$
5 less than c	$c - 5$

(Be careful. In subtraction, the order of the numbers is important.)

Phrases That Mean MULTIPLICATION

5 times a number	$5x$ or $5 \times x$
twice a number	$2n$ or $2 \times n$
the product of 4 and b	$4b$ or $4 \times b$

(When a number and a variable are written with no space between them, they are multiplied. For example, $5x$ means 5 times x.)

Phrases That Mean DIVISION

the quotient of y and 7	$y \div 7$ or $\frac{y}{7}$
a number divided by 6	$x \div 6$ or $\frac{x}{6}$
half of a number	$n \div 2$ or $\frac{n}{2}$

(The fraction bar in a fraction means that the numerator is divided by the denominator. So, $x \div y$ is the same as $\frac{x}{y}$.)

EXAMPLE 1

Write an expression for the following expression.

a number divided by 4

STRATEGY

Use key words to translate the words into an expression.

STEP 1   Choose a variable to stand for the unknown number.

Let n represent the unknown number.

STEP 2   Show the number (n) divided by 4.

$n \div 4$ or $\frac{n}{4}$

SOLUTION

An expression for "a number divided by 4" is $\frac{n}{4}$ or $n \div 4$.

EXAMPLE 2

Write an expression for the following:

twice as much as t

STEP 1   Find the key words.

Twice is the key word.

Twice means to multiply a number by 2.

STEP 2   Identify the variable that stands for the unknown number.

t represents the unknown number.

STEP 3   Write the expression.

$2t$ or $2 \times t$

SOLUTION

An expression for "twice as much as t" is $2t$.

CHECK IT OUT *with the* Coach™

How would you translate the phrase below into a mathematical expression?

n less 5

Let's check it out.

What is the key word in this phrase?

The key word is _____.

Which operation does that key word tell you to use?

The operation to use is _____.

Write an expression that includes that operation.

The expression for this phrase is _____.

Sample Test Questions

1 What is the variable in this algebraic expression?

$$5 + y + 8$$

A 5

B $+$

C y

D 8

2 What is the constant in this algebraic expression?

$$6 + a \times b$$

F 6

G $\times$

H a

J b

3 Which expression has the same value as this phrase?

10 more than a number

A $10 \times n$

B $n + 10$

C $10 - n$

D $n \times 10$

4 Which expression has the same value as this phrase?

twice as much as v

F $2 + v$

G $2 \times 2 \times v$

H $2 \times v$

J $v + 2$

5 Which expression represents this phrase?

half as much as y

A $y \div 2$

B $2y$

C $y + \frac{1}{2}$

D $y - \frac{1}{2}$

6 Which expression represents these words?

a number divided by 4

F $\frac{4}{n}$

G $\frac{n}{4}$

H $4n$

J $4 \div n$

7 Write an expression that represents these words.

the product of 4 and b

Answer _____

8 Write an expression that represents this phrase.

the sum of 6 and x

Answer _____

Short-Response Question

9 Look at this phrase.

eight more than a number

Part A

Write an algebraic expression to represent this phrase.

Answer _____

Part B

Explain how you determined your answer for Part A and why you took the steps that you did.

_____

_____

_____

LESSON 57

Evaluating Expressions Using the Order of Operations

5.A.3 Substitute assigned values into variable expressions and evaluate using order of operations

Evaluating an algebraic expression means finding the value of the expression. To find the value of an algebraic expression, substitute specific numbers for the variables and do the math.

When you evaluate an algebraic expression that has two or more operations, you must know in what order to compute. Let's review the Order of Operations, which you also used in Lesson 27.

RULES FOR ORDER OF OPERATIONS

Rule 1: Do what is inside the parentheses first.

Rule 2: Multiply and divide before you add and subtract.

Rule 3: Next, multiply and divide in order from left to right.

Rule 4: Finally, add and subtract in order from left to right.

EXAMPLE 1

If $x = 5$, what is the value of $(10 + x) \div 3$?

STRATEGY

Substitute 5 for x in the expression. Then follow the rules for the Order of Operations.

STEP 1   Substitute 5 for x in the expression.

$$(10 + x) \div 3 = (10 + 5) \div 3$$

STEP 2   Which rule applies first?

Use Rule 1: Do what is inside the parentheses first.

$$10 + 5 = 15$$

STEP 3   Now, divide.

$$15 \div 3 = 5$$

SOLUTION

If $x = 5$, the value of the expression is 5.

EXAMPLE 2

If $z = 6$, what is the value of this expression?

$$14 - 2 \times z + 7$$

STRATEGY

Substitute 6 for z in the expression. Then follow the rules for the Order of Operations.

STEP 1   Substitute 6 for z.

$$14 - 2 \times z + 7 = 14 - 2 \times 6 + 7$$

STEP 2   Which rule applies first?

Rule 2 applies first: Multiply and divide before you add and subtract.

$$2 \times 6 = 12$$

STEP 3   Rewrite the expression.

$$14 - 12 + 7$$

STEP 4   Only addition and subtraction remain, so use Rule 4 next.

Add and subtract in order from left to right.

$$14 - 12 + 7 = 2 + 7 = 9$$

SOLUTION

The value of the expression, when $z = 6$, is 9.

CHECK IT OUT with the Coach™

How would you evaluate $8 \times 9 \div a$ when $a = 3$?

Let's check it out.

First, substitute 3 for a in the expression.

$8 \times 9 \div$ _____

Then, follow the rules for the Order of Operations.

Which rule applies first?

Rule _____ applies first.

That rule says that I should _____.

So, the first step would be to _____.

The second step would be to _____ the remaining numbers.

Sample Test Questions

1   If $m = 2$, what is the value of $6 \div m \times 3$?

   A   1

   B   9

   C   10

   D   12

2   If $a = 4$, what is the value of $8 - a + 2$?

   F   2

   G   4

   H   6

   J   8

3   If $x = 5$, what is the value of $5x - 10$?

   A   0

   B   10

   C   15

   D   35

4   If $n = 18$, what is the value of $\frac{n}{2} + 7$?

   F   16

   G   15

   H   13

   J   2

5   If $k = 2$, what is the value of $63 \div 9 - k + 2$?

   A   7

   B   8

   C   11

   D   12

6   If $t = 10$, what is the value of $t - 3 \times 2 + 11$?

   F   14

   G   15

   H   25

   J   27

7   If $z = 3$, what is the value of $7z - (8 + 3)$?

   Answer _____

8   If $y = 4$, what is the value of $\frac{8}{y} \times (7 - 2)$?

   Answer _____

Short-Response Question

9   Look at this expression.

$$4n + 3 \times (4 - 1)$$

If $n = 2$, what is the value of this expression?

Show your work.

Answer _____

LESSON 58

Strand 2: Algebra

Solving Equations

5.A.4 Solve simple one-step equations using basic whole-number facts

5.A.5 Solve and explain simple one-step equations using inverse operations involving whole numbers

An **equation** is a number sentence with an equal (=) sign. Solving an equation means finding the value of the variable in the equation.

One way to solve an equation is to isolate the variable. Isolating the variable means getting the variable by itself on one side of the equation.

EXAMPLE 1

Solve for z: $6z = 30$

STRATEGY

Get z by itself.

STEP 1   Write the equation.

$6z = 30$

STEP 2   Decide which operation will isolate the variable.

$6z$ is the same as $6 \times z$.

Since 6 is multiplied by z, divide by 6 to get x by itself.

STEP 3   Do the math.

Divide both sides by 6 to find the value of z.

$6z \div 6 = 30 \div 6$

$z = 5$

STEP 4   Check your answer by substituting 5 for z in the original equation.

$6 \times z = 30$

$6 \times 5 = 30$ ← This equation is true, so $z = 5$.

SOLUTION

$z = 5$

Example 1 shows that different equations require that you use different operations to isolate the variable. A good rule is: use the **inverse operation**, or the opposite operation, of the one that appears in the equation.

When a number is *added* to the variable, you *subtract* to find the answer. Addition and subtraction are inverse operations.

In Example 1, a number was *multiplied* by the variable, so you *divide* to find the answer. Multiplication and division are inverse operations.

EXAMPLE 2

Solve for y: $y - 7 = 3$

STRATEGY

Get y by itself.

STEP 1 Write the equation.

$y - 7 = 3$

STEP 2 Decide which operation will isolate the variable.

Since 7 is subtracted from y, add 7 to get y by itself.

STEP 3 Do the math.

Add 7 to both sides of the equation.

$y - 7 + 7 = 3 + 7$

$y + 0 = 10$

$y = 10$

SOLUTION

$y = 10$

EXAMPLE 3

Solve for k: $k \div 3 = 6$

STRATEGY

Get k by itself.

STEP 1 Write the equation.

$k \div 3 = 6$

STEP 2 Decide which operation will isolate the variable.

Since k is divided by 3, multiply by 3 to get k by itself.

STEP 3 Do the math.

Multiply both sides of the equation by 3.

$\frac{k}{3} \times 3 = 6 \times 3$

$k \div 1 = 18$

$k = 18$

SOLUTION

$k = 18$

CHECK IT OUT with the Coach™

Which operation should you use to isolate the variable in this equation?

$h + 9 = 18$

Let's check it out.

You need to use the inverse operation.

Since 9 is added to h, you need to _____ 9 from both sides of the equation to get h by itself.

This works because _____ is the inverse operation of addition.

Sample Test Questions

1 How could you isolate the variable, g, in this equation?

$$g - 6 = 12$$

A Add 6 to both sides of the equation.

B Subtract 6 from both sides of the equation.

C Multiply both sides of the equation by 6.

D Divide both sides of the equation by 6.

2 How could you isolate the variable, x, in this equation?

$$4x = 8$$

F Add 4 to both sides of the equation.

G Subtract 4 from both sides of the equation.

H Multiply both sides of the equation by 4.

J Divide both sides of the equation by 4.

3 Solve for f: $5 + f = 12$

A 2

B 7

C 17

D 60

4 Solve for z: $8z = 16$

F 2

G 3

H 8

J 24

5 Solve for n: $\frac{n}{2} = 7$

A 5

B 9

C 10

D 14

6 Solve for y: $y - 2 = 6$

F 3

G 4

H 8

J 12

7 Solve for c: $4 \times c = 24$

Answer _____

8 Solve for b: $b + 3 = 12$

Answer _____

Short-Response Question

9   Samera solved an equation for a. Her solution is shown below.

$$9a = 18$$
$$9a - 9 = 18 - 9$$
$$a = 9$$

Part A

Her solution contains an error. Solve the equation $9a = 18$ and determine the correct answer.

Show your work.

Answer _____

Part B

Explain what error Samera made and what she could have done differently to solve the problem.

_____

_____

_____

LESSON
59

Strand 3: Geometry

Plotting Points on a Grid

5.G.12 Identify and plot points in the first quadrant

Sometimes you may need to plot a point on a **coordinate grid**.
A coordinate grid is made of two number lines that meet at a point called
the **origin**.

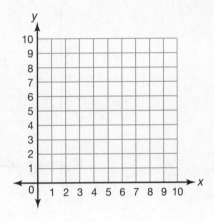

The horizontal (left to right) number line is called the **x-axis**. The vertical
(up and down) number line is called the **y-axis**.

To plot a point on a coordinate grid, you use an **ordered pair** of numbers.
An ordered pair is a set of two numbers, such as (5,2).

• 5 is the first number. It tells you the x-coordinate.

• 2 is the second number. It tells you the y-coordinate.

Each ordered pair can be represented by a point on the coordinate grid.

Rules for Locating Ordered Pairs on a Coordinate Grid

• Start at the origin.

• Use the x-coordinate to determine how many units to move to
the right.

• Use the y-coordinate to determine how many units to move up.

EXAMPLE 1

Locate a point in the coordinate plane for the ordered pair (5,2).

STRATEGY

Follow the rules for locating ordered pairs on a grid.

STEP 1   Start at the origin (where the *x*- and *y*-axes meet).

STEP 2   Move to the right along the *x*-axis the same number of units as the *x*-coordinate.

The *x*-coordinate is 5, so move 5 units to the right.

STEP 3   From the 5 on the *x*-axis, move up the same number of units as the *y*-coordinate.

The *y*-coordinate is 2, so move up 2 units.

Place a point at that location.

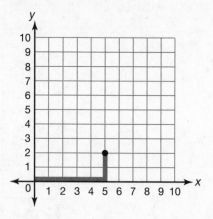

SOLUTION

The point shown in Step 3 is at (5,2).

EXAMPLE 2

Locate and connect these points on the coordinate grid:

(3,2), (5,4), and (7,6)

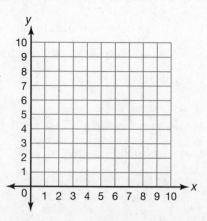

328

STRATEGY   **Follow the rules for locating ordered pairs on a grid.**

STEP 1   Plot (3,2) on the coordinate grid.

Start at the origin. Move 3 units to the right on the *x*-axis.
From 3 on the *x*-axis, move up 2 units. Plot a point there at (3,2).

STEP 2   Plot (5,4) on the coordinate grid.

Start at the origin. Move 5 units to the right on the *x*-axis.
From 5 on the *x*-axis, move up 4 units. Plot a point there at (5,4).

STEP 3   Plot (7,6) on the coordinate grid.

Start at the origin. Move 7 units to the right on the *x*-axis.
From 7 on the *x*-axis, move up 6 units. Plot a point there at (7,6).

STEP 4   Draw a line segment connecting the three points.

Connect the points in the order that you drew them. Draw a
line segment from (3,2) to (5,4). Then continue the line segment
from (5,4) to (7,6).

SOLUTION   **When the points have been plotted and connected, they will look like this:**

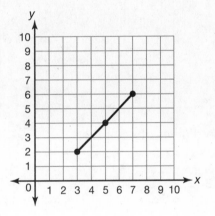

How could you plot the point for (4,9) on a coordinate grid?

Let's check it out.

First, start at the origin.

Then, move _____ units to the right along the *x*-axis.

From that point on the *x*-axis, move up _____ units.

Plot a _____ there to represent the ordered pair (4,9).

Sample Test Questions

1 What are the coordinates of point *X*?

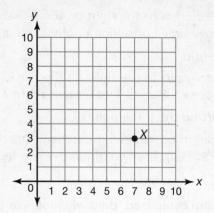

A (3,7)

B (7,2)

C (7,3)

D (8,3)

2 What are the coordinates of point *A*?

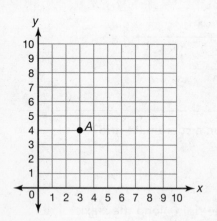

F (3,4)

G (3,5)

H (4,3)

J (5,3)

3 What are the coordinates of point *Z*?

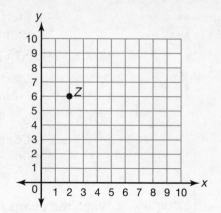

A (1,6)

B (2,6)

C (6,1)

D (6,2)

4 Which point is located at (9,7)?

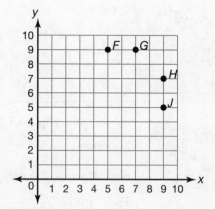

F point *F*

G point *G*

H point *H*

J point *J*

5 Line segment *MN* has endpoints at *M* and *N*. What are the coordinates of point *N*?

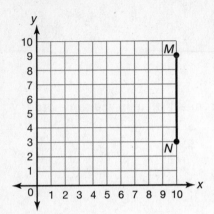

A (9,10)

B (10,9)

C (3,10)

D (10,3)

6 Makota used a coordinate grid to make this map of his town. What coordinates did he use to show the location of the school?

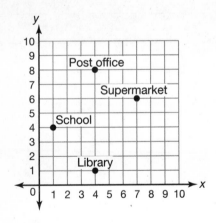

F (7,6)

G (4,8)

H (4,1)

J (1,4)

7 What are the coordinates of the point that is farthest from point *S* on the grid?

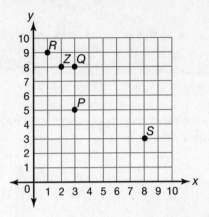

Answer _____

8 The gray circle shows the bull's eye of a toss game. What coordinates show the location of the center of the bull's eye?

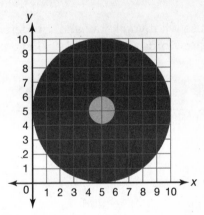

Answer _____

Short-Response Question

9   Look at the ordered pairs shown below.

(3,1)   (6,3)   (10,6)

Part A

Plot those points on the coordinate grid below. Then connect them in the same order you plotted them.

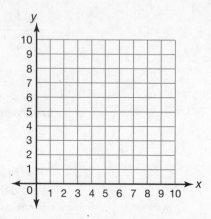

Part B

Use what you know about ordered pairs to explain why your drawing is correct. Use words and/or numbers in your explanation.

_____

_____

_____

LESSON 60

Strand 3: Geometry

Drawing Figures and Finding Perimeter on a Grid

5.G.13 Plot points to form basic geometric shapes (identify and classify)
5.G.14 Calculate perimeter of basic geometric shapes drawn on a coordinate plane (rectangles and shapes composed of rectangles having sides with integer lengths and parallel to the axes)

PLOTTING GEOMETRIC FIGURES ON COORDINATE GRIDS

The coordinate plane is useful for plotting points. You can also use it to plot and form geometric figures, like polygons.

EXAMPLE 1

The points plotted on this coordinate plane show three vertices of a square. What would be the coordinates of the fourth vertex of the square?

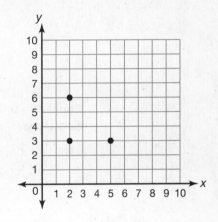

STRATEGY

Figure out where the fourth vertex will be located. Then find the coordinates for that point.

STEP 1   Where will the fourth vertex be located?

Each side of a square is the same length. Since (5,3) is 3 units to the right of (2,3), the fourth vertex will be 3 units to the right of (2,6).

Plot the point and connect the vertices to make sure it looks like a square.

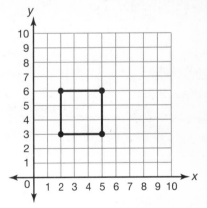

STEP 2   What are the coordinates of the fourth vertex?

The *x*-coordinate for that point is 5.

The *y*-coordinate for that point is 6.

The coordinates are (5,6).

SOLUTION

The coordinates for the fourth vertex are (5,6).

FINDING PERIMETERS OF FIGURES ON COORDINATE GRIDS

When geometric figures are plotted on the coordinate plane, you can use the grid lines to find the perimeter of the objects. Just count the units (spaces) to find the length of each side. Then add the lengths of the sides to find the perimeter.

EXAMPLE 2

Andrew made this L-shaped figure by putting two rectangles together. What is the perimeter of the figure?

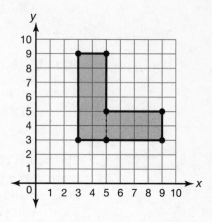

STRATEGY

Count the units to find the lengths of the sides. Then add those lengths to find the perimeter.

STEP 1   Count the units to find the length of each side.

             Since this is not a rectangle or other familiar shape, you must count the lengths of all the sides.

             The lengths of the sides, in units, are 2, 4, 4, 2, 6, and 6.

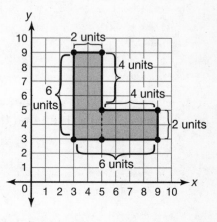

STEP 2   Add to find the perimeter.

$$P = 2 + 4 + 4 + 2 + 6 + 6 = 24$$

SOLUTION

The perimeter of the L-shaped figure is 24 units.

CHECK IT OUT *with the* **Coach**™

A square is plotted on a coordinate grid. How could its perimeter be determined?

Let's check it out.

Squares have all sides the same _____.

So, count the units along _____ side(s) of the square.

To find the perimeter of the square, _____.

Sample Test Questions

1 Three vertices of a rectangle are plotted below. What would be the coordinates of the fourth vertex?

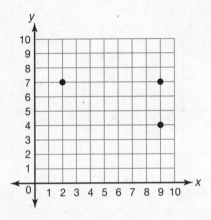

- **A** (2,3)
- **B** (2,4)
- **C** (4,2)
- **D** (4,4)

2 What kind of figure is plotted on the grid below?

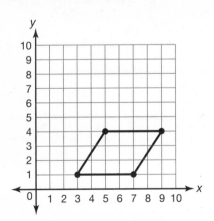

- **F** rectangle
- **G** trapezoid
- **H** parallelogram
- **J** pentagon

3 Two vertices of a square are plotted below. Which pair of coordinates could name the other two vertices of this square?

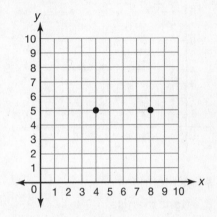

- **A** (4,2) and (8,2)
- **B** (4,1) and (8,1)
- **C** (4,2) and (7,2)
- **D** (4,1) and (7,1)

4 What is the perimeter of the rectangle plotted on the coordinate plane?

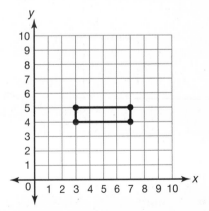

- **F** 4 units
- **H** 8 units
- **G** 5 units
- **J** 10 units

5 Two vertices of a polygon are plotted on this grid. Suppose a third vertex is plotted at (8,6) and the vertices are connected to form a triangle. What kind of triangle will the three vertices form?

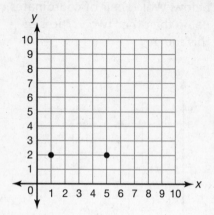

A acute triangle

B right triangle

C obtuse triangle

D equilateral triangle

6 What is the perimeter of the square plotted on this grid?

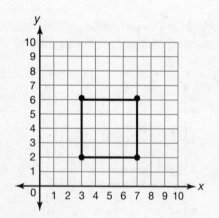

F 16 units

G 14 units

H 12 units

J 8 units

7 Two squares were combined to make the shaded figure shown on the grid. What is the perimeter of the shaded figure?

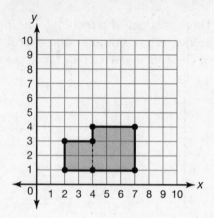

Answer _____

8 Two rectangles were combined to make the T-shaped figure shown on the grid. What is the perimeter of the T-shaped figure?

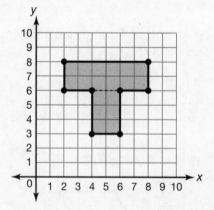

Answer _____

Short-Response Question

9   The two points plotted below show two vertices of a right triangle.

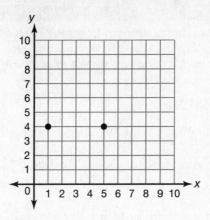

Part A

Plot a third point that could be the third vertex of this right triangle.
Then connect the points to show the right triangle.

Part B

Explain how you decided where to plot the third vertex and how you know that the triangle
you created is a right triangle.

_____

_____

_____

LESSON

61

Strand 5: Statistics and Probability

Probability

5.S.5 List the possible outcomes for a single-event experiment
5.S.7 Create a sample space and determine the probability of a single event, given a simple experiment (i.e., rolling a number cube)

OUTCOMES

Imagine flipping a coin. What could happen?

The coin could land on heads, or it could land on tails. Heads and tails are the two possible results or **outcomes** of flipping a coin.

It is sometimes helpful to list all the possible outcomes of an event. This list is called the **sample space**.

EXAMPLE 1

If you roll this number cube with faces numbered 1 to 6, how many possible outcomes are there? List them all.

STRATEGY

List all the possible numbers you could roll.

On this number cube, you could roll a 1, 2, 3, 4, 5, or 6.

So, there are 6 possible outcomes.

SOLUTION

There are 6 possible outcomes. The list of all possible outcomes is: 1, 2, 3, 4, 5, and 6.

EXAMPLE 2

There are 3 red tiles, 3 blue tiles, and 1 green tile in a box. Imagine an experiment in which you reach into the box and draw a tile without looking. What is the sample space for this experiment?

STRATEGY

List all the possible tiles you can draw from the box.

There are 3 red tiles, 3 blue tiles, and 1 green tile in the box.

So, the sample space is: {red, red, red, blue, blue, blue, green}.

Notice that braces, { }, are often used to show a sample space.

SOLUTION

The sample space for this experiment is {red, red, red, blue, blue, blue, green}.

PROBABILITY

It is sometimes not enough to know what the possible outcomes are. You might want to know how likely it is that a particular outcome will occur. You can do this by finding a **probability**.

A probability is expressed as the ratio of favorable outcomes to total possible outcomes.

$$\text{probability} = \frac{\text{favorable outcomes}}{\text{total possible outcomes}}$$

You can find the number of total possible outcomes by listing the sample space.

EXAMPLE 3

Suppose you have a bag of 5 marbles. Here are the colors of the marbles:

1 red   **1 blue**   **3 yellow**

You will reach into the bag and draw a marble without looking. What is the probability that you will draw a yellow marble?

STRATEGY

Write a ratio comparing the favorable outcomes to the total possible outcomes.

STEP 1   What is the sample space for this experiment?

The sample space is {red, blue, yellow, yellow, yellow}.

STEP 2   How many total possible outcomes are there?

There are 5 outcomes in the sample space, so there are 5 total possible outcomes.

STEP 3   How many favorable outcomes are there?

The question asks for the probability of drawing a yellow marble, so drawing a yellow marble is a favorable outcome.

There are 3 yellow marbles in the bag, so there are 3 favorable outcomes.

STEP 4   Write the probability.

$$\text{probability} = \frac{\text{favorable outcomes}}{\text{total possible outcomes}} = \frac{3}{5}$$

SOLUTION

The probability of drawing a yellow marble is $\frac{3}{5}$ or 3 out of 5.

EXAMPLE 4

This spinner is divided into 6 equal-sized sections. If you spin the spinner, what is the probability that the arrow will land on a 3?

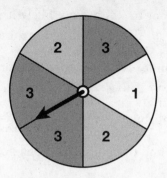

STRATEGY   **Write a ratio comparing the favorable outcomes to the total possible outcomes.**

STEP 1   How many total possible outcomes are there?

There are 6 sections on the spinner, so there are 6 total possible outcomes.

STEP 2   How many favorable outcomes are there?

The number 3 is in 3 of the sections.

So there are 3 favorable outcomes.

STEP 3   Write the probability.

$$\text{probability} = \frac{\text{favorable outcomes}}{\text{total possible outcomes}} = \frac{3}{6}$$

Simplify: $\frac{3}{6} = \frac{3 \div 3}{6 \div 3} = \frac{1}{2}$

SOLUTION   **The probability of spinning a 3 is $\frac{1}{2}$ or 1 out of 2.**

CHECK IT OUT *with the* **Coach**™

There are 10 boys and 11 girls in a class. If each student's name is placed in a hat and one name is drawn at random, what is the probability that a boy's name will be picked?

Let's check it out.

How many total possible outcomes are there?

There are 10 boys and 11 girls in the class, so there are a total of

_____ students in the class.

This means that there are _____ total possible outcomes.

How many favorable outcomes are there?

The number of boys in the class is _____, so the number of

favorable outcomes is _____.

Write the probability: $\frac{\text{favorable outcomes}}{\text{total possible outcomes}} =$ _____

So, the probability that a boy's name will be picked is _____.

Sample Test Questions

1 There are 6 cubes in a box: 3 yellow cubes, 1 orange cube, and 2 purple cubes. If a cube is picked from the box at random, what is the sample space for this experiment?

A {yellow}

B {yellow, orange, purple}

C {yellow, yellow, yellow, orange, purple}

D {yellow, yellow, yellow, orange, purple, purple}

2 Which shows all the possible outcomes of spinning this spinner?

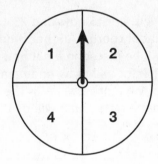

F 1, 2

G 1, 2, 3

H 1, 2, 3, 4

J 1, 2, 3, 4, 5

3 There are 8 cards in a box. They are numbered 1, 2, 3, 4, 5, 6, 7, and 8. What is the probability of picking a 3 from the box?

A $\frac{1}{8}$

B $\frac{1}{7}$

C $\frac{1}{3}$

D $\frac{3}{8}$

4 What is the probability of spinning this spinner and having the arrow land on a section labeled blue?

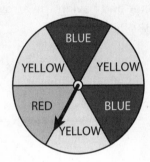

F $\frac{1}{6}$ H $\frac{2}{5}$

G $\frac{1}{3}$ J $\frac{1}{2}$

5 Bill takes 10 cards and numbers them from 11 to 20. He plans to shuffle the cards and pick one from the deck without looking. What are all the possible outcomes of this event?

A 1, 2, 3, 4, 5, 6, 7, 8, 9, 10

B 11, 20

C 11, 12, 13, 14, 15, 16, 17, 18, 19, 20

D 10, 11, 12, 13, 14, 15, 16, 17, 18, 19, 20

6 Gerilyn will reach into this bag and draw a letter without looking. What is the probability that she will choose an N?

F   1 out of 7

G   1 out of 6

H   2 out of 7

J   2 out of 5

7 What is the probability of spinning this spinner and having the arrow land on the unshaded area?

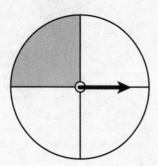

A $\frac{1}{4}$

B $\frac{3}{4}$

C $\frac{3}{1}$

D $\frac{4}{1}$

8 There are 3 white (W) tiles, 2 gray (G) tiles, and 4 black (B) tiles in a box. Sierra will reach into the box and pick a tile without looking. Which could represent the sample space for this event?

F   {W, W, W, G, G, B, B, B, B}

G   {W, W, G, G, G, B, B, B, B}

H   {W, W, W, G, G, G, B}

J   {W, G, B}

9 Sylvia has cards numbered from 1 to 10. She will shuffle them and pick a card at random. What is the probability that she will choose a prime number?

Answer _____

10 There are 15 boys and 25 girls in the school chorus. All the students' names will be placed in a hat and the chorus director will draw one name at random to win a prize. What is the probability that a girl's name will be drawn?

Answer _____

Short-Response Question

11 The spinner below is divided into eight equal-sized sections.

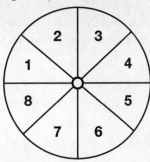

Part A

What is the probability of spinning the spinner and having the arrow land on an odd number? Write your answer as a fraction in simplest terms.

Answer _____

Part B

Use words and/or numbers to explain how you determine your answer and why you took the steps you did.

_____

_____

_____

Strand 5: Statistics and Probability

Displaying Probability Experiments

5.S.6 Record experiment results using fractions/ratios

You can investigate probability by doing experiments. For example, you can flip a coin 50 times and record how many times you get heads and how many times you get tails. You can use fractions or ratios to show the actual number of times an outcome occurred in your experiment.

EXAMPLE 1

Students in Mr. McCormick's class performed a probability experiment. They used this spinner.

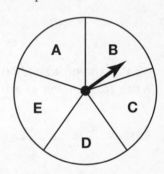

The students spun the spinner 20 times. This table shows their results.

Write ratios to show the actual number of times each outcome occurred in the experiment.

Experiment Results

Letter	Number of Times Spun
A	4
B	3
C	5
D	2
E	6

STRATEGY   **Write ratios for each outcome.**

STEP 1   Write a ratio to show how many times the students spun the letter A.

$$\text{ratio} = \frac{\text{number of times it landed on A}}{\text{total number of spins}} = \frac{4}{20} = \frac{4 \div 4}{4 \div 4} = \frac{1}{5}$$

So, the ratio was $\frac{1}{5}$. In other words, the spinner landed on the letter A about 1 out of every 5 times it was spun, or $\frac{1}{5}$ of the times it was spun.

STEP 2   Write a ratio to show how many times they spun the letter B.

$$\text{ratio} = \frac{\text{number of times it landed on B}}{\text{total number of spins}} = \frac{3}{20}$$

STEP 3   Write a ratio to show how many times they spun the letter C.

$$\text{ratio} = \frac{\text{number of times it landed on C}}{\text{total number of spins}} = \frac{5}{20} = \frac{5 \div 5}{20 \div 5} = \frac{1}{4}$$

STEP 4   Write a ratio to show how many times they spun the letter D.

$$\text{ratio} = \frac{\text{number of times it landed on D}}{\text{total number of spins}} = \frac{2}{20} = \frac{2 \div 2}{20 \div 2} = \frac{1}{10}$$

STEP 5   Write a ratio to show how many times they spun the letter E.

$$\text{ratio} = \frac{\text{number of times it landed on E}}{\text{total number of spins}} = \frac{6}{20} = \frac{6 \div 2}{20 \div 2} = \frac{3}{10}$$

SOLUTION   **Write the ratios of how many times each letter was spun in the table.**

Experiment Results

Letter	Number of Times Spun	Ratio
A	4	$\frac{1}{5}$
B	3	$\frac{3}{20}$
C	5	$\frac{1}{4}$
D	2	$\frac{1}{10}$
E	6	$\frac{3}{10}$

Look at the spinner in Example 1. The probability of the spinner landing on the letter A was:

$$\text{probability} = \frac{\text{favorable outcomes}}{\text{total possible outcomes}} = \frac{1}{5}$$

That's the same ratio that was found in the experiment.

But notice that the probability of the spinner landing on the letter C was also $\frac{1}{5}$, even though the ratio that was found in the experiment was $\frac{1}{4}$. The ratio was not exactly the same as the probability because in real life, probabilities do not predict exactly what will happen.

EXAMPLE 2

Mr. McCormick's class conducted the same probability experiment the next day. They used the same spinner, but spun it 100 times instead of 20 times. Their results are shown in this graph.

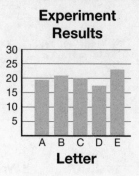

Experiment Results

Write a ratio to show the actual number of times that the letter C was spun in this experiment.

STRATEGY

Write a ratio for the favorable outcome.

According to the graph, the letter C was spun 20 times.

$$\text{ratio} = \frac{\text{number of times it landed on C}}{\text{total number of spins}} = \frac{20}{100} = \frac{20 \div 20}{100 \div 20} = \frac{1}{5}$$

Notice that this time the result was the same as the probability of spinning the letter C, $\frac{1}{5}$.

SOLUTION

The ratio was $\frac{1}{5}$. So, the letter C was spun 1 out of every 5 times, or about $\frac{1}{5}$ of the time.

In general, the more times you perform an experiment, the closer the ratio of your outcomes will get to the probabilities you would expect.

CHECK IT OUT *with the* **Coach**™

Luther flips a coin 20 times and it lands on heads 11 times. How could you use ratios to show the results of this experiment?

Let's check it out.

First, write a ratio to show how many times the coin landed on heads.

$\text{ratio} = \dfrac{\text{number of times it landed on heads}}{\text{total number of flips}} =$ _____

Next, determine how many times the coin landed on tails.

Subtract the number of times the coin landed on heads from the total number of flips.

Since $20 - 11 =$ _____, the coin landed on tails _____ times.

Write a ratio to show how many times the coin landed on tails.

$\text{ratio} = \dfrac{\text{number of times it landed on tails}}{\text{total number of flips}} =$ _____

So, the results were that the coin landed on heads _____ of

the times it was flipped and it landed on tails _____ of the times it was flipped.

Sample Test Questions

Jenna conducted a probability experiment. She spun this spinner 24 times.

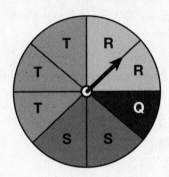

Then she recorded her results in this table.

Experiment Results

Letter	Number of Times Spun
Q	4
R	5
S	6
T	9

Use these data for Questions 1 and 2.

1 What fraction of the 24 spins landed on the letter Q?

A $\frac{4}{9}$ C $\frac{1}{5}$

B $\frac{1}{4}$ D $\frac{1}{6}$

2 Which shows the ratio of the number of times she spun the letter T to the total number of spins?

F $\frac{1}{9}$ H $\frac{9}{24}$

G $\frac{1}{8}$ J $\frac{3}{5}$

Emilio conducted a probability experiment. He put 2 red marbles, 1 blue marble, and 2 green marbles in a bag. Then he picked a marble without looking, recorded its color, and replaced it in the bag. He did this 30 times. The tally chart below shows his results. Use this tally chart for Questions 3 and 4.

Experiment Results

Color	Number of Picks
red	~~||||~~ ~~||||~~ ||
blue	~~||||~~ |||
green	~~||||~~ ~~||||~~

3 Which shows the ratio of the number of times he picked a blue marble to the total number of times he picked a marble in the experiment?

Answer _____

4 Which fraction of the 30 picks resulted in a red marble being chosen?

Answer _____

Short-Response Questions

For Questions 5–7, you will conduct your own probability experiments and record your results.

5 Conduct a probability experiment by rolling a number cube 36 times.

Part A

Fill in a table to show how many times you rolled each number during the experiment. Then write the ratio of the actual number of times you rolled each number to the total number of rolls.

Experiment Results

Number	Number of Times Rolled
1	
2	
3	
4	
5	
6	

Part B

Choose one of the ratios you wrote for Part A and explain how you determined it.

_____

_____

_____

6 Use the circle below as a spinner. Take a small paperclip and place one end of it on the center of the circle. Then put the point of your pencil on the center of the spinner so that it is holding that end of the paperclip in place. To spin your spinner, flick the other end of the paperclip with your finger and watch it spin.

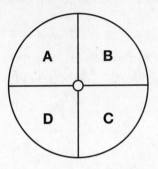

Part A

Spin the spinner 40 times. Record your results in a tally chart.

Experiment Results

Letter	Number of Times Spun
A	
B	
C	
D	

After you have collected your data, write ratios of the actual number of times you spun each letter to the total number of spins.

Part B

Choose one of the ratios you wrote above and explain what that ratio means. (For example, does it mean that you spun that letter 1 out of every 2 times, or that $\frac{1}{2}$ of the 40 spins landed on that letter?)

_____

_____

_____

7   How many letters are in your first name? Take that many index cards and write each letter of your name on one index card.

Shuffle the cards and place them face down. Then randomly pick a card from the deck, record its letter, and replace it back into the deck. Do this 25 times.

Part A

On a grid, make a bar graph to show the number of times you picked each letter. Give your bar graph a title, label each axis, and choose an appropriate scale.

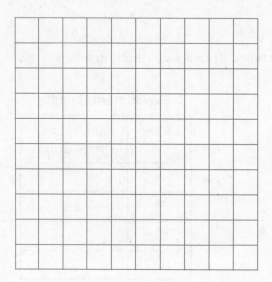

Part B

After you have collected your data, write ratios showing the actual number of times you picked each letter to the total number of picks. Then choose one of the ratios and explain how you determined it.

_____

_____

_____

Progress Check for Lessons 56–62

1 What is the perimeter of the square plotted on this grid?

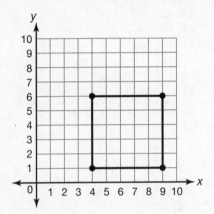

A 9 units

B 10 units

C 20 units

D 25 units

2 Which operation isolates the variable in the equation $n - 8 = 5$?

F add 8 to both sides of the equation

G subtract 8 from both sides of the equation

H multiply both sides of the equation by 8

J divide both sides of the equation by 8

3 Which expression has the same value as this phrase?

6 less than g

A $g - 6$ **C** $6 \div g$

B $6 - g$ **D** $6g$

4 What are the coordinates of point V?

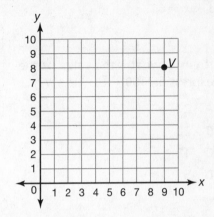

F (8,9)   **H** (9,9)

G (8,8)   **J** (9,8)

5 Cole has these six cubes in a bag.

If he reaches into the bag and picks a cube without looking, what is the probability that he will choose a cube with an odd number on it?

A $\frac{2}{3}$ **C** $\frac{1}{3}$

B $\frac{2}{5}$ **D** $\frac{1}{4}$

6 Solve for x:

$$6x = 54$$

F $x = 8$

G $x = 9$

H $x = 48$

J $x = 60$

7 If $x = 5$, what is the value of the expression $100 \div 10 - x + 7$?

A 27

B 20

C 12

D 5

8 Russell will reach into a bag that has 2 green tiles, 1 red tile, and 3 gold tiles. Which of the following shows the complete sample space for this event?

F {green, red, gold}

G {green, green, red, gold, gold}

H {green, green, green, red, gold, gold}

J {green, green, red, gold, gold, gold}

9 Three vertices of a rectangle are shown on the grid below. What are the coordinates of the fourth vertex?

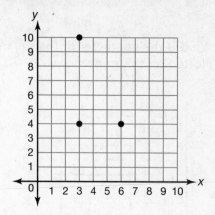

A (6,10)

B (7,10)

C (10,6)

D (10,7)

10 Roy recorded the number of times the pointer from a spinner landed on certain letters. What fraction of the 20 spins landed on the letter L?

Experiment Results

Letter	Number of Times Spun
K	4
L	5
M	9
N	2

F $\dfrac{1}{4}$

G $\dfrac{1}{5}$

H $\dfrac{1}{6}$

J $\dfrac{1}{10}$

Short-Response Questions

11 A rectangle and a square were combined to make the shaded figure on the grid below.

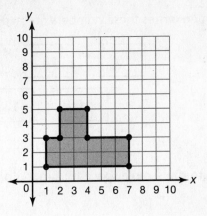

Part A

What is the perimeter of this figure?

Answer _____ units

Part B

Use what you know about finding the perimeter of figures on a grid to explain how you know your answer is correct. Use words, numbers, and/or pictures in your explanation.

_____

_____

_____

12 Bobby solved this equation for *x*. His solution is shown below.

$$x + 3 = 9$$
$$x + 3 + 3 = 9 + 3$$
$$x = 12$$

Part A

Bobby's solution contains an error. Solve the equation $x + 3 = 9$ and determine the correct value for *x*.

Answer _____

Part B

Explain what error Bobby made and what he could have done differently to solve the equation.

_____

_____

_____

Extended-Response Question

13   Armen writes these numbers on cards.

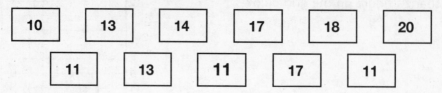

Part A

Write the sample space for picking one card at random.

Answer _____

Part B

Suppose Armen shuffles the cards and draws a card from the pile without looking. What is the probability that Armen will **not** draw a prime number?

Answer _____

Part C

Explain how you determined your answer for Part B and why you took the steps you did.

_____

_____

_____

_____

_____

Glossary

acute angle an angle that measures less than 90 degrees (Lesson 43)

acute triangle a triangle that has three acute angles (Lesson 43)

algebraic expression a mathematical expression that includes one or more variables (Lesson 37)

angle a figure formed by two rays or two line segments that have a common endpoint, called the vertex (Lesson 40)

bar graph a graph that uses bars of different heights to represent and compare data (Lesson 52)

common denominator a number that is a common multiple of the denominators of two or more fractions (Lesson 18)

compatible numbers approximate values that make it easier to compute an estimated answer (Lesson 35)

composite number a counting number that has more than two factors

Example: 9 has three factors (1, 3, and 9) so 9 is a composite number. (Lesson 23)

congruent having the same shape and size (Lesson 41)

constant a value that does not change in a mathematical expression or sentence (Lesson 37)

coordinate grid a 2-dimensional grid with two perpendicular axes, the x-axis and y-axis; also called the coordinate plane (Lesson 59)

data information that is collected (Lesson 52)

decimal a number with a decimal point (Lesson 20)

denominator in a fraction, the number below the fraction bar (Lesson 17)

dividend a number that is being divided

Example: In 8 ÷ 2 = 4, 8 is the dividend. (Lesson 26)

divisor a number that divides the dividend

Example: In 8 ÷ 2 = 4, 2 is the divisor. (Lesson 26)

double-line graph a line graph that shows two lines that represent related data (Lesson 53)

elapsed time The amount of time that passes between two events (Lesson 49)

equation a mathematical sentence with an equal (=) sign (Lesson 58)

equilateral triangle a triangle that has three congruent sides (Lesson 43)

equivalent fractions two or more fractions that have equal values (Lesson 17)

estimate a number that is close to the exact amount (Lesson 34)

expression a collection of numbers and/or variables connected by an operation or operations (Lesson 27)

factor a number that divides another number evenly; one of the numbers that is multiplied to give a product

Example: The factors of 6 are 1, 2, 3, and 6 because $1 \times 6 = 6$ and $2 \times 3 = 6$. (Lessons 24 and 25)

formula an equation that shows a mathematical relationship (Lesson 38)

fraction a number that names part of a whole or part of a set of objects (Lesson 17)

geometric pattern a pattern made up of shapes (Lesson 39)

greatest common factor (GCF) the greatest number that evenly divides two or more numbers (Lesson 24)

hexagon a polygon with six sides and six angles (Lesson 40)

improper fraction a fraction with a numerator that is greater than or equal to the denominator (Lesson 28)

inverse operations operations that are opposites of one another

Example: addition and subtraction are inverse operations (Lesson 58)

irregular polygon a polygon that is not a regular polygon; not all sides of the polygon are the same length and/or not all angles are the same measure. (Lesson 40)

isosceles triangle a triangle that has two sides of the same length (Lesson 43)

least common denominator (LCD) the smallest number that is a multiple of the denominators of two or more fractions (Lesson 18)

least common multiple (LCM) the smallest number that is a multiple of two or more numbers (Lesson 24)

line graph a graph representing data with connecting line segments; often used to show changes over time (Lesson 53)

line of symmetry a line on which a figure can be folded such that the two halves of the figure will match exactly

Example: A rectangle has two lines of symmetry. (Lesson 45)

line segment a part of a line that has two definite endpoints (Lesson 38)

line symmetry A figure has line symmetry if it can be folded along a line such that its two halves match exactly

mean the sum of the numbers in a set of data divided by the number of addends in the set. Also called *average*. (Lesson 54)

mixed number a number consisting of a whole number and a fraction (Lessons 14 and 28)

multiple the product of a number and a counting number (Lesson 24)

numerator in a fraction, the number above the fraction bar (Lesson 17)

obtuse angle an angle that measures more than 90 degrees and less than 180 degrees (Lesson 43)

obtuse triangle a triangle that has one obtuse angle (Lesson 43)

octagon a polygon with eight sides and eight angles (Lesson 40)

operation a process, such as addition, subtraction, multiplication, or division, performed on numbers or expressions (Lesson 27)

Order of Operations a set of rules used to evaluate numerical expressions
1) Do what is in parentheses first, starting with the innermost set; 2) Multiply and divide before you add and subtract; 3) Multiply and divide in order from left to right; 4) Add and subtract in order from left to right. (Lessons 27 and 57)

ordered pair a set of two numbers used to locate a point on a coordinate plane

The first number (the x-coordinate) tells the horizontal location, and the second number (the y-coordinate) tells the vertical location. (Lesson 59)

origin the point where the x-axis and the y-axis meet

The ordered pair that describes the origin is (0,0). (Lesson 59)

outcome the result of a probability experiment (Lesson 61)

parallel lines that never intersect (Lesson 38)

parallelogram a quadrilateral with both pairs of opposite sides parallel (Lesson 38)

pattern a predictable arrangement or configuration of numbers or figures (Lesson 39)

pentagon a polygon with five sides, five angles, and five vertices (Lesson 38)

percent a ratio of a number to 100

Example: $17\% = \frac{17}{100} = 0.17 = 17$ hundredths (Lesson 22)

perimeter distance around a polygon (Lesson 38)

place-value chart a chart used to show the values of the digits in a number (Lesson 15)

polygon a closed figure made up of line segments that meet at their endpoints (Lesson 38)

prediction a statement of something that may happen in the future (Lesson 55)

prime number a counting number that has exactly two different factors, itself and 1

Example: 3 has only two factors (1 and 3), so 3 is a prime number. (Lesson 23)

probability the likelihood that an event will occur (Lesson 61)

protractor a tool for measuring the number of degrees in an angle (Lesson 48)

quadrilateral polygon that has four sides, four angles, and four vertices (Lesson 38)

quotient the result of division (Lesson 26)

ratio a comparison of numbers (Lesson 19)

ray a part of a line that has one definite endpoint and goes on and on in one direction (Lesson 48)

rectangle a parallelogram with four right angles (Lesson 38)

regular polygon a polygon that has all sides the same length and all angles the same measure (Lesson 40)

rhombus a parallelogram with all sides the same length (Lesson 43)

right angle an angle that measures 90 degrees (Lesson 43)

right triangle a triangle with one 90° angle (Lesson 43)

rounding a process used to approximate a value (Lesson 32)

sample a small part of a larger group that is used to make predictions about the larger group (Lesson 55)

sample space the set of all the possible outcomes of a probability experiment (Lesson 61)

scalene triangle a triangle with no two sides the same length (Lesson 43)

similar having the same shape, but not necessarily the same size (Lesson 42)

square a rectangle with all sides equal in length (Lesson 38)

trapezoid a quadrilateral with exactly one pair of parallel sides (Lesson 43)

triangle a polygon with three sides, three angles, and three vertices (Lesson 38)

variable a letter or symbol that stands for a number in a mathematical expression or sentence (Lesson 37)

vertex of a polygon the point where two sides of a polygon meet (Lesson 43)

vertex of an angle a point that is common to both sides of an angle (Lesson 48)

x-axis the horizontal number line in a coordinate system (Lesson 59)

y-axis the vertical number line in a coordinate system (Lesson 59)

Punch-Out Tools

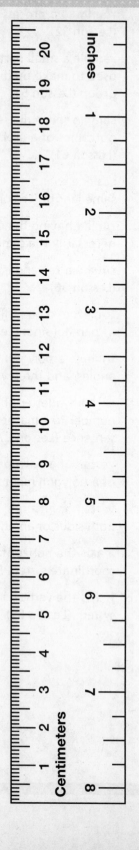

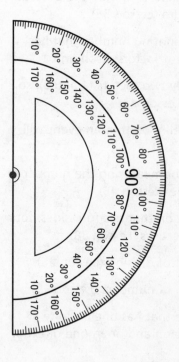

Notes

Notes

Notes

Notes

Notes

Notes

Notes

Notes